*Critical Perspectives
on Early Childhood
Education*

Critical Perspectives on Early Childhood Education

Edited by
Lois Weis
Philip G. Altbach
Gail P. Kelly
Hugh G. Petrie

Foreword by Mary A. Jensen

State University of New York Press

The editors gratefully acknowledge the publishers of *Educational Policy*; *Teaching and Learning*: *The Journal of Natural Inquiry*; Falmer Press, and the American Psychiatric Press for permission to reprint articles contained in this volume.

Most of these chapters have appeared in *Educational Policy*, Vol. 3, Number 4 (1989).

OTHERS

Chapter 2

Deborah Phillips and Marcy Whitebook, "The Child Care Provider: A Profile." in WORKING, PARENTING, AND DAY CARE, Shahla Chehrazi, ed., American Psychiatric Press.

Chapter 3

William Ayers, "Teaching and Being: Connecting Teachers' Accounts of Their Lives with Classroom Practice," *Teaching and Learning: The Journal of Natural Inquiry*, Spring, 1989, Vol. 3, No. 3.

Chapter 5

Bronwyn Davis, "The Accomplishment of Genderedness in Pre-school Children." In CHILDREN AND THEIR PRIMARY SCHOOLS, Andrew Pollard, ed., Falmer Press, 1987.

Published by
State University of New York Press, Albany

© 1991 State University of New York

For information, address State University of New York
Press, State University Plaza, Albany, N.Y., 12246

Production by M. R. Mulholland
Marketing by Fran Keneston

Library of Congress Cataloging-in-Publication Data

Critical perspectives on early childhood education / edited by Lois
    Weis . . . [et al.].
        p.   cm. — (SUNY series, frontiers in education)
    Includes bibliographical references and index.
    ISBN 0-7914-0697-0 (alk. paper). — ISBN 0-7914-0698-9 (pbk.:
alk. paper)
    1. Early childhood education—United States.   2. Child care—
United States.   I. Weis, Lois.   II. Series.
LB1139.25.C75   1991
372.21—dc20   90-43396
                                                                    CIP

10 9 8 7 6 5 4 3 2 1

Contents

Acknowledgments

The editors gratefully acknowledge the assistance of Edith Hoshino, who copyedited all of the papers that previously appeared in *Educational Policy;* Helen Kress, Sharon Smith, and Cyndy Boyd who copyedited manuscripts and handled numerous tasks associated with the editing of this volume; and Jeanne Ferry, who provided much-needed secretarial assistance.

Foreword

Early childhood education is experiencing dramatic changes. Multiple spheres of influence have contributed to these changes. The large increase in numbers of working mothers has created a need for expanding child care services. A growing number of employers have responded with child care assistance benefits. The media has recognized the need with regular coverage of child care issues. Recent research has documented the benefits of high quality early childhood programs for young children. Professional groups have defined specific guidelines for good early childhood education practices. Finally, recent introduction of hundreds of early childhood bills into Congress and state legislatures indicates a pervasive concern about early education and care in our society and among our elected officials. These changes have brought not only growth to the field but complex challenges to policymakers and advocates at local, state and national levels.

Without reflective policy development, rapid growth can put the field of early childhood education at risk. Such circumstances demand a comprehensive set of principles to guide policy making decisions. The opening chapter of *Critical Perspectives on Early Childhood Education* details six principles that frame key policy issues represented by articles in the book.

Please understand that I am not suggesting every article adopts all six principles. Rather, each article offers a provocative perspective. The mix of perspectives is valuable in that it challenges static assumptions about early childhood education and facilitates shifts in our thinking as we compare and contrast various perspectives. Dogmatic beliefs and unexamined practice will not produce either healthy professionals or programs and policies consistent without democratic values. Of course, you will find that the writers are not always in accord. And, I am not saying that you should agree with all the authors; instead, question and discuss the basis of fact and opinion as you read.

Although *Critical Perspectives on Early Childhood Education* includes diverse perspectives and suggestions for policy making, it also offers examples of various approaches to research. Awareness of these different methods of inquiry is useful to anyone interested in the knowledge base of early childhood education, and the lines of inquiry taken may suggest new directions for research.

The editors have grouped the articles into three sections. Part I examines the nature and issues of work and professionalism in early childhood education, often from teachers' perspectives. Because staff retention and training are critical challenges for the health of the field at this time, this section demands our careful attention. Part II looks at the underbelly of early childhood curriculum: sex-role development, social integration in children's interactions, work/play distinctions, rough and tumble play and aggression, and evaluation. These aspects of the curriculum, although often overlooked, have profound influences on children's learning experiences. I also was delighted that many authors in this section incorporated the views of children in their analyses of experienced curriculum. Part III places the issues of Part I and II into broader research and social perspectives. Review of research on motivation reveals limitations of emphasis on cognitive development in curriculum development and evaluation. Historical analysis reveals longstanding inequities in goals and staff training of early childhood programs aimed at low-income families. An analysis of economic outcomes indicates that high quality preschool programs primarily benefit society and not the family leading the author to conclude that public funds should support high quality early childhood programs. Finally, a cross-cultural examination of early childhood policies for family-based support and extra-familial care suggests possible directions for policy development.

The strength of this book lies not in any one article or section but in the themes that weave in and out of articles throughout the book and engage the reader in puzzling out the significance of these themes for good early childhood education. The authors and editors are to be congratulated for their efforts to put current policy issues in early childhood education into perspective. I believe that teachers, policymakers, advocates, administrators, and researchers can learn and profit from this book.

Mary A. Jensen
State University of New York—Geneseo

Introduction

Early childhood education encompasses day care, nursery, kindergarten, and primary school years. There has been a great deal of ferment in the field in the United States recently, and a number of social trends are turning national attention increasingly in this direction. To begin with, many more children than ever before attend these programs. In 1966, for example, fewer than 30 percent of three- to five-year-olds were enrolled.[1] By 1980, 53 percent were in attendance, and well over that are enrolled today. There has been a steady increase in enrollments in early childhood programs of all types since the mid-1960s, and kindergarten has become nearly universal. Today more women with young children are working in the paid labor force, either out of choice or by necessity. About one-third of women with preschool children work full time outside the home, and this rises to more than one-half when part-time workers are included. Thus the need for some type of early childhood programs has increased significantly.

While it certainly is the case that many early childhood programs have a distinctly developmental focus, the role of such programs in broadening inequality in educational outcomes cannot be overlooked. By the time children reach grade three, the gap in achievement between minority and majority, rich and poor, and suburban and urban children is strikingly apparent. These differences only tend to be exacerbated during later years, leading to differences in track placements in high school, entrance to different sectors of tertiary-level education, and, ultimately, differential occupations and incomes. While it is certainly not the responsibility of early childhood educators to close the achievement gap by themselves, these educators are taking much more seriously the notion that they must do their part in lessening the gap by providing all students with a sound emotional and academic beginning. Thus potential inequalities in the early grades of elementary school, for example, are being scrutinized, and numerous programs being put in place in order to redress perceived problems.

Unfortunately it is becoming apparent that the early childhood sector as a whole may itself be contributing in an active way to these inequalities

1

despite what are at times the best intentions of early childhood teachers and caretakers. Although the number of licensed day-care centers has grown rapidly within recent years, for example, this growth has not been sufficient to meet the needs of the growing number of two-earner or single-earner families in the U.S., causing many families to turn to nonlicensed centers or unlicensed family day care. In addition, many licensed day-care centers are well beyond the financial means of low-income families. Thus there is widespread inequality in the provision of day care, with poor children often in unlicensed settings, or those supported by federal assistance, and middle-class children attending relatively expensive, high-quality day-care centers and half- or extended-day private nursery schools. The very fact that children are being socialized in widely different settings serves to bring the early childhood sector into the debate on education and inequality in spite of the fact that the primary goal of many of these programs is not centered around academic achievement.

Currently there are a variety of key issues relating to early childhood education. It would be impossible for all such issues to be discussed in this volume. Rather, we have tried to touch upon a select number of such issues, ever mindful of the facts that important questions need to be asked in other areas and that some excellent work is being done that we have not included here. Important areas not covered here, for example, include compensation for early childhood teachers (how can we get the *best* for so little money?); the role and impact of family day care; and community participation in the definition, organization, and implementation of early childhood programs. We have not, in other words, tried to cover the field so much as present exemplary work in certain key areas.

Edward Zigler and Matia Finn-Stevenson offer an overview of the "problem" of childcare in America and suggest ways of remedying this problem. Deborah Phillips and Marcy Whitebook; William Ayers; and Kelvin Seifert and Laura Atkinson examine issues related to the early childhood teaching force, including the gendered nature of such teaching. Seifert and Atkinson examine specifically the way in which home and school combine in teachers' lives and they contrast the experiences of male and female teachers. Ayers draws from his larger study of preschool teachers to introduce us to the way in which teachers connect self and practice within the context of the preschool setting.

Bronwyn Davies, beginning the section of the book entitled "Within the Schools," explores the construction of genderedness, and Beth Swadener examines peer interactions in two day-care centers, focusing on the issues of race, gender, and exceptionality as they shape such interactions. Anthony Pelligrini and Mariajosé Romero focus on play in early childhood settings—Pelligrini from the standpoint of the utility of "rough-and-tumble play'' as distinct from aggressive behavior, and Romero from a critical perspective, in that she examines emerging definitions of work and play among preschoolers. Carol Hodges asks whether current standardized achievement tests ought to be used to measure instructional outcomes in kindergarten and suggests that alternative forms of assessment be sought.

In the last section of this volume, ''Early Childhood Education in Broader Social and Economic Context,'' Wendy Grolnick provides a rationale for reexamining the importance of affective goals in early childhood education, and Julia Wrigley explores the creation of various early educational programs for different clientele historically, suggesting that early childhood education is inherently unequal in its conception and distribution. Steve Barnett examines four issues related to early childhood education policy, with a focus on economic considerations. Sally Lubeck, in the final chapter, examines family policies in other countries and compares them to proposed United States legislation.

The editors of this volume are not in early childhood education. We came upon this issue out of a sense that the education of young children is an important area and that persons like ourselves, who are researchers in social and educational policy matters, ought to become more familiar with it. We do not claim, therefore, to be experts in the field and did not embark upon this volume with the intention of codifying the field. Rather, we wish to introduce others like ourselves to issues surrounding the education of young children and, at the same time, provide a volume which offers research on young children conducted by those in early childhood education as well as those in areas such as sociology of education and policy studies. We hope this serves to introduce researchers and practitioners to work conducted by persons in areas other than their own, thus broadening and strengthening the research agenda in this critically important area.

Lois Weis

EDWARD F. ZIGLER and MATIA FINN-STEVENSON

Chapter One

Overview
Child Care in America:
From Problem to Solution

During the past year we have witnessed unprecedented attention to the nation's child care problem. Virtually everyone, from working parents to the chief executives of major corporations, is discussing the lack of good quality, affordable child care services. The media is covering the topic diligently, with stories about and analyses of the child care crisis appearing in daily newspapers and in such diverse publications as the *American Psychologists, Elementary School Principal, Newsweek,* and *U.S. News & World Report.* In addition, various ways to address the issue are being proposed at every level of government. President George Bush put forth a $2.2 billion child care plan while he was campaigning for the presidency. Members of the U.S. Senate and House of Representatives have introduced close to 200 different proposals in an attempt to create legislation and to dcfine the federal government's role in the solution to the child care problem.

This recent attention belies the fact that the child care issue is hardly new; it has been a major social problem in this country for nearly two decades. During the 1970 White House Conference on children, the lack of affordable, good quality child care was identified as the number one priority issue for the nation to address. In 1971, Congress passed the Child Development Act, which called for expanding the number of child care facilities, subsidizing the child care costs of families on welfare, and allowing tax

5

deductions to families using child care services. At the time, however, public recognition of the problem was limited, and the opposition to any form of out-of-home care was enormous and powerful and led to presidential veto of the bill.[1] Since then the problem has become worse, but as a nation we have come no closer to instituting a solution.

THE MAGNITUDE OF THE PROBLEM

The emphasis on child care we are now witnessing is not surprising given the magnitude of the problem and the fact that changes in work and family life have created an increased demand for child care services. Two decades ago, family life and work were regarded as separate worlds, but since then these two contexts have become increasingly more interdependent with aspects of one affecting the functioning of the other.[2] Although there is a great deal of interdependence between the family and the work place, no social supports exist to facilitate work and family life, resulting in conflict, stress, and loss of productivity.[3] Workers, particularly those with young children, are experiencing difficulties as they try to juggle work and family responsibilities. Employers recognize that stressful conditions at home contribute to loss of productivity at work, but many are slow in responding to the familial demands of their employees.

One major contributing factor to the changes in work and family life and to the growing demand for child care has been the movement of women into the paid labor force. In 1950 the percentage of women with children under six who were working outside of the home was 11.9 percent; by 1987 it was 56.8 percent.[4] Even more dramatic has been the increase in the number of working women with very young children. Whereas a decade ago only 31 percent of mothers with infants under the age of one were working, in 1987 that figure increased to 51 percent, creating an enormous demand for child care services.[5] It is projected that 93 percent of women of childbearing age will become pregnant while they are working; thus the number of mothers who return to work while their children are very young will increase, creating yet a greater need for child care.

Other factors that have contributed to the growing need for child care stem from the transformation of the American family—in particular, the growth in the number of single parent families.[6] Although single parent families are not necessarily a homogeneous group, they are generally characterized by female heads of household, poverty, and the presence of children under the age of five.[7] This profile of the single parent family is particularly evident among minorities: 50 percent of all poor, black children live in a single parent family headed by a woman. In addition to the growing numbers of single parent families, ours has become a highly mobile and scattered society.[8] Families no longer live near their kin, and working parents with children can no longer depend on the support and assistance of relatives who traditionally could be counted upon to help with child care either on a regular basis or during emergencies such as the illness of the child.

The economy is another important factor that has contributed to changes in family life and the associated need for child care. The median annual income for families in the United States has fallen steadily over the past 16 years. When the figures are adjusted for inflation, it is revealed that families have less income today than they did in 1973, and more families are dependent on dual incomes. As noted in the Joint Economic Committee's 1986 report, although the median family income in America fell by 3.1 percent between 1973 and 1984, the drop in median family income would have been more severe (9.5 percent), had women not joined the labor force to help supplement the family income.[9] According to the U.S. Bureau of Labor, 40 percent of married women who are working have to supplement their family's income because their husbands earn less than $15,000 annually. Among single parent families, the economic need for work is even more acute. If the mother in these families does not work, family income is approximately $4500; if she does work, it is only $9000 more.[10] It is evident that in both single parent and two-worker families, many women are working primarily out of economic necessity.

UNDERSTANDING THE PROBLEM

Despite the fact that an increasing number of families depend on out-of-home care for their children, child care has been, and continues to be, regarded as an individual family problem, to be addressed by parents. This is evident, for example, in the fact that the majority of businesses in America do not make provisions for facilitating work and family life by making available parental leaves of absence, flexible work schedules, or child care services.[11] The same attitude is also evident in the lack of initiatives on the part of the government to address the problem.

Although child care is an issue that families are of necessity addressing on an individual basis, given the fact that so many of the nation's families need child care and given the discrepancy between the demand for and supply of care,[12] this problem is truly national in scope. In attempting to resolve the problem it is important at the outset to define its various constituent units[13] and ascertain what barriers exist that may prevent our reaching a solution to the problem.

Public awareness of the need for child care, for example, is a prerequisite to any national action on the issue because no society acts until it has a sense of the immediacy of a problem.[14] Much progress has been made in this regard. As noted earlier in this article, a child care system would have been put in place in the early 1970s had President Richard Nixon not vetoed the 1971 Child Development Act. At the time, however, awareness of the need for child care was not universal and there were many who spoke about the dangers of out-of-home care rather than of its need.[15] Although for several years thereafter there was no forum for highlighting children's issues nor any media interest in topics related to families,[16] this state of affairs is changing. Many states have convened commissions and task forces for the purpose of studying and/or promoting the needs of children, and state legislatures are creating committees to address issues related to family life. (An example is the Family and the Workplace Committee in the Connecticut state legislature.) At the federal level there is the bipartisan House Select Committee on Children, Youth, and Families, which has produced numerous reports that highlight child care as a national problem.[17] There is also the Senate Subcommittee on Children, Youth, Families, Drugs, and Alcoholism, which has been holding hearings on child care and related issues. Perhaps even more important has been the media coverage of the problem that has resulted in the widespread recognition that the child care problem is a national crisis.

The Cost of Care

Besides public awareness that a problem exists, there is need for educating the public about various associated issues, one of these being the high cost of care. Many parents choose child care in part on the basis of cost. The cost of care is related to quality, and high quality care tends to be too expensive for most parents. Precise data on what families spend on child care are not yet available, but it is known that child care costs between $1500 and $10,000 per year,[18] depending on the quality of care and the age of the children. It is estimated that full-time child care for preschoolers costs an average of $3000 a year, and for infants the costs can exceed $9600 a year.

The high cost of child care is significant for at least two reasons. First, child care costs are a major expenditure for families, and the amount of money families spend on child care is directly related to their incomes. Low-income families spend less on child care in absolute terms than do higher-income families, but the proportion of the family budget that is taken up by child care costs is far greater among low-income families, who must allocate as much as 25 to 30 percent of their earnings to child care.[19] Second, since cost and quality of care are related, we are witnessing the emergence of a two-tier system of child care in which the choices of care for low-income children are limited to low-cost—and, therefore, low-quality—care.

The Quality of Care

The fact that good quality care is a privilege that only some children are enjoying is of concern because child care is an environment in which children spend a large portion of their day, every day. As such, child care has a significant effect on the development of children. The issue of the effect of child care on children is controversial, and the research on the topic, discussed in more length later in this article, is as yet inconclusive. Although, as will become apparent, the research yields conflicting findings and opinions, there is consensus that no matter what type of care they are in—center-based or family day care—children will not be adversely affected by the child care experience as long as they are in good quality settings.[20]

Good quality care is a value-laden term that is likely to differ depending on people's attitudes about what constitutes good care. In defining good quality, child care specialists differentiate between developmentally appropriate care that is responsive to the individual needs of children and care that is mere baby sitting or basic supervision. In studies of different child care settings, researchers found that an important indicator of quality child care is an appropriate staff/child ratio and group size for the age of the children involved. Another determinant of good quality care is the child care provider; those providers who receive training in child development are more likely than others to interact with the children, to provide the children with experiences conducive to optimal growth and development, and to understand the needs of children at different ages.[21]

Having the ability to distinguish the needs of children at different age levels is important in determining the kinds of experiences children need to undergo. During the first year of life, children experience rapid physical growth and developmental changes; they require constant supervision to ensure their safety and well-being.[22] Moreover, they have no ability to tolerate discomfort for long periods of time. Therefore they should be cared for by a flexible and responsive adult who can attend to their needs. Another requirement during infancy is consistency of care. This is a factor in the care of older children as well, but it is crucial during infancy since during this period the parent and child become acquainted with and attached to one another. Infants can and do form multiple attachments. However, in the first few months of life they can only relate to a limited number of people because they are still learning the cues and conventions that govern human behavior. They need to spend time becoming acquainted with their parent or caregiver. Frequent changes in caregivers may inhibit the infant's ability to get to know and rely on the responsivity of any one caregiver and thus may serve as a barrier to the formation of attachment.

As toddlers, children become increasingly better able to interact with a greater number of people, and they begin to broaden their sphere of social relations to include other children of their age. It is important during this period of life to facilitate a sense of autonomy in children and to care for them in a manner that will encourage independence but at the same time place limits to ensure their safety. During the preschool years, as children come to rely on and enjoy the company of their peers, they benefit from having the time and the opportunity to explore their environment and to play since through play children develop the social and cognitive skills that form the foundation for later learning.[23]

During the school-age years, children spend the majority of their time in school and are in child care for only a few hours a day. Good quality child care for school-age children should provide them with supervision that allows them the freedom and opportunity to choose among various physical activities, play, or time alone for homework or reading if they so choose. One mistake often made by providers of child care for school-age children is to insist that children engage in creative activities that often resemble what the children experience during the school day, thus not enabling the children to take the needed time off from mental tasks.

Availability of Care

Good quality care, as described above, is often difficult to find. There is little information on the number of child care facilities and on the quality of their programs and staffs. The information on the demand side—that is, who uses child care—is better; however that database is also inadequate, so there is some confusion and disagreement on the issue of availability of care. Some claim that there is no shortage of child care facilities.[24] Others contend that the demand far exceeds the supply.[25] There is agreement on several points, however. It is commonly accepted that the demand for child care is going to increase not only because of the growing presence of mothers in the labor force and the growing numbers of two-earner and single parent families but also because: (1) there are more young children to be cared for since the *baby boom* generation is having children, and (2) as the following generation (referred to as the *baby bust* generation because of their small numbers) comes of age, there will be fewer workers in a variety of fields, including child care, thus widening the gap between the need for and availability of care.[26] It is also agreed that, although many parents who need child care are not finding it, there is no guarantee that they are finding good quality care. As we noted earlier, the quality of care children receive is determined in large part by the provider, with good quality care more likely to be given by providers who have an educational background and training in child development. However, the child care field is beset with problems of low salaries, virtually nonexistent benefits, and the low status of the child care providers.[27] Staff turnover in the child care field is more than twice as high as the turnover in other professions and approximately 40 percent of providers are being replaced each year just to maintain the present child care work force.[28] The tightening labor market noted earlier will only intensify the problem; with increased competition for workers, people who may have chosen to go into, or stay in, the child care field will be in a position to choose other, higher-paying jobs.[29]

RESEARCH ON THE EFFECT OF CHILD CARE ON CHILDREN'S DEVELOPMENT

Even more important than understanding the issues of cost, quality, and availability of care is understanding the effects of child care on the development of children.

This research is limited in part because of methodological problems and the focus on center-based care, which is a setting for only some of the children who are in out-of-home care; many others are in family day-care homes, about which not much data exist.[30] Nevertheless some information can be gained from the available research, which indicates that since the needs of children differ at different stages of development (infancy, the preschool period, and the school-age years), any viable child care must at the outset address the varied needs of children at different stages of development.[31]

As stated earlier, the infancy period is of particular concern. Infants are dependent on sensitive care that is responsive to their individual needs, and they require the consistent and loving attention of a caregiver who not only takes care of the infants' physical needs but also engages the infants in playful social interactions.[32] The younger the infants, the more vulnerable they are to any disturbances in their routine care and the more important it is that they be cared for by a primary caregiver.[33] T. B. Brazelton notes that during the first few months of life the opportunity for the baby and the parents to spend time together learning about one another is important not only for the baby but also for the parents since the birth of the baby is a stressful life event necessitating the adjustment of all family members.[34]

Since it is so crucial for infants and parents to be together during the first years of life, the question of the effects of out-of-home care on infants has been raised. In a review of the research on the topic, J. Belsky found cause for concern, noting that infants who are placed in child care before the age of one may evidence insecure attachment, aggression, noncompliance, and social withdrawal during the preschool years.[35] Although other researchers[36] have refuted Belsky's conclusions, some reviews of the research indicate that some infants may be adversely affected by the day care experience, especially if they experience stressful conditions at home.[37] The National Center for Clinical Infant Programs convened a number of leading researchers in the field who agreed that as long as the infants are in stable, high-quality day care, they will not be adversely affected by their child care experiences. Nonetheless the younger they are, the more vulnerable the children are to negative consequences associated with the environment. Because of the vulnerability of the young infant and also because of the need for the parents to adjust to the birth of the child, the Blue Ribbon Committee on Infant Care Leave has recommended a national parental leave policy that would enable parents to take a paid leave of absence from work for the first few months after birth.[38]

The effect of out-of-home care on preschoolers presents less concern since by the time children are three years of age they are developmentally prepared to interact with peers and to benefit from participation in group care. For preschoolers, good quality child care does not seem to have any adverse effects, and it can be a valuable experience since the opportunity to interact with peers is not only desirable but is in fact a necessary aspect of normal social development.[39] Also, some children, notably those from low-income families, evidence benefits in terms of social and intellectual development from their participation in child care.[40]

Although much of the research on the effects of child care focuses on younger children, close to half of those who need child care are between the ages of 5 and 12. The need for child care services is particularly acute for children in this age group since many of them, because of lack of child care, are left alone at home before and after school and during vacations. There are disagreements as to how children are affected by this experience. Some researchers have found no differences in locus of control, self-esteem, and social and interpersonal competence between children who are in self-care and those who are supervised before and after school.[41] Other researchers contend that self-care can be beneficial because it has the potential of enabling the growth of independence in children. Many others are concerned that children who are alone at home are often afraid, lonely, and at risk of injury.[42] Two researchers who have reviewed the research on the topic have found links between self-care and juvenile delinquency.[43]

CURRENT RESPONSES TO THE PROBLEM

The Role of Government

Since child care is an environment that can have either negative or positive effects on children's development, depending on the quality of care that is being offered, the lack of good quality, affordable child care is a major social problem that must be addressed. To date the federal government has played a limited role in helping parents deal with the child care problem. The only comprehensive child care legislation passed by Congress was the one noted earlier, which was vetoed by President Nixon in 1971. Since that time, advocacy groups have challenged the federal government to provide leadership, particularly in the area of federal child care standards. Such standards would provide a baseline for the safe care of children in centers and family day care homes by specifying minimum child to staff ratios, group size, provider training, and other requirements that address good quality care.[44] There is no guarantee that such standards would result in good quality care across the board because their enforcement could become prohibitively costly. Federal standards, however, would help ensure that all states issue a license for the operation of a child care facility on the basis of criteria that have been examined in light of their applicability to good quality care facilities with extreme variations among these states' requirements for staff to child ratios, group size, and training,[45] and specific measures that address the health and safety of children.[46]

Although to date advocates have not succeeded in realizing their goal for federal child care standards, they have met with a small measure of success in having the government partially address the high cost of care. Currently the cost issue is addressed in a two-pronged approach: the dependent care income tax credit and subsidies to low-income families through the Title XX Social Services Block Grant. Neither provision is adequate. The dependent care tax credit represents the largest source of federal assistance to families with child care needs, amounting in 1985 (the latest years for which data are available) to $3.2 billion, which benefited 8.5 million families,[47] the majority of whom earned more than $25,000 a year. Since the tax credit is not refundable, it is only applicable to those who owe taxes and thus cannot be used by families with very low incomes, who are most in need of help.[48] In order to enable low-income families to benefit from a tax credit, President Bush has proposed a refundable tax credit of up to $1000 a year for children ages four and under.

The other source of federal support for child care, Title XX, is limited because it was hit hard by the extensive federal domestic budget cuts of 1981; whereas in fiscal year 1980 the federal government appropriated nearly $3 billion for Title XX, the funding for fiscal year 1988 was less than half that amount, after adjusting for inflation.[49] Title XX as a source of support for child care is further limited because the funds are not earmarked specifically for child care. Rather, states decide how much they should spend for child care and how much for other social services. It is reported that the amount of Title XX money states allocate to child care varies greatly from state to state.

Patchwork System

States also vary in their commitment to addressing the child care needs of families. A few states have been able to piece together funding from various sources in an attempt to fill the gaps left by the Title XX cutbacks. Some states have also been able to adopt innovative child care programs apart from those that come under the welfare system. The New York legislature, for example, has recently allocated $12 million to improve the salaries and benefits of staff working in nonprofit child care facilities. California has established an impressive statewide resource and referral network, which provides subsidies and/or vouchers for child care, information and referral services, and provider training and recruitment. Even in California, however, where the response to the child care problem has been the most progressive among the states, government funds alone were not sufficient and had to be used to leverage private sector funds in order to meet local child care needs. Thus a consortium of corporations and local and state government agencies in California was created, which was able to raise $700,000 to fund six pilot projects designed to expand the supply of child care in one area of the state and to train family day-care providers, also in the same area, in order to upgrade the quality of care.

Several other demonstration programs exist in communities across the nation, which are funded by foundations or by corporate support, and there are also some 3500 corporations operating or supporting the operation of child care facilities or information and referral services for their employees. These initiatives represent a grass roots attempt to address some of the child care problems, but they remain scattered and operate with no assurance of long-term funding.

Besides child care demonstration projects, a variety of child care services exist including family day-care homes, church- and corporate-sponsored day care, for-profit day care, and other services operated by nonprofit, community-based organizations. As such, what currently exists represents a patchwork system that is hard to access and to work within in order to achieve needed improvements.

Toward a Realistic Solution to the Problem

In an attempt to create a more coherent child care structure, there have been calls for both lesser and greater government involvements. Some groups advocate limiting the role of government to tax credits; other groups argue for increased government involvement, for example, in the regulation of child care. These and other views are represented in the legislation introduced in Congress this year. Although the existence of legislative proposals on child care shows that as a nation we are ready to address the child care problem, the fact that so many different proposals were introduced is also an indication that there is no consensus on the approach we should take.

Guiding principles

Several principles have been identified to serve as a guide to action on a child care policy. The first such principle is the need for child care that is stable and reliable and of good quality and that becomes part of the very structure of society. Such child care, if it is to be accessible to all children, must be tied to a known, widely used social institution, and it must become a national priority.

Although child care should be a national priority, the question remains of whether it should be a state- or federal-based system. Child care, like education, is not mentioned in the Constitution; thus—like education—it may be conceived as a state-based system. The constitutional factor, however, is only one relatively small part of the argument that child care should be a state-based system. Another important consideration is the lack of initiative to address the issue on the part of the federal government. Although we believe that child care should be primarily a state-based system, the federal government has an important role to play in funding research on child care and subsidizing the care of low-income children—as it currently does through Chapter 1 of the Elementary and Secondary Education Act and Public Law 94–142.

Another principle is that every child should have access to good quality care and that all ethnic and socioeconomic groups should be integrated as fully as possible in order to eliminate the possibility of a two-tier child care system.

The third principle is that child care in this country must be based on the optimal development of children; it should focus not on any one developmental domain but rather on all aspects of development, including physical, social, emotional, and intellectual development. Within this principle, it is important to underscore the fact that child care, although it is a service that enables parents to work, is actually an environment, the quality of which is likely to affect the children's development and well-being.

The fourth principle is that child care must be predicated on a partnership between parents and providers. This principle of parent involvement, essential for the optimal development of children,[51] is derived from the Head Start program, which owes its success to the fact that parents take an active role in the program.

A fifth guiding principle underscores the crucial role providers have in the quality of care children receive. In order to ensure good quality care, we must recognize and support child care providers, provide them with training, and enable them to receive pay upgrades in accordance with their experience and training.

Finally, any solution to the child care problem must appreciate the heterogeneity of children and parents. Families have differing child care needs, and it would be unfair to deprive them of choices as they make arrangements for child care. Any child care proposal must therefore ensure that we have a system for child care that is flexible and adaptable to the varying needs of children and parents.

The above-cited principles underscore the fact that, given the continuing need for child care, we have to put in place a child care system that, like education will be affordable and accessible to all children who require child care. Such a child care system, however, should not be viewed as compulsory; it should also provide appropriate services to children of varying ages.

In the case of newborn infants, one of the parents should have the option of staying home to care for the child for the first few months of life. During the rest of the infancy period, until the child is three, appropriate out-of-home care is a good quality family day-care home or other forms of individualized child care either in the child's own home or in the home of a relative.

Using the Schools

In the case of preschool and school-age children, a cost-effective way to provide universally available child care to those children who may need it would be to use the existing school system. We have a $2 trillion investment in public schools supported by tax dollars. By capitalizing on this investment and adding a child care system within the already existing public school system we will be able to increase the supply of good quality care as well as ensure equitable and affordable child care.

Toward this end, the first author conceptualized a plan for school-based child care and support services. Referred to as the School of the Twenty-First Century program, the plan calls for specific provisions for schools to adopt.[52] These include two child care services that would be delivered in the school building—one an all-day child care for children ages 3 to 5, the other a before- and after-school and vacation care for children ages 5 to 12. In some school districts, children of age 5 are in kindergarten for a full day; thus, they would have before- and after-school and vacation care as do the older children. In other districts, kindergarten children attend school for only half a day, in which case they would join the child care program for the rest of the day.

The fact that the child care services are delivered in the school does not mean that they should adhere to an academic curriculum. In order to provide good quality care, these programs would have to be developmentally appropriate. Preschool child care, like early education programs for preschool children, should not focus on academics but rather on play and social interactions and should be staffed by providers with training in child development. School-age child care programs should encourage opportunities for physical and recreational activities and should enable children to choose among these.

Besides the child care services, the School of the Twenty-First Century calls for three outreach services. One of these is home visitation to parents from birth until the child has reached the age of 3. Modeled after the Missouri program known as Parents as First Teachers, the home visitation outreach service would send parent educators to the home several times a year to enhance parents' parenting skills, to provide them with information about their children's development, to ascertain if the parents or the child need specific services or assistance, and to help them locate these. Although this is not specifically a child care service, the home visitation component is an important support service that can facilitate positive parent-child interactions and prevent later educational and developmental problems.

Another outreach service is support and technical assistance to family day-care providers in the neighborhood of the school. Family day-care homes generally provide care to a small group of infants and toddlers (sometimes also to school-age children) in the provider's home. Among the many benefits associated with care in a family day-care home are the home setting and the small group size appropriate for infants and toddlers. Moreover if the care provided is of good quality, the family day care home experience can be conducive to children's development. Although they now provide the bulk of child care services in this country,[53] family day care providers are generally isolated from the child care community; they lack the opportunities for training and social support, and many of them operate *underground*. The School of the Twenty-First Century program can serve as a support mechanism by creating a network of family day-care providers in the neighborhood of the school and providing them with the support and assistance they need.

The third outreach service is an information and referral service so that parents who need nighttime care or other specialized child care services may seek referrals from the school.

The School of the Twenty-First Century program would be supported by parental fees and would include provisions for a sliding scale fee system according to the families' income. Participation in the program would be voluntary; parents satisfied with their current child care arrangements or parents with no need for child care would not have to enroll their children in the School of the Twenty-First Century program.

Schools may choose whether they want to administer and manage the program or subcontract with a community-based organization to manage the program. In either case, the program should be administered as a separate system within the school system and coordinated by an individual with training and experience in child development.

There are several benefits associated with the School of the Twenty-First Century program: (1) Locating some of the community's child care services in the schools can help increase the supply of services. (2) Using the school building may be cost effective since rent, overhead expenses for janitorial and other services, and utilities may be absorbed by the school board budget. (3) Since every community has a school, school-based child care can ensure access to child care close to the child's home. Perhaps even more important, school-based child care provides the opportunity for continuity of care, which is an important developmental consideration.[54]

Besides these benefits, locating child care in the schools is a step toward the goal of institutionalizing child care and creating a child care system within which to address such issues as staff pay upgrades and training that may enhance the professionalization of the child care field.

Precedents for the School of the Twenty-First Century program exist in numerous communities that have developed and implemented school-based child care. In many communities, day-long programs for four-year-olds have also been implemented. Although many of these are early intervention efforts rather than day care, they address the child care needs of some families and are indicative of schools' growing interest in prekindergarten children. In addition, the School of the Twenty-First Century program, although it is a relatively new idea, has been implemented in several school districts in Missouri[55] and Connecticut.[56] In both cases the programs are supported by parental fees, but there are variations in the start-up funds. Missouri used foundation funds for building renovations and state Department of Education funds for training, whereas the Connecticut programs used state funds specifically appropriated for the development of the programs and Title XX funds to subsidize the care of low-income children.

Legislative proposals for funding school-based child care programs are currently being considered in Congress. In the Senate, Sen. Christopher Dodd (D-Conn.) introduced the School Child Care Demonstration Projects Act, which focuses on initiating pilot School of the Twenty-First Century programs in each state. In the House, Rep. Augustus F. Hawkins (D-Calif.) introduced the Child Development and Education Act, which earmarks a significant amount of money for the development of school-based child care programs.

In addition, school districts in several communities across the nation are in the process of planning the implementation of School of the Twenty-First Century programs. It is evident that the idea of this program is feasible and that school board members and administrators are not only ready to accept young children into the school but also recognize that assisting parents with child care is an important service likely to facilitate the development of children and to prepare them for school success. As one of the principals in Missouri noted,

> I feel that putting child care in my building has been one of the most important contributions I have made in my tenure as principal. It is helping parents and children; ultimately, it will help us educators because we will have a group of children who are happy and well-adjusted and who are familiar with the school environment.[57]

Since the nation is reorganizing the need for child care and since schools are responsive and ready to help resolve the child care problem, we are now at a turning point at which we can capitalize on the momentum for action and, using the schools, begin to build a comprehensive, on-going system to provide support and child care to parents and children.

NOTES

1. J. R. Nelson, "The Politics of Federal Day Care Regulations," in *Day Care: Scientific and Social Policy Issues*, ed. E. Zigler and E. Gorden (Boston: Auburn, 1982), pp. 267–306.

2. R. M. Kanter, *Work and Family Life in the United States: A Critical Review and Agenda for Research* (New York: Russell Sage Foundation, 1977).

3. U. Bronfenbrenner, "Strengthening Family Systems," in *Infant Care and Infant Care Leave*, E. Zigler and M. Frank (New Haven, Conn.: Yale University Press, 1988), pp. 143–160.

4. U.S. Department of Labor, *Child Care: A Workforce Issue* (Washington, D.C.: Government Printing Office, 1988).

5. Ibid.

6. U.S. Bureau of the Census, "Money, Income, and Poverty Status of Families and Persons in the U.S.," *Current Population Reports*, series P–60 (Washington, D.C.: U.S. Bureau of Census).

7. H. A. Mendes, "Single Parent Families: A Typology of Lifestyles," *Social Work* 24, no. 3 (March 1979): 193–200.

8. E. Zigler and M. Finn-Stevenson, "A Vision of Child Care in the 1980's," in *Facilitating Infant and Early Child Development*, ed. L. A. Bond and J. M. Joffe (Hanover, N.H.: University Press of New England, 1982), pp. 443–465.

9. Joint Economic Committee, *Family Income in America* (Washington, D.C.: Joint Economic Committee, 1986).

10. U.S. Department of Labor, *Child Care: A Workforce Issue.*

11. Zigler and Frank, *Infant Care and Infant Care Leave.*

12. Child Care Action Campaign, *Child Care: The Bottom Line* (New York: Child Care Action Campaign, 1988).

13. E. Zigler and P. Ennis, "Child Care: A New Role for Schools," *Principal 68* (September 1988): 10–13.

14. E. Zigler and M. Finn, "From Problem to Solution: Resolving the Problems of Children and Families," *Young Children* 36, no. 4 (May 1981): 31–32, 55–59.

15. Nelson, "The Politics of Federal Day Care Regulations."

16. E. Zigler and S. Muenchow, "A Room of Their Own: A Proposal to Renovate the Children's Bureau," *American Psychologist* 40 (March 1985): 953–959.

17. Select Committee on Children, Youth, and Families, *Child Care: Improving the Options,* no 39–146–0 (Washington, D.C.: Government Printing Office, 1984).

18. D. Friedman, *Corporate Financial Assistance for Child Care,* Research Bulletin no. 177 (New York: The Conference Board, 1985).

19. Ibid.

20. National Center for Clinical Infant Programs, *Who Will Mind the Babies?* (Washington, D.C.: National Center for Clinical Infant Programs, 1988).

21. R. Roupp, J. Travers, F. M. Glanz, and C. Coelen, *Children at the Center,* (Cambridge, Mass.: Abt Associates, 1979).

22. D. Phillips, ed., *Quality in Child Care: What Does the Research Tell Us?* (Washington, D.C.: The National Association for the Education of Young Children, 1987).

23. E. Zigler and M. Finn-Stevenson, *Children: Development and Social Issues* (Lexington, Mass.: Heath, 1987).

24. R. Haskins, "What Day Care Crisis?" *AEI Journal on Government and Society Regulations,* no. 2 (February 1989).

25. Child Care Action Campaign, *Child Care: The Bottom Line.*

26. D. Bloom and T. Steen, "The Labor Force Implications of Expanding the Child Care Industry," paper prepared for the Child Care Action Campaign (New York: CCAC, 1988).

27. H. Hartmann and D. Pearce, "Wages and Salaries of Child Care Workers: The Economic Reality," paper prepared for the Child Care Action Campaign (New York: CCAC, 1988).

28. W. Johnson, *Workforce 2000: Work and Workers for the Twenty-First Century* (Indianapolis: Hudson Institute, 1987).

29. Child Care Action Campaign, *Child Care: The Bottom Line.*

30. A. Kahn and S. Kamerman, *Child Care: Facing the Hard Choices* (Boston, Mass.: Auburn, 1987).

31. K. McCartney, S. Scarr, D. Phillips, S. Grajek, and J. C. Schwartz, "Environmental Differences Among Child Care Centers and Their Effects on Children's Development," in Day Care: *Scientific and Social Policy Issues,* ed. Zigler and Gordonn pp. 126–151.

32. D. Stern, *The First Relationship: Infants and Mothers* (Cambridge: Harvard University Press, 1977).

33. M. Rutter, "Protective Factors in Children's Responses to Stress and Disadvantage," in *Promoting Social Competence in Children,* ed. M. W. Kent and J. E. Rolf (Hanover, N.H.: University Press of New England).

34. T. B. Brazelton, "Issues for Working Parents," *American Journal of Orthopsychiatry* 56 (January 1986): 14–25.

35. J. Belsky, "Infant Day Care: A Cause for Concern?" *Zero to Three* 6, no. 5 (May 1986): 1–7.

36. D. Phillips, K. McCartney, S. Scarr, and C. Howes, "Selective Review of Infant Care: A Cause for Concern," *Zero to Three* 6, no. 6 (June 1987): 18–24.

37. T. J. Gamble and E. Zigler, "The Effects of Infant Day Care: Another Look at the Evidence," *American Journal of Orthopsychiatry* 56 (September 1986): 26–42.

38. P. Hopper and E. Zigler, "The Medical and Social Science Basis for a National Infant Care Policy," *American Journal of Orthopsychiatry* 58 (July 1988): 324–338.

39. Zigler and Finn-Stevenson, *Children: Development and Social Issues.*

40. C. Howes, "Current Research on Early Day Care—A Review," paper presented at a meeting of the San Francisco Psychoanalytic Institute, 20–21 September 1986.

41. H. Rodman, D. Pratto, and R. Nelson, "Child Care Arrangements and Children's Functioning: A Comparison of Self-Care and Adult-Care Children," *Developmental Psychology* 21 (May 1985): 413–418.

42. L. Long and T. Long, *Latchkey Children* (Washington, D.C.: National Institute of Education, 1982), contract no. 400–76–0008.

43. E. Zigler and N. Hall, "Day Care and Its Effects on Children: An Overview for Pediatric Health Professionals," *Journal of Developmental and Behavioral Pediatrics* 9 (February 1988): 38–46.

44. D. Phillips, et al., "Selective Review of Infant Day Care."

45. K. Young and E. Zigler, "Infant and Toddler Care: Regulations and Policy Implications," *American Journal of Orthopsychiatry* 56 (January 1986): 43–55.

46. M. Finn-Stevenson and B. A. Ward, "Children in Day Care: Do State Regulations Ensure Their Health and Safety?" (forthcoming).

47. L. B. Lindsey, "Better Child Care, Cheaper," *Wall Street Journal,* 5 July 1988.

48. Ibid.

49. Children's Defense Fund, *A Children's Defense Budget* (Washington, D.C.: Children's Defense Fund, 1987).

50. J. Sugarman, "A Proposal to Create the Children's Trust Fund" (Olympia, Wash.: Department of Social and Health Services, 1988).

51. E. Zigler and P. Turner, "Parents and Child Care Providers: A Failed Partnership?" in *Day Care: Scientific and Social Policy Issues,* ed. Zigler and Gordon, pp. 174–182.

52. E. Zigler, "A Solution to the Nation's Care Crisis: The School of the Twenty-First Century," paper delivered at the 10th Anniversary of the Bush Center for Child Development and Social Policy, New Haven, Conn., 1987.

53. Kahn and Kamerman, *Child Care: Facing the Hard Choices.*

54. Zigler and Finn-Stevenson, *Children: Development and Social Issues.*

55. Zigler and Ennis, "Child Care: A New Role for Schools."

56. C. Hall, "Family Resource Centers," paper prepared by the Connecticut State Department of Human Resources, Hartford, Conn., 1989.

57. Interview with author.

Part I

Teachers as Child Care Providers
Select Issues

DEBORAH PHILLIPS and MARCY WHITEBOOK

Chapter Two

The Child Care Provider: Pivotal Player in the Child's World*

INTRODUCTION

Medical and mental health professionals frequently rely on critical information provided by school teachers in diagnosing children. By enlisting the assistance of these educators, child psychiatrists, psychologists and social workers develop and implement enhanced treatment plans for their young clients. With increasing numbers of preschool and school-age children now spending a substantial portion of their day in child care, it behooves professionals working with families to establish relationships with equally pivotal, but often overlooked, players in the child's world—the child care providers.

Unfortunately, this task is far more challenging than it may appear. Most elementary and secondary school teachers are readily accessible, work in familiar environments, and have received training that sensitizes them to the value of children's mental health. Not so for child care providers, whose workplace may be a private home, a large public or private institution, or a moderate-sized facility in a church or community center. Some are regulated by the state and are thus publicly visible; others operate underground. Some child care providers hold master's degrees in early childhood education; others have not completed high school. Effective collaborations between mental health practitioners and child care providers must begin, therefore, with an understanding of child care work and of those who make it their profession.

CHILD CARE TODAY

Contemporary social forces have led to the increasing amalgamation of the day nursery and the nursery school.[1] World War II provided the impetus to change. Child care centers staffed by nursery school teachers were established for women war workers, thus linking child care to mainstream, nonpoor families. Head Start and the emphasis on preschool education in the 1960s again challenged the autonomous traditions of the nursery school and day nursery. Although such programs are exclusively a service for disadvantaged children, emphasis is placed on education in the preschool tradition as well as on socialization. Child care remains a secondary function of these largely part-day intervention programs.

The relentless growth in the number of mothers with young children who work outside their homes has further contributed to the blurring of boundaries between day nurseries, nursery schools, kindergartens, and even some family day care homes. Many nursery schools now have extended-day programs to meet the needs of the middle-class working family. Similarly, many child care centers and family day care homes envision their roles as providing a preschool or kindergarten experience while providing care for children of working parents.

Perhaps nowhere does the controversy about services for young children emerge as clearly as in a discussion of what to call the child care practitioner. Is he or she a teacher or an educator? A babysitter or custodian? A professional? Some practitioners claim "day care" in their title and reject "teacher" in their efforts to demonstrate the wide range of services they perform for children.[2] Others prefer "teacher," assuming this title includes caregiving functions but offers higher social status. Other "teachers" are insulted by being expected to perform tasks that are not strictly educational in nature.

The U.S. Department of Labor's Dictionary of Occupational Titles reflects this confusion over titles and job descriptions for child care providers.[3] Child care workers "read aloud," "organize activities of prekindergarten children," "teach children simple painting, drawing, and songs," "direct children in eating, resting, and toileting," "maintain discipline," and "help children to remove outer garments." Prekindergarten teachers "plan group activities to stimulate learning," "instruct children in activities designed to promote social, physical, and intellectual growth," and "prepare children for primary school." The Dictionary notes that the use of the term "instruct" is restricted to preschool teachers, and descriptions of nonacademic responsibilities are reserved for child care workers.[4]

This debate about nomenclature reflects strong differences of opinion related to philosophical and functional dimensions of the services provided by child care workers. Depending on how the service is envisioned, different ideas about preparing practitioners emerge. For some, the informal route of female socialization is thought to provide adequate training for the work. For those who view the work as skilled and who assume an educational component in the service, a more formal route involving specialized education is recommended. Bachelor degrees in early childhood education, child development, or home economics are frequently required for head teachers in public centers and many nursery schools. More recently, two-year college certificates in early childhood-related fields have gained widespread acceptance as criteria for teaching jobs. Lying between the more formal educational route and the informal path is a third mode of occupational socialization, best embodied in the Child Development Associate (CDA) credential. The CDA is an on-the-job training and certification program now available to family day care providers as well as center workers.[5]

THE SIGNIFICANCE OF CHILD CARE WORK

Most seasoned child care consumers recognize that the quality of their children's child care hinges on the adults who provide the care. Too few adults for the number of children, too many changes in caregivers, and poorly trained or untrained staff are cause for concern. Parents often make such comments as "There didn't seem to be anything going on for the children," "I was worried that the provider couldn't handle an emergency," or "My child doesn't want to talk about her teacher."

Research lends support to parents' worries. Extensive empirical evidence has identified the skill, structure, and stability of staff in child care programs as primary ingredients of child care quality.[6] Positive cognitive, social, and emotional development in child care are directly attributable to adult caregivers who are trained in early childhood education or child development, who establish consistent attachments with the children in their care, and who are responsible for a manageable number of children.

State regulations, the sole source of quality monitoring in governing child care, have largely ignored these research findings. Twenty-eight states require neither prior experience in child care nor training in child development for family day care providers. Twenty-seven states have no education or training requirements for child care teachers prior to employment. Some states mandate continuing education or in-service training, but others require as few as three hours annually. Neither preservice education nor ongoing training is required of center staff in seven states.[7] Staff must only meet an age requirement (as low as sixteen years in some states) and have no criminal record. Consequently, some providers are far better equipped to plan appropriate programs for children and facilitate the efforts of other professionals concerned about individual children.

A DESCRIPTION OF CHILD CARE WORK

Regardless of how child care practitioners label themselves, what the public calls them, or what their occupational socialization has been, all partake to some extent of the low status, poor compensation, and stressful working conditions endemic to early childhood jobs.

For those with little direct experience with young children, child care work is considered unskilled. Because young children spend much of their time playing, it is assumed that the adults in their midst function in a similar carefree manner. And because the work of caring for children has long been performed by women without pay, it is regarded as something natural and unlearned, an outgrowth of female nurturing, rather than skilled work that requires training and deserves adequate compensation.

A wide range of skills is required to perform the diverse functions involved in caring for young children. The image of a jack-of-all-trades replaces that of the unskilled babysitter. An examination of typical responsibilities included in job descriptions for center personnel sheds more light on the actual tasks child care providers perform: curriculum planning and implementation, parent contacts (meetings and conferences), meal preparation, janitorial services, clerical tasks, administrative duties (budgeting, fund raising, and staff supervision), indoor/outdoor supervision of children, and staff meetings.[8] Listing responsibilities, however, gives only a partial picture of what caregivers actually do.

Consider curriculum planning and implementation. In order to perform these tasks, good caregivers must begin by assessing the children and the program environment. They must be keen observers of behavior and must be able to recognize appropriate and inappropriate responses for children of different ages. Additionally, they must have an understanding of the range of needs within the population of children under their care. Which activities are appropriate for facilitating the particular skills one is seeking to build? Of those activities, which will be most engaging for this particular group of children? Are there sufficient materials and staff to implement the planned activities? Additionally, caregivers must have alternate activities prepared in case of a weather change or another unpredictable occurrence. The time actually spent implementing curriculum constitutes only a small portion of the work; preparatory tasks consume a large part of the caregiver's day.[9]

Of course a caregiver's activities are not restricted to creating a rich environment for learning and development. Attending to the physical needs of children over the course of a long day also consumes a great deal of energy. And the younger the children, the more physically demanding the caregiving.[10]

Keeping the program financially afloat is a task that would tax the most experienced corporate executive. Although the burden of activity in this arena falls most heavily on the director or administrative staff, teachers and family day care providers may find themselves embroiled in budgeting, fund raising, purchasing insurance, seeking legal advice, or scrounging for goods and services in the local community.

Staff relations and management may pose the most serious challenges caregivers face. Some facility in training or supervising other adults is essential to effective communication with coworkers. Staff must also manage relationships with parents, which often involves intense feelings.[11]

Negotiating these myriad responsibilities requires flexibility and careful organization. The work of caring for children, like other household chores, is never done. One cannot prepare for a snack, help a child to sleep, comfort a distraught parent or coworker, or change wet clothes and assume that these chores can be permanently crossed off this week's "to do" list. Not only are these demands likely to be repeated frequently, but they are likely to compete with equally compelling pleas, perhaps in the midst of a carefully planned, not easily interrupted project—such as cooking corn bread with seven impatient four-year-olds. Although there are moments of calm during the day, they too are unpredictable.

Differences in caregiver experiences emerge, of course, depending on the setting, the ages of the children served, job responsibilities, and funding options. For example, the pace of a day with infants is quite different from one with older children. With babies, workers typically experience several slow times in a day, but seldom do all children rest simultaneously. Preschoolers, on the other hand, maintain high energy throughout the morning with little opportunity for breaks before the afternoon nap.

For center workers, one's role as aide, teacher, director, or support staff (cook, nurse, social worker, etc.) further shapes the caregiving experience. A San Francisco study found that aids, teachers, and teacher-directors all performed the same range of duties.[12] Job title reflected no differences in paid or unpaid time spent in curriculum planning and implementation, maintenance, and meal or snack preparation, but it did suggest differences in time spent communicating with parents and performing clerical or administrative chores. Similar results were obtained by Kontos and

Stremmel based on interviews with forty center-based staff in northeastern Pennsylvania. Regardless of job title, indoor/outdoor supervision of children and curriculum implementation were the most time-consuming tasks for all staff.[13] Directors and assistant directors were almost exclusively responsible for clerical, budget, and administrative duties. Daily parent communication was shared equally among all staff.

Job titles also indicate differences in power and control over major policy decisions and day-to-day decision making. In the Kontos and Stremmel study, for example, decision-making was almost exclusively reserved for directors.[14]

THE CHILD CARE WORK FORCE TODAY

Overall, it is estimated that the number of child care workers providing direct service to children lies between 2.8 and 3.4 million.[15] The number of child care workers grew by 13 percent between 1983 and 1985 alone. The most dramatic growth is among child care workers who work outside private home settings, increasing by 90 percent since 1972 and 43 percent since 1982. This child care work force remains predominantly female, with women comprising 95–99 percent of employees, compared to 44 percent in the total labor force.[16]

The available evidence on child care providers consists of three relatively independent literatures. One relies on survey methods to examine the demographic characteristics of child care workers, including their age and sex composition, their salaries, their preparation, and job turnover. The second, more empirical, literature examines the relationship of staff training and stability to child care quality.[17] The third, which examines job satisfaction among child care workers, is among the newest areas of child care research.

Demographic Characteristics of Child Care Providers

According to the national day care study (Coelen, Glantz, and Calore 1978), the 200,000 center-based child care workers in the United States in the mid-1970s were primarily female and under forty years of age. About one-third were ethnic minorities. In 1984, the Department of Labor reported 677,000 child care workers (excluding those who work in private households) and an additional 330,000 workers who define their employment as prekindergarten or kindergarten teacher.[18] Assuming these numbers are comparable, they indicate that the number of nonhousehold child care workers has tripled in the last decade.

The National Day Care Home Study described the family day care provider population ten years ago as predominantly female and 25–55 years of age.[19] About 60 percent were ethnic minorities. Interesting patterns emerged when the age, race, and site of the family day care providers were examined together. White women providing informal care outside the regulatory system were substantially younger (median age: 30.4 years) than any other group of providers (median age for total sample: 41.6 years). Most of these mothers chose to provide family day care during the early years of their own children's lives, and they tended to come from households with relatively high household incomes. Black and Hispanic caregivers, by contrast, were older and were typically not living in high income households. The modal annual income category for the total sample was $6,000. No comparable current data exist for family day care providers, but it is known that since 1977 there has been a 46 percent increase in the number of registered or licensed family day care homes.[20] In light of consistent growth in the demand for child care over the last decade (Hofferth and Phillips, 1987), it is likely that a similar growth pattern has occurred in unregulated family day care and other forms of home-based care such as baby sitting, thus further expanding the less visible child care work force.

A recent study by the National Committee on Pay Equity ranked child care teachers and providers as the second most underpaid workers in the nation (only the clergy earned less).[21] The earnings of child care workers fall below those of animal caretakers, bartenders, parking lot attendants, and amusement park workers (see Table 1).

In 1984, 58 percent of non-household child care workers earned poverty level wages, with median annual incomes of $9,204. The poverty level in 1984 for a four-person household was $10,610 a year (National Association for the Education of Young Children 1986b). By 1986, the median annual income of child care workers remained under $10,000, whereas the poverty level rose to $11,200.[22] For workers who care for children in private homes, the median annual income was $4,732 in 1986.

Although many believe these low wages typically supplement the higher earnings of spouses, this case is far from the truth. In 1977, 30 percent of center-based child care providers were the sole income earners for their families, and 70 percent provided more than half their families' income.[23]

These striking salary data are not solely attributable to lack of education or training among the child care work force. In 1977, family day care providers had, on the average, 11.3 years of education; the majority (57 percent had completed high school, and about 30 percent had received some post-secondary education. In 1977 center-based providers had, on the average, 14–15 years of formal education. Close to 30 percent had 16+ years of

TABLE 1

Earnings and Education of Child Care Workers Compared to Other Occupations

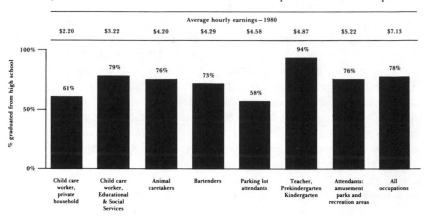

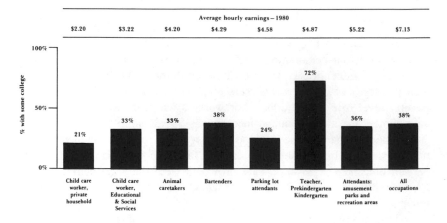

Source: *1980 Census of the population, Vol. 2*, subject reports, Earnings by Occupation and Education (May 1984). PC80-2-8B, U.S. Bureau of the Census.

education—twice the percentage among all employed females in the United States at that time.[24] Anecdotal evidence, however suggests that there has been a general decline in both the level and appropriateness of the training among child care workers in the 1980s.

Moreover, the low wages of child care workers are compounded by the unpaid overtime work that this profession entails. A majority of the workers in San Francisco study reported several unpaid hours spent each week in curriculum planning and preparation, staff meetings, parent contacts, and general center maintenance. Almost half received no compensation for these extra hours worked. Kontos and Stremmel found that center-based staff reported an average of 59.73 hours spent on center responsibilities per week, compared to their paid work weeks of 37 hours.[25] Only seven of the forty staff members were compensated for overtime. Annual wages, therefore, fail to reflect the true hourly wage of child care workers.

Low salaries are not offset by excellent benefits. Kontos and Stremmel report that 42.5 percent of the 40 percent of the center-based staff in their study had no medical insurance and 70 percent had no dental insurance.[26] Unpaid maternity leave was available to 45 percent of the sample. The majority of the staff (75 percent) received some paid vacation days, averaging nine days per year. Other state and local data from isolated staff surveys (National Association for the Education of Young Children 1986) reveal that the 42.5 percent estimate for no health care coverage is typical,[27] and further, that at most 20 percent of child care workers report participating in a retirement plan. Staff working in publicly funded centers are usually the highest paid child care workers in any community and those most likely to receive benefits.

With respect to job turnover, child care workers have among the highest turnover rates of any occupation tracked by the Department of Labor. The department estimates that 42 percent of all non-household child care workers and 59 percent of private household workers will need to be replaced each year between 1980 and 1990 just to maintain the current supply of child care providers. These rates, which may underestimate actual turnover rates according to studies done in several local communities reporting 60 percent turnover rates, are more than double the average replacement rate of 19.4 percent for all occupations.[28] Low pay, lack of benefits, and stressful working conditions are the major reasons child care workers leave their jobs in such high numbers.[29]

Staff turnover is an important source of inconsistent child care. Initial research suggests that caregiver stability is related to children's adjustment in child care.[30] In a similar vein, found that career-committed caregivers interacted with young children in more age-appropriate and stimulating ways than did caregivers who approached their work as a temporary job.[31]

This brief demographic profile of child care workers reveals remarkable growth in a work force that is predominantly female, receives very low wages and few benefits, despite levels of education that match national averages, and that exhibits extremely high turnover rates. The data on which this profile is based, however, are seriously flawed and outdated. The federal databases on child care workers are based on outmoded definitions of the child care work force, rely heavily of self-reported information, and fail to tabulate data to permit, for example, an examination of wages for workers with different levels of education or varying levels of experience.[32] The National Day Care Study and the National Day Care Home Study, the only other sources of national data on child care workers, were conducted ten years ago when the supply of child care was about half of what it is today. Despite the significance of this profession, we have, at best, only sketchy information about the adults who provide child care in this country.

EMPIRICAL STUDIES OF RELATIONS AMONG TRAINING, JOB SATISFACTION, AND CHILD CARE QUALITY

After an initial wave of child care research that compared children reared at home with those who attended child care centers, growing recognition of the wide diversity of child care environments prompted a new emphasis on studies of variation in child care quality and its effects on child development.[33] This second wave of child care research identified several staff-related factors as central ingredients of high quality child care: training, ratios, stability, and staff-child interaction.[34]

In a study conducted by Pettygrove, Howes and Whitebook, variations in costs related to staffing requirements were analyzed for twenty-five state-funded infant/toddler programs in California.[35] Programs with a larger share of their budget devoted to staff reported lower turnover rates and shorter delays in finding substitute and replacement staff. In 1986, Olenick analyzed quality reviews for sixteen state-funded preschool programs in California, and found that quality positively related to budget allocations for teacher salaries and benefits and negatively related to costs for supervisory personnel. These California studies found that the percentage of total budget spent on personnel—not the total cost of care—was related to quality and to staff turnover qualifications (*Child Care Employee News* 1987).[36]

In sum, characteristics of child care staff, particularly their child-related training, workload as assessed by staff-child ratios, stability and job commitment, and competence to engage in stimulating verbal interaction with children have been linked directly to the quality of care received by children and to children's healthy development in child care. The next question concerns factors that predict and promote these staff characteristics. Surprisingly, this issue is largely unexplored, despite its apparent significance.

JOB SATISFACTION AMONG CHILD CARE WORKERS

Although job satisfaction is among the most widely researched topics in psychology (Moos 1979), child care workers are only beginning to be studied in this context.[37] Yet the job turnover statistics for child care workers, combined with evidence that the training and commitment of this work force has major implications for the children in child care, has highlighted the need for research on factors that enhance job satisfaction in child care.

Anecdotal evidence suggests that low morale, stress, and job burnout are not uncommon among child care workers.[38] The same literature, however, suggests that these workers find the day-to-day challenges of their work highly satisfying. For example, the forty center-based staff studied by Kontos and Stremmel reported contact with children and coworker relations as the most satisfying aspects of the jobs.[39] The study also reported that wages and benefits were the most dissatisfying aspect. When asked to make recommendations for improving their jobs, about one-third of the staff cited reducing the child-staff ratios and one-fifth mentioned better pay and better administration. It is clear that job satisfaction in child care is a complex, multifaceted issue requiring multi-dimensional measurement.

Preliminary work in this area suggests that caregiver job satisfaction is related positively and significantly to such caregiver behaviors as encouragement, development of verbal skills, and age-appropriate instruction.[40] Alternatively, low levels of satisfaction are related to greater limit-setting and disparagement of children on the part of the caregivers. Berk's study also differentiated intrinsic (e.g. feelings of accomplishment) and extrinsic (e.g., pay, employee policies) sources of job satisfaction and found generally stronger links between extrinsic satisfaction and caregiver behavior. Finally, caregivers with higher levels of career commitment were found to be more educated, more satisfied with their work, show fewer restrictive encounters with children, and to place more emphasis than less committed caregivers on the development of children's verbal skills.[41]

A second empirical study of job satisfaction among child care workers yielded results that contradict those of Berk. Specifically, caregivers with higher levels of education were found to be less satisfied with their salaries and promotion opportunities. Length of time on the job also showed a negative relation to satisfaction with pay and promotion opportunities.

Kontos and Stremmel reported a nonsignificant correlation between staff job satisfaction and center quality assessed with the Early Childhood

Environment Rating Scale (Harms and Clifford 1980), although significant relations were found for two more refined measures.[42] High-quality centers had staff who reported receiving compensation for overtime work and who spent more time with curriculum planning than did low-quality centers. The lack of a relation between overall job satisfaction and quality may be attributable to the minimal variation in satisfaction yielded in this study. Most staff were satisfied with their jobs.

Although implying a link between job satisfaction, caregiver background, working conditions, and quality of care, this area of research is in its infancy. These initial results require replication and extension to other settings and to a more diverse sampling of providers. Studies of child care as an adult work environment need to develop more differentiated conceptions of job satisfaction and to relate worker perceptions to characteristics of the child care programs, to staff stress and career commitment, and to the development of children in child care. Staff-parent relations examined in the context of employment issues constitute additional unexplored territory.[44]

GAPS IN THE RESEARCH LITERATURE ON CHILD CARE STAFF

In addition to the problems of timeliness and reliability, the available data on child care staff are limited by three additional unaddressed issues. First, the three focuses of information on child care staff reviewed here have remained as largely independent paths of inquiry. Yet several of the most pressing issues concerning child care staff require that these literatures be interwoven into a single study. For example, how do the family structure and income of a child care staff interact with job satisfaction and commitment to child care work? How do caregiver characteristics interact with characteristics of program clientele? Do indicators of caregiver satisfaction vary reliably with other indicators of program quality such as ratios, group size, and quality of the physical environment?

Second, with the single exception of the National Day Care Study, the literature that includes caregiver measures within studies of child care quality have been restricted to single-site investigations, which fail to reflect national diversity in the child care market. This diversity becomes particularly significant in light of the large differences in state child care regulations pertaining to staff qualifications. Similarly, regional variation in economic conditions is also expected to affect the basic parameters of child care work, such as pay schedules, alternative job opportunities, and the financial means of the families who use child care.

Third, other than the flawed Department of Labor Data, no research addresses trends in the child care work force. Have the basic characteristics of this work force changed over the last decade? Have wages kept up with inflation? Have changes in the nature of the children in care, such as the growing number of infants, prompted higher salaries or greater demands for trained staff? A National Child Care Staffing Study currently in progress is returning to the cities examined in the National Day Care Study so that several of these important issues can begin to be addressed.[45]

POLICY IMPLICATIONS

Almost every news story about child care begins with statistics describing the rapidly expanding percentage of mothers in the work force. These figures conjure up a variety of images of women on the job—some with briefcase in hand, others wielding heavy equipment, and of course, clerical and factory workers, nurses, school teachers, and waitresses. Seldom imagined, however, are the child care providers who enable millions of women and men to balance, however precariously, the dual roles of worker and parent.

At this time of increasing demand for child care services, coupled with growing recognition of the developmental value of preschool education, the field of early childhood education faces a severe shortage of qualified, trained providers. Child care centers throughout the country report difficulty in recruiting and retaining adequately prepared staff. In many communities, extensive efforts to recruit family day care providers are underway (Lawrence 1987).[46] Without adequate numbers of providers, expansion of the child care supply is severely hampered. Programs either simply cannot be developed, or those that emerge are forced to hire inadequately trained or uncommitted personnel—both of which severely compromise the caliber of services. Recruitment and retention of multiple cohorts of untrained staff drain program budgets. Yet increases in salaries and benefits needed to attract and retain qualified staff generally require increased fees for families, many of whom already find child care costs unmanageable.

Several factors have converged to constrain the rapid growth of a qualified, stable work force of child care staff. First the rising demand for teachers in the elementary grades and recent efforts to enhance the salaries of public school teachers have created competitive pressures that place those seeking to recruit and retain child care staff at a distinct disadvantage. Given that starting salaries for a nine-month school position exceed twelve-month earnings for most child care teachers after years on the job, it is not surprising that early childhood teachers with bachelor's degrees and/ or credentials find public schools a relatively more attractive option.[47]

Second, decreasing interest in educational careers among college students and the declining size of the young adult population further aggravate the problem. And third, growing interest among young women in fields traditionally closed to females further limits the pool of potential applicants. The low pay in child care offers little economic incentive for people to pursue, let alone make a long-term commitment to, a child care career. Sadly, the better trained staff, however, are precisely those who are meeting the rising need for public school teachers.

To keep child care an attractive option entails substantially higher salaries and benefits, and thus higher costs to parents. Increased salaries also decreases the number of spaces supported by government dollars at current funding levels. Thus, efforts to rectify the child care staffing crisis are in direct conflict with the equally pressing need for affordable services for families.

The convergence of rising demand for child care and trends that appear to be eroding the child care work force has implications for each of the three primary issues identified with child care: supply, quality, and costs. As child care services continue to play a major role in the lives of growing numbers of American children, the question of who will care for them becomes increasingly important. As Young and Zigler point out: "When a family chooses day care, it is not buying a service that permits both parents to work, but rather it is purchasing an environment that influences the development of its child".[48] As the research evidence accumulates that caregivers with child-related training are indeed the backbone of quality environments for young children, it becomes imperative that mechanisms be developed to attract and retain qualified staff despite the economic implications.

With the cost of child care in some areas now as high as $4,000–$6,000 a year for just one child, it is easy for us to see why high-quality child care is beyond the financial capabilities of most American families. Unfortunately, there are those who will argue that the way to keep child care affordable and to respond to the shortage of child care teachers is to lower regulations and standards—standards that in some states already frighteningly inadequate.[49] The argument put forth is that with lower qualifications and higher adult to child ratios, child care programs will be able to hire fewer providers and pay them less to care for the same number of children. Thus the cost of child care can be held relatively steady.

But can we afford to use low standards as a means of containing costs? In raising the question of affordability we must not only ask what parents can afford to pay but also what will be the consequences for children if we continue to rely on teachers and providers to subsidize the cost of child care. What will be the short- and long-term effects on the education and development of children if they are cared for in programs with insufficient numbers of adults and in which the adults are not trained in early childhood development? Ultimately, what is the cost if children experience a constantly changing group of adult caregivers during their early years?

Others are looking for ways to balance parents' needs for affordable care with those of providers for fair and decent employment without compromising quality. Massachusetts allocated close to $10 million between 1985 and 1987 to raise day care salaries in publicly funded programs. When advocates realized that wage-upgrading efforts led to higher fees in centers for families who had not simultaneously received state-supported services, they fought and won funds for an affordability project to expand the economic range of families receiving subsidies.

In Toronto, Canada, government grants to centers for the sole purpose of raising salaries have been awarded annually for the last four years. These grants are explicitly intended to help programs attract and retain qualified workers without raising parent fees at a higher rate than the cost-of-living. The success of this program is evidenced by a recent decision by the Provincial government to assume responsibility for the grants program and to extend it to other communities. Day care workers holding an A.A. degree in non-profit centers in Toronto now average $17,200 a year, a several thousand dollar increase since the program began.

Senator Dodd (D: Connecticut) recently sponsored legislation to provide scholarships to employed providers pursuing the Child Development Associate (CDA) credential, a national on-the-job training program. Although this project doesn't increase salaries per se, it minimizes the drain of training costs from child care providers' meager incomes. Expanding eligibility to child care workers for college loan deferments, now available through both state and federal sources to students who pursue K12 teaching careers, would also constitute a potential incentive for young adults to enter the child care profession. Miller describes the various legislative efforts that are evolving and clarifies the role of government in child care.[50]

CONCLUSION

Because most families cannot afford to pay the real cost of child care, staff are expected to subsidize parent fees and accept salaries that are far below the value of the job they perform. Sadly, we are beginning to understand the consequences of this form of subsidy. By relying on early childhood professionals to keep the cost of child care affordable, we are running the risk of exhausting a valuable national resource—a resource that is critical to the future education and development of our young children. However, if we recognize the importance of giving our children the highest quality care and education in their earliest years, then we must value the people who are providing that care and compensate them accordingly.

As medical and mental health professionals establish working relationships with child care workers, the disparity between the actual value of this profession and its economic and social position will become readily evident. Perhaps some will join other advocates who are seeking reforms to enable child care to become an economically viable and socially respected career.

NOTES

* This chapter also appears in Shahla Chehrazi, ed., *Working, Parenting and Daycare*, American Psychiatric Press (in press).

1. M. Almy, "Day Care and Early Childhood Education," *Day care: Scientific and Social Policy Issues*, ed. E. Zigler and E. Gordon, (Boston, Auburn House, 1982); S. Scarr and R. A. Weinberg, "The Early Childhood Enterprise: Care and Education of the Young," *American Psychology* 41 (1986): 1140–1146.

2. L. Katz, *Teacher's developmental stages. Talks with teachers: Reflections on Early Childhood Education*, ed. L. Katz (Washington, D.C.: National Association for the Education of Young Children, 1977).

3. US Department of Labor, *Dictionary of Occupational Titles* 4th Ed. (Washington, D.C.: US Government Printing Office, 1977).

4. D. Phillips and M. Whitebook, "Who are the Child Care Workers? The Search for Answers," *Young Children* 41 (1986): 14–20.

5. E. Zigler and Freeman in *Working, Parenting and Daycare*, ed. Shahla Chehrazi (American Psychiatric Press, in press).

6. C. Howes, "Caregiver Behavior in Center and Family Day Care," *Applied Developmental Psychology* 57 (1986): 202–216; C. Howes and M. Olenick, "Family and Child Care Influences on Toddlers' Compliance," *Child Development* 57 (1986): 202–216; D. Phillips, *Quality in Child Care. What Does Research Tell Us? Research Monographs of the National Association for the Education of Young Children*, Vol 1 (Washington, D.C., 1987); D. Phillips, S. Scarr and K. McCartney, "Child Care Quality and Children's Social Development," *Developmental Psychology* 23 (1987): 537–543; R. Ruopp, J. Travers, F. Glantz, et al., *Children at the Center: Final Results of the National Day Care Study* (Cambridge, MA: ATB Associates, 1979).

7. G. Morgan, *The National State of Child Care Regulations 1986* (Washington D.C.: National Association for the Education of Young Children, in press.)

8. M. Whitebook, C. Howes, J. Friedman, et al., "Caring for Caregivers; Burnout in Child Care," *Current Topics in Early Childhood Education,* ed. L. Katz, vol. 4 (New York: Albex, 1982).

9. M. Almy, *The Early Childhood Educator at Work* (New York: McGraw-Hill 1975).

10. L. Katz, *Teacher's developmental stages. Talks with Teachers: Reflections on Early Childhood Education,* ed. L. Katz (Washington, D.C.: National Association for the Education of Young Children, 1977).

11. S. Kontos, and W. Wells, "Attitudes of Caregivers and the Daycare Experience of Families," *Early Childhood Research Quarter* 1 (1986): 47–67, D. Powell, *Toward a Sociological Perspective of Relations Between Parents and Child Care Programs. Advances in Early Education and Day Care,* ed. S. Kilmer, vol. 1 (CT: JAI Press, 1980).

12. M. Whitebook, C. Howes, J. Friedman, et al, "Caring for Caregivers: Burnout in Child Care," *Current Topics in Early Childhood Education.*

13. S. Kontos and A. J. Stremmel, "Caregivers' Perceptions of Working Conditions in a Childcare Environment," *Early Childhood Research Quarterly* (in press).

14. S. Kontos and A. J. Stremmel, "Caregivers' Perceptions of Working Conditions in a Childcare Environment."

15. National Association for the Education of Young Children, *The Child Care Boom. Growth in Licensed Children from 1977 to 1985* (Washington, D.C.: 1986b).

16. US Department of Labor. Bureau of Statistics, *Annual Report for 1984* (Washington, D.C., 1985).

17. C. Howes in *Working, Parenting and Daycare,* ed. Shahla Chehrazi (American Psychiatric Press, in press).

18. US Department of Labor. Bureau of Statistics, *Annual Report for 1984.*

19. S. Fosburg, *Family Day Care in the United States: Summary of Findings. Final Report of the National Day Care Home Study,* vol. 1 (Washington, D.C.: Department of Health and Human Services, 1980).

20. National Association for the Education of Young Children, *The Child Care Boom. Growth in Licensed Childcare from 1977 to 1985.*

21. National Committee on Pay Equity, *Pay Equity: An Issue of Race, Ethnicity and Sex* (Washington, D.C., 1987).

22. *Child Care Employee News* 1, 2, 3, (1987).

23. C. Coelen, F. Glantz, and F. Calore, *Day Care Centers in the United States: A National Profile 1976–1977* (Cambridge, MA: Abt Associates, 1978).

24. C. Coelen, F. Glantz, and F. Calore, *Day Care Centers in the United States: A National Profile 1976–1977.*

25. S. Kontos and A. J. Stremmel, "Caregivers' Perceptions of Working Conditions in a Childcare Environment."

26. S. Kontos and A. J. Stremmel, "Caregivers' Perceptions of Working Conditions in a Childcare Environment."

27. *Child Care Employee News,* 1, 2, 3, (1987); National Association for the Education of Young Children, *The Child Care Boom. Growth in Licensed Child Care from 1977 to 1985* (Washington, D.C., 1986b).

28. A. Eck, "New Occupational Separation Data Improve Estimates of Job Replacement Needs," *Monthly Labor Review* 107 (3), (1984): 3–10; *Child Care Employee News* 1, 2, 3, (1987).

29. S. Kontos and A. J. Stremmel, "Caregivers' Perceptions of Working Conditions in a Childcare Environment," *Early Childhood Research Quarterly* (in press); M. Whitebook, C. Howes, J. Friedman, et al., "Caring for Caregivers: Burn-out in Child Care," *Current Topics in Early Childhood Education,* ed. L. Katz, vol. 4 (New York: Abex, 1982).

30. E. Cummings, "Caregiver Stability and Day Care," *Developmental Psychology* (1980): 31–37.

31. L. Berk, "Relationships of Educational Attainments, Child Oriented Attitudes, Job Satisfaction, and Career Commitment to Caregiver Behavior Toward Children," *Child Care Quarterly* 14 (1985): 103–129.

32. D. Phillips and M. Whitebook, "Who are the child care workers? The Search for Answers."

33. J. Belsky, "Two Waves of Day Care Research. Developmental Effects and Conditions of Quality," *The Child and the Day Care Setting,* ed. R. C. Anslie, (New York: Praeger, 1984), pp. 1–34.

34. C. Howes in *Working, Parenting and Day care,* ed. Shahla Chehrazi (American Psychiatric Press, in press).

35. W. Pettygrove, C. Howes, and M. Whitebook, "Cost and Quality of Child Care: Reality and Myth," *Child Care Information Exchange* (in press).

36. *Child Care Employee News* 1, 2, 3, (1987).

37. L. Berk, "Relationships of Educational Attainments, Child Oriented Attitudes, Job Satisfaction, and Career Commitment to Caregiver Behavior Toward Children,"; P. Jorde-Bloom, "Teacher-Job Satisfaction: a Framework for Analysis," *Early Childhood Research Quarterly* 1 (1986): 167–183.

38. M. Hyson, "Playing with Kids: Job Stress in Early Childhood Education," *Young Children* 37, 2, (1982): 25–31; P. Jorde, *Avoiding Burnout in Early Childhood Education* (Washington, D.C.: Acropol, 1982); S. Kontos and A. J. Stremmel, "Caregivers' Perceptions of Working Conditions in a Childcare Environment,"; M. Whitebook et al., "Caring for Caregivers: Burn-out in Child Care," *Current Topics in Early Childhood Education.*

39. S. Kontos and A. J. Stremmel, "Caregivers' Perceptions of Working Conditions in a Childcare Environment."

40. L. Berk, "Relationships of Educational Attainments, Child Oriented Attitudes, Job Satisfaction, and Career Commitment to Caregiver Behavior Toward Children".

41. L. Berk, "Relationships of Educational Attainments, Child Oriented Attitudes, Job Satisfaction, and Career Commitment to Caregiver Behavior Toward Children."

42. P. Jorde-Bloom, "Factors Influencing Overall Job Commitment and Facet Satisfaction in Early Childhood Work Environments," Paper presented at the meeting of the American Educational Research Association (Washington, D.C., 1987).

43. S. Kontos and A.J. Stremmel, "Caregivers' Perceptions of Working Conditions in a Childcare Environment."

44. S. Kontos and W. Wells, "Attitudes of Caregivers and the Daycare Experiences of Families," *Early Childhood Research Quarterly* 1 (1986): 46–67; D. Powell, *Toward a Sociological Perspective of Relations Between Parents and Child Care Programs. Advances in Early Education and Day Care,* ed. S. Kilmer, vol. 1, (CT: Jai Press, 1980).

45. M. Whitebook, D. Phillips, and C. Howes, *National Child Care Staffing Study,* (Berkeley, CA: Child Care Employee News, 1987).

46. M. Lawrence, *California Child Care Initiative, Year End Report* (San Francisco, CA: Resource and Referral Network, 1987).

47. M. Whitebook, "The Teacher Shortage: Professional Precipice," *Young Children* 41 (1986): 10–11.

48. K. T. Young and E. Zigler, "Infant and Toddler Day Care Regulations and Policy Implications," *Journal of Orthopsychiatry* 56 (1977): 43–55.

49. D. Phillips and E. Zigler, "The Checkered History of Federal Child Care Regulation. *Review of Research in Education,* ed. E. Rothkoph, vol. 14 (Washington, D.C.: American Educational Research Association, 1987); E. Zigler and Freeman in *Working, Parenting and Daycare.*

50. Miller in *Working, Parenting and Daycare,* ed. Shahla Chehrazi (American Psychiatric Press, in press).

WILLIAM AYERS

Chapter Three

*Teaching and Being: Connecting
Teachers' Accounts of Their Lives
with Classroom Practice*^{*}

Let me introduce you briefly to six teachers:

Anna is a teacher in an infant-toddler program. She has been a kindergarten teacher and a teacher in day care for twelve years. When her own
daughter was born, she decided to take two years away from work. From
her daughter she learned the importance of those first years in a child's
growth and development and, upon returning to work, she chose infant
care. Anna is well-known by parents and teachers in her community as an
outstanding teacher.

Chana is a group family day care provider. She began taking children
into her home while she was caring for her own two children and has carried
that work on even after her youngest son went on to elementary school several
years ago. Chana cares for twelve children with the help of two assistants.
Chana's day care home is exemplary and she is often asked to speak about
day care issues at community and professional gatherings. Chana has a
master's degree from Bank Street College of Education, and she is a leader
in the effort to obtain official recognition for group family day care.

Michele teaches in a pre-kindergarten program in a public elementary
school. She has three daughters, the eldest in college and the youngest in
kindergarten. Michele went to City College of New York, taught in day

care for ten years, and has taught in an innovative public school for three years. Her husband teaches in the same school and they share a commitment to urban, public education as well as a deep investment in a child-centered approach to teaching. Michele is widely recognized among her peers as an outstanding teacher.

JoAnne has worked in child care for over ten years as founder, director, and now collective member of JoAnne's Child Care Community. JoAnne is largely self-educated, having read widely and deeply in child development and early childhood education. The fact that she never attended college surprises colleagues and associates because of her broad knowledge of and huge reputation in the field. She often speaks at early childhood conferences, and was profiled in a national magazine for developing an exemplary non-sexist and non-racist program.

Darlene is the mother of four children, and is organizer and director of a unique and astonishing day care center for the children of homeless families. Darlene began teaching in day care in 1978, and has been director or head teacher in several settings. Besides teaching and parenting, Darlene is a graduate student in educational administration and special education. Darlene is well-known and highly regarded among early childhood professionals.

Maya teaches kindergarten in a school that was founded in the heady days of the progressive education movement. She is a mother and a grandmother; both roles she relishes. Maya has taught young children for over twenty years, and has also spent part of her time in recent years teaching teachers. Maya has been approached many times to move to adult education, but she resists, feeling that her best work is with youngsters. She balances her professional life, continuing to be a kindergarten teacher, and offering workshops and classes to other teachers throughout the year.

These are the main characters of a story I wrote recently about teachers and autobiography. Because of my training and the context of my work with these teachers, I should say these are the subjects of my study and, of course, that is true also. If I used those words, many readers would be comforted and reassured, while a few might be put off. In either case, we would share in a sense of familiarity, for the language of the social scientist, of the technician and the expert, is not only the common sense language of educational research, but increasingly the everyday language of our modern world.

My project was not, however, a study in the traditional sense, and the language of the report was not expert, not technical. What I attempted, rather, was an unfolding of life narratives and an opening of meaning in which teachers' voices became central. As these teachers examined the dailiness and the ordinariness of their lives with children, and as they looked backward and forward in an attempt to understand the present reality as a moment in an unfinished story, we identified themes and patterns together, and we began to get a clearer focus on the choices, conflicts, contradictions, tensions, dilemmas, and joys of their lives with children. The talk was everyday teacher talk, and so it was also value-talk and feeling-talk. It was talk of the ordinary and the mundane, and yet it was talk that was frequently eloquent, consistently thoughtful, and always infused with a sense of care and connection.

Some have criticized this inquiry for its seeming lack of scientific rigor. My brief response to the charge of being unscientific is to plead guilty. This work is not based on a positivistic model. It makes no claim to general rules nor to having great predictive value. There is no attempt to couch these words in the assumed bloodless objectivity of data-driven empiricism.

Rather, there is an attempt to recast the subjective experiences and the personal feelings of these teachers as valuable in their (as well as our) understanding of teaching. There is an embracing of the unique, the particular, the possible. There is a search (perhaps this is a better choice of word than "research" here, pointing as it does to the singular quest and the specific challenge) for detail, for the unique signature of each teacher. Looking back at the brief introductions, note what we have gained and what we have missed thus far. We know, for example, that JoAnne has no formal education, and that Chana has a master's degree from Bank Street College. We assume that JoAnne has no children. We could, if we chose, find out more information of this type: age, IQ, anything you like. We could search for patterns in these data, patterns that might define good teaching, for example, from the outside.

What we don't know yet, and precisely what this work aimed at, is the insider's perspective. What does any of this mean to these teachers themselves? What significance does it hold? What value does any of it have in their worlds? How does it impact their teaching? Clearly our introductions, each a sketch of objective information, are inadequate to answer these other kinds of questions. This initial information may pique our interest, and it may play a role in our growing understanding, but it is as forgettable as cocktail party conversation unless we find a way to go beyond, to pierce the veil of facts. If we want to discover things like meaning, value, significance, and context in our search for understanding, we must move into other areas and probe more deeply. We certainly must find a way to hear the teachers' voices.

I chose in this work to discover a lot about a few teachers, rather than a little about a lot of teachers. Instead of aggregating teachers in order to research the common teacher, the point here was to celebrate the particular, the uncommon, and the unpredictable. This choice was based on a strong belief that it is in the lived situations of actual teachers and children—

rather than in, for example, the educational commissions, policy panels, or research institutions—that the teaching enterprise exists and can best be understood. This requires seeing the reality of teaching and teachers in as full a context as possible. The "secret" of teaching after all is in the detail of everyday practice, the very stuff that is washed away in attempts to generalize about teaching. The goal here was not to predict, but perhaps to extend our sense of the possible by portraying some of the breadth and scope of what preschool teaching can be. We do not, of course, end up with truth, but perhaps more modestly with a burgeoning sense of meaning and knowing grounded in real people and concrete practices. I aimed at understanding, not explanation.

Since reform proposals, curriculum units, and administrative directives ultimately live or die in the hands of individual teachers, it is to individual teachers that we must ultimately turn if we are to understand teaching. It is true, of course, that no teacher is an island, none is a perfectly free agent. Teachers are shaped by powerful social and economic forces, forces that coerce and constrain, prod and bombard, push and pull. Teachers particularly are formed by their relationships to power and their role in a bureaucracy geared to reproducing the social relations of society.

But it is also true that teachers finally decide what goes on in classrooms. When the door is closed and the noise from outside and inside has settled, a teacher chooses. She can decide to satisfy distant demands or not, accommodate established expectations or not, embrace her narrowest self-interest or not. She can decide whether to merely survive another day of inexhaustible demands and limited energy or she can decide, for example, to interpret and invent, resist and rebel. She can decide to link up with others and create something different. There are all kinds of ways to choose, all kinds of ways for people to invent their teaching in a world that is often resistant and always problematic, and in this work I saw six ways in vivid detail.

So, while we note that powerful forces in society have serious and intricate designs on schools, we also acknowledge that any designs must finally be filtered through the minds and the hearts and the hands of teachers and students. And, while teachers may be cajoled or fooled or, as in these times, threatened or punished into accepting and implementing certain practices, they also might not. In looking at teachers we are looking at the base of the educational pyramid (and in looking at preschool teachers we are at the lower end of the bottom). Ironically, if we look closely enough, we are also looking at the peak of power and possibility.

I tried to look closely enough, working simultaneously to construct ethnographic and autobiographical texts. I felt that by observing these teachers and then asking them to help me better understand some of the detail of their work—both phenomenologically and from the perspective of historical precedent—we could construct honest and textured portraits of teachers. This kind of exercise, I thought, had the potential to become a powerful tool in teacher education as well as teacher renewal. In creating self-portraits, I thought teachers would become more self-aware, more self-conscious. In becoming more self-conscious, I figured, teachers could also become more intentional, freer, more able to endorse or reject aspects of their own teaching that they found hopeful or contrary, more able to author their own teaching scripts.

Part of the time I functioned as a participant observer, collecting detailed notes, mapping spaces, diagramming and describing each teacher in the context of a specific setting, and attempting to move from broad to more focused and selected accounts of practice. The participation and observations were guided by my own intuition and experience as an early childhood teacher, as well as those things these teachers and their children brought to my attention. Observations focused on the structures and routines of each setting, the interactions among the children as well as between the adults and the children, the actions of the teacher, the explicit and implicit goals of each program, and the feeling-tone of each group. Part of the time I was an interviewer, and interviews tended to be informal, open-ended situations. My goal was to develop a meaningful narrative text that described and linked together influences, events, people, and experiences that contributed to the creation of the teacher as she finds herself today. Probing the significance of current activity and reconstructing a meaningful past created the conditions for each teacher, speaking in her own voice, to critically examine teaching practices and locate them in a continuum from past to future. What emerged was a kind of autobiography, although the word "autobiography" seemed too heavy, too loaded with earth-shaking expectations for all of us. My work was "co-biography" in an attempt to highlight the collaborative aspect of this project, but that word seemed awkward and unreal too. "Life-narratives" was the handy and unanimous usage for what we were constructing, and it was the life-narratives combined with the ethnographic accounts that emerged as the portraits of preschool teachers.

The most interesting area of inquiry was the use of "non-linear" or "interpretive" activities.[1] Focused interpretive activities explore the same ground as interviews or questionnaires or vignettes but without the heavy reliance on speaking or writing. They involve working with familiar materials (paper, clay, and paint, for example) to represent or symbolize salient experiences. Interpretive activities can disengage people from conscious thought and provide insight and significant discoveries. One interpretive activity that I used, for example, involved teachers using clay to depict

particularly successful moments in teaching. This is not unlike being asked
in an interview to describe a successful moment in teaching, but it offers
the possibility of opening to this question in new and surprising ways, of
disengaging intellectually and discovering a different pathway to meaning.
An example of a non-linear activity that many people engage in spontane-
ously is doodling, and an interesting case of doodling providing a turning
point in an autobiographical project is offered by Alex Haley describing his
work on *The Autobiography of Malcolm X*.[2] Malcolm X had wanted his
autobiography to be a classic conversion model, the testament of a saved
person, and so he refused to talk about anything of a personal nature and
offered only the most formal statements about his life. Haley felt that this
refusal was disastrous as far as writing a meaningful narrative was concerned. He noticed, however, that as Malcolm X spoke, he often doodled
on napkins. Haley took to collecting and reading the napkins, and eventually even to providing Malcolm X with blank paper and pens. It was from
the "private utterances of the napkins" that Haley formulated the first
probing, personal questions that began Malcolm X's powerful telling of his
social and political goals in the context of his own life-situation.[3]

In interviews, vignettes, and interpretive activities, the goal was to
build up a store of reflective information about practice and background, to
develop the beginnings of a thoughtful narrative. While the effort ranged
widely, I eventually grouped questions for convenience into three broad areas of concern:

1. The Reflective Practitioner.

What do you like most about teaching? What are the rewards for you?
When do you feel best as a teacher? What are your favorite moments?

What is most difficult about teaching? Do you ever feel like leaving?
Why? Why do you stay? If you could, what things would you change in
your work?

Which children appeal to you? Why? Which ones make your work problematic?

What is the role of parents in your work? What is your role in the lives
of children and families?

What should it be? Why is your space arranged the way it is? Why do
you follow particular routines?

Why do you teach as you do? What criteria do you have in mind? What
do you take to be valuable in your teaching? What other teachers do you

admire? Why? What are your goals for children? How do you meet these goals?

2. The Autobiographer.

When did you decide to become a teacher? What did your decision mean to you at that time? What about teaching interested or attracted you?

What role, explicitly or implicitly, did your family play in your decision to teach? Do you remember any early experiences that affected your decision to teach?

Do you remember any outstanding teachers from your years as a student? What do you remember? Did this influence your decision in any way?

What was your formal teacher education like? Did it prepare you for the realities of teaching? Is teaching pretty much what you'd expected? When you first taught, were there any colleagues or mentors who influenced you? How?

Can you remember when you felt comfortable as a teacher, confident with your own philosophy and practical knowledge?

Can you think of early experiences that continue to influence what and how you teach now? Can you describe the central teaching ideas that guide your work and how you came to adopt them?

Are you sometimes surprised to see what you have become?

Have you changed as a teacher over the years? How?

3. The Whole Person.

What is of value to you beyond teaching? Are you involved in any social or political groups?

What concerns you most about children and families today? About the state of society or the world?

Are there any conflicts between your goals for children and the school's goals? Society's goals? If so, do the conflicts affect the children? How?

Are you involved in any other projects or interests outside of teaching? What? How are they important to you?

What have you read recently that was significant to you?

What do you imagine you'll be doing in five years? In ten years?

We were all, of course, looking at an enterprise that is complex, idio-syncratic, and largely mysterious, something David Denton describes as a "world of intentional action, individuated and shared meanings, affectional ties, tensive relationships, in which there is always the possibility of one's saying no".[4] We were looking at people who are assumed to be moral, self-determining agents even as they are entangled and constrained by a host of pressures and factors. And we were looking at people's lives—not categories or summaries—being lived in a shared world. We were attempting to hear teachers' voices, to attend to teachers' stories with care and hope.

CHANA

Following is an excerpt from a portrait of Chana:

Chana is a group family day care provider. "Don't call me a teacher," she insists. "I run a group family day care home. People who say they 'teach' kids eighteen months to four years old are doing something I don't do. I don't have a credential and I don't identify with it. I could teach, and believe me, life would be easier, but then I would have abandoned something I've fought for years." I continue to use the word "teacher" occa-sionally, but I mean it in the broadest sense of someone who engages whole people—mind, body, emotion, culture, spirit—in learning. But each time I say "teacher" in her presence, I am immediately corrected.

Her apartment is not only home for her, her husband, and their two sons, it is also the home-away-from-home for seventeen toddlers who attend on a complexly staggered schedule. The apartment reflects both realities: a large and comfortable home with a lovely old breakfront, a grand piano, crowded bookshelves, and walls adorned with paintings, pictures, and family photographs including ancient relatives and cousins in Israel; and a well-organized day care center with changing table and potty chairs, step-stools and booster seats, art materials, and manipulatives. Except for Chana's bedroom which is off limits and behind the only closed door in the apart-ment, the entire space flip-flops every day and serves two complementary but very different needs. On one visit her younger son was home from school with the flu, and so he was in his parents' room. He slept and read and played quietly. Daniel, eight years old, had been part of the day care as a toddler himself, and now seems to take the constraints of the toddler in-vasion in stride: "I keep my stuff put away and it's not a big deal. If there's a big mess I don't like it, but it's usually ok."

"I was born in Philadelphia," Chana says, "and raised in a Jewish neighborhood after the war. It was a striving, middle-class environment with clean, new schools. Everyone I saw was rising together, and everyone

I knew was very much alike. By junior high school and high school there were always so many of us and we were the smartest and belonged to all the clubs so that I never felt outside of anything. I can see the problems and limitations of that life now. But it was at that time a safe harbor for me—a place from which to grow up with confidence and feeling.''

Characteristically, as soon as Chana reads this her objections begin. ''I guess I am uncomfortable with the beginning of this portrait because we devote so few words to a whole community's experiences. It make my view seem trivial.'' She is a substantial woman, combining elements in equal measure that would seem contradictory in another person: she is opinionated and open, caring and demanding, understanding and convinced. She is also self-assured, dependable and unequivocal. ''I am not wispy. I am not airy,'' she says by way of self-description. ''I met a Torah Scribe recently who told about his craft and taught calligraphy to teachers in Jewish schools. Many of us did not have Hebrew names—especially those of us born before Israel existed. We came from a shtetl tradition with Yiddish names. I was asked for my name in preparing forms for my son's Bar Mitzvah. The Torah Scribe had a list and told me Chana Matanah is my Hebrew name. I like it.'' Chana Matanah means gift and Chana is a solid and undivided gift.

Chana and her sister were raised in an old-fashioned extended family. Her mother started working during the war, and her father was often away on business. ''In a sense my grandmother raised me, and she was a wonderful mother. On top of that I had an aunt who looked exactly like my mother (her identical twin) and her husband, and my mother's brother—and all of us living under one roof.'' It was a nurturing set of people for a child to have, and that felt good. ''The daily separations from my mother were so early in my life and so natural that I'm not sure we felt them as separations at all. We all lived together and lots of people were in charge of me. I wasn't bundled and dropped. No vital toys or bottles were left behind. All objects stayed the same. No guilt. No conflicts that I can remember. When we moved to our own house, the first thing I learned to do was to take the bus to grandma's. My grandfather was ill and a shut-in, and I spent my weekends with them.'' Her most powerful early memories involve time with her grandfather—making ice cream in a freezing tray, drinking tea with lots of milk and sugar, collecting pictures of automobiles from magazines and the faces of movie stars that came as a promotion in the bread they bought; and her grandmother—singing Russian songs, organizing efforts for the ILGWU, helping to sort her piece work and collect tickets for ''a partial,'' the partial unemployment benefits available to part-time workers.

Chana's parents had a small accounting firm and her mother had an office in the house. Now there is a small crack in the almost perfect picture just described. Chana remembers that her sister complained about the family business because there was a sense of their mother divided and preoccupied. There was often something to do in the office, and their mother would go there after dinner or on Sundays. There were clients coming and going in the evenings. Chana says that she and her sister grew up respecting their parents' involvement in the community, an involvement that sometimes drew them away. And they had their child's complaint: "We thought if she had a regular job then when she was home she would be completely there for us. It's a laugh to me now, because I sometimes think my own kids experience a similar problem with my work. They must sometimes think that if I had a real job at least I could call in sick or take vacation once in a while."

Today Chana's building is solid, the lobby spacious and clean with mirrors and ornament tiles, the elevators speedy and efficient. It is not difficult to find Chana's apartment on the sixth floor: the visitor simply follows the sounds of childrens' voices and laughter and tears around a corner and down the end of a corridor where there is a parking lot of carriages and strollers. "The neighbors put up with a lot," Chana admits sympathetically. "And they say encouraging things to me all the time." The building and the neighborhood are traditionally German-Jewish. There are many older people. "They all seem to like the kids." she says.

On the door to apartment 6C is a cardboard sign with a plastic cylinder taped to it and in large letters a message: "No-choke testing tube—a simple test for safety—$1.00." Next to the sign is a clipboard with note saying, "We are going to the nursing home this morning." Inside the door is a closet and a short corridor leading to the dining room. Along the length of the corridor is a bulletin board for parents, and directly below and parallel to it a long mirror at knee level (toddler eye-level). The bulletin board is busy with information for parents: an article entitled "12 Alternatives to Whacking Your Kid," a list of neighborhood social services, a pamphlet called "What You Can Do to Stop Disease in Your Child's Day Care Center," an envelope of voter registrations forms, a xeroxed page with a large heading "HEAD LICE," an information sheet about library programs, an advertisement for automobile restraints, a pamphlet about a parenting center run out of the Y, an article about reading to your young child, a notice about children's television, and an envelope of notes concerning frequent activities or announcements for use when appropriate on the front door, for example, "We are planting today." "Painting with Florence." "In the playground." "Movement today with Joanne." "Welcome back." "We need paper." "Music today with Toby."

Opposite the mirror and down into the dining room a bit is a low, long set of pegs for coats and hats. Under each peg rests a cardboard square for boots or shoes with a set of silhouetted feet cut from colorful, patterned paper, and a child's name pasted to each. The dining room table is covered with plastic, and on top of the plastic is a pile of construction paper, some magic markers, several rolls of brightly colored tape, and three varieties of age-appropriate scissors: the classic small, dull round-nosed type, a space-age spring-action set to be gripped as if shaking hands, and an ingenious pair with small finger holes for a young child snuggled beneath large finger holes for an adult hand.

"Oh, it's hard to wait," Chana empathizes with Oren who is spinning anxiously in his seat while another child chooses which tape to use. Two children are working busily, seated on booster chairs. Oren doesn't want a booster and he's shifting this way and that in the grown-up dining room chair. "Here, Oren, it's your turn. I'm going to turn you around so you're more comfortable. If you don't want a booster then move around here on your knees so you can reach the table." Oren begins to cut tape and stick it gleefully on the paper.

The dining room is the central room and off of it is a den, the kitchen, the living room, and a corridor leading to the bathroom and the bedrooms. The den is a beehive of early childhood energy and purpose. Iliusha is working on a puzzle with great animation. He is large and loud and he exclaims as he fits each piece together with bursts of heart and spit and great dramatic gestures accompanied by powerful Russian phrases. Two children are going on a make-believe shopping trip with little red and yellow plastic shopping cards piled with dolls and stuffed animals. One child has a hat on and a jangling row of bracelets up one arm. "We're going to the supermarket," she says, "I'm the super-mommy and you're the super-daddy."

In the kitchen JoAnne, one of Chana's assistants, oversees the making of apple crisp for a special snack. Three children on booster chairs are pulled up to the long kitchen table and are cutting apples like mad into all imaginable shapes and sizes from massive chunks to tiny slivers. A lot of apple makes it into a large mixing bowl, and a lot is eaten by the cooks themselves. JoAnne talks about the recipe and how they will proceed as she works alongside the children. She doesn't mind their eating, but she reminds the children several times not to put the dull plastic knives into their mouths. "Serious cooks don't put knives in their mouths." The children nod and chop and chew.

The bell sounds and JoAnne answers the intercom and then buzzes in a new arrival. In a few minutes Gina bursts through the door followed by her mother. Gina is two, bundled in coat and scarf and hat with just a bit of round face and sparkling eyes peeking out. Chana greets them and kneels down alongside to chat as Gina's mother unbundles her, revealing a sturdy, smiling girl. After a trip to the bathroom and some last instructions, Gina's mom is ready to leave. Chana lifts Gina up for a last hug and then tries to interest her in an activity in the den. Gina is comfortable in Chana's arms, her body and face relaxed, but she insists, "One more hug!" and Chana easily agrees. Gina suggests they walk mommy to the door, and they do. Chana proposes they go in now, but Gina wants to walk mommy to the elevator. Chana goes along and they say goodbye again. Chana now asks, "Do you want to wave from the window?" and Gina does. So they wait a minute and then open the hall window and Gina stands on the sill holding onto the child protection gate and yells goodbye. "The kids love it, and I only worry about the neighbors when the kids dance on the radiator too enthusiastically and make too much noise." From six floors below Gina's mother waves and blows kisses and Gina laughs and jumps down, heading eagerly back to Chana's.

Just as Gina joins the cooking crew Carolyn arrives. She only comes two mornings a week and she is not really settled in on this day when her mother hurries off. Chana holds her and rocks her but she sobs and sobs. "I want mommy." Soon her face is puffy and red and dripping. Chana, wiping nose and eyes, rocks her and softly chants, "Mommies go away, and mommies come back; Mommies go away, and mommies come back." The sobbing recedes a bit, and then returns full force. "I want her. I want her." Chana comforts and affirms. "You want your mommy," she says softly. "Mommy will come back after lunch. Mommy's working."

"No, she's not working."

"Well, she's working on something. Remember she told you she'd be back after lunch and she told me to take good care of you and to check your Pamper and to put Desitin on your rash? Let's check it now." Chana's soothing chant becomes a kind of mantra.

(Later, when reading this, Chana commented, "It's all true, but me? A mantra? Cute.")

After a time Chana moves into the den and pulls a large shoe box from a shelf. In it are well-handled, contact-covered photographs of mommy and daddys, grandmas and grandpas, dogs, friends and vacations, and happy Chana-care moments like trips to the playground and the nursing home. She finds Carolyn's pictures and they look at them together. A couple of other children clamber onto the couch and sort through the pictures finding their own photographs. Soon photographs are strewn in all directions and Carolyn has found one that she clutches tightly to her stomach.

Chana moves Carolyn off her lap for the first time and gets down an audio tape from another shelf and puts it into the tape player. The tape is Carolyn's mommy reading a favorite book. Carolyn listens for a time and then cries a bit more. "I can't hear." Sarah complains. "Well," Chana responds gently, "She's having a personal cry, and it's hard for her to do it quietly."

Chana lies on her side on the floor with a box of small letter blocks. "Which block would Mommy like?"

"She likes both," Carolyn says seriously. It is the first authentic response of the morning, a real answer, engaged and thoughtful. Chana sets her to building a pile of blocks that Mommy would like. She works methodically, but she is still low-keyed and without enthusiasm. Her language begins to blossom some: "I need this one. I like this." But she is not yet herself.

"Separation is the curriculum," Chana explains later. "It's the whole program. And I think it's the central issue in child care. I'm very explicit about it with parents and with other providers. When parents come and see my home, it looks like such a wonderful place to visit, so many interesting things for kids to do, so inviting. And for parents who are anxious about academics they see the letterboard for example, right away, even though I thing it's stuck way off in the other room. They see the pre-school experience that they think will get their kid ready to read. But I'm very clear. I'm not promising anything. They're not going to read; they probably won't know their letters by the time they leave me. 'But she's so bright!' They're all bright. Fine. All I commit to, and what I work on, is that a child will feel okay here without her parents, that she'll be able to acknowledge the difficulties and still participate fully in life here. That's the whole program."

When Chana interviews parents she describes why separation is such a critical issue for young children. She discusses the tension between connectedness and autonomy and she gives them materials to read. "We expect more than a change of clothes from parents," Chana says. "We want parents to be prepared to spend enough time here in the beginning to allow the child to feel comfortable, we want photographs and tapes from home, we want to create a comfortable bridge for kids. We do home visits and we go with small groups of kids to visit each home during the year. Of course, people interpret it differently. Some people do it in the way we had hoped they would, others say, 'But I have to be some place at 10 o'clock and I hope my kid isn't one who needs more time!' We have to live with that. There's bound to be a tension between what would be ideal and the realities of people's lives. Anyone who can spend the kind of time we would like working on separation until it is really comfortable for everyone is certainly privileged."

The audio tapes of parents and grandparents talking and reading favorite stories is inventive. There are two tape players, and children can listen in two rooms. "It's something I had done with my own kids," Chana explains. "But in a different way. My in-laws live far away and so I asked them to make tapes for my kids. I saw that it was meaningful to them, even to laugh at grandpa's accent, at his mispronunciations. My kids know 'Frog and Toad' backwards and forwards, and when grandpa says 'Frog and Todd' we can listen and laugh and also have a pleasant memory. I also miss my own grandfather, and when I recommend that parents tape grandparents reading and talking I think about what a treasure it will be.''

Chana first used tapes in her teaching when she began to get children whose first language was not English. These children were having the same separation difficulties as everyone else, but they were compounded by being unable to communicate in English with some important adults. ''I asked these parents for tapes, and I got 'The Carrot Seed' in Nepali and 'Goodnight Moon' in Serbo-Croatian, and I thought, 'This is great!' They were a comfort. It was an easy step from there to using that with all kids.''

There are a lot of non-working telephones for the children and they play a lot at calling mommy and telling her what they need. ''Kids use them because their parents use them and the telephone is a meaningful instrument in today's life,'' Chana explains. ''We also tell parents who can stay in the beginning to go out for an hour and then call to check in. When they call, if all is well they're so relieved and they don't want to talk because that could be upsetting. I usually say, 'Look, if it's upsetting, let's let her get it out. Why should she have to hold herself together?' I mean it's like the parents who try to distract the kid in the morning and then sneak out. I'm against that. I think you need honest, reliable messages, and you need to allow for some honest upset. Some people are very much afraid of that crying. I think I'm pretty good at suffering the sadness and the let-down of separation, and then really enjoying the reunion, perhaps because my early separations weren't dreadful for me and I learned in my own extended family to trust separation. In any case I'm not torn up about separation questions and in a sense that makes me the perfect person for what I do.''

Chana remembers a powerful separation from her own life. Her grandfather was housebound, then bound to one floor, one room, and one chair. ''As his world constricted, the TV, radio, telephone, and newspapers became his connectors,'' she says. ''I always thought he was the smartest man in the world. Now as I am writing I realize that he was no intellectual. He never had books brought in, didn't subscribe to magazines, and didn't express deep political commitments. Yet he seemed to me to be bright, exciting, interested in everything. He was interested in me and that's what makes me cry when I let myself remember him. He was sure I was the best—and so proud. His support was uncomplicated. His agenda was to spend as much time together as possible—and to enjoy it all we could. I think we watched the A's on TV. I am sure we heard the games on the radio. We listened to all the old-time radio stories—Suspense, Johnny Dollar, Henry Aldrich, Beulah, Amos and Andy. We listened to news and watched Dave Garroway. We discussed everything we saw. We ate candy and peanuts from a can and ice cream.'' When he died Chana felt a certain and deep loss, but she also felt prepared. Morning in the supportive circle of her family allowed her to see his death as a natural part of life, and allowed her own life to go on.

In a way this memory makes Chana feel sorry for her own children. "We are all so busy that no one is just for them—absolutely delighted in teaching and listening to them. How interesting that I remember hours on end of full and complete attention and today we scratch to find one hour per week. Could more be tolerated? Is my memory a distortion?"

Chana brings the conversation back to child care saying, "It is good child development practice to acknowledge the pain and loss of separation for both sides. We do that here easily and naturally. We use pictures, tapes, and telephone calls to help parent and child through the experience. Events of the day and photos are posted on the front door—to prepare, build links, remember and remind. Perhaps we reflect our own experiences in the special commitment we give to whatever part of good practice we really feel. In a sense I feel well prepared to share in easing separations. I am comfortable with tears, special transitional objects, and talking about anger and loss." Later, when asked to make an image of a successful moment in her teaching out of clay, Chana makes a small figure holding hands with two larger figures. "That's a child, Rachel in this case, and her mother and me making a bridge." Chana sometimes thinks of herself as a bridge for children, sometimes as a life raft for families.

Chana and JoAnne begin to change, toilet, and bundle up a group of children for the trip to the nursing home. They work steadily and purposefully, describing the trip, reminding kids of their visit last week, solving crises, overcoming obstacles, and in twenty minutes the parade of double strollers and care givers and hand-holding walkers head out the door. In the elevator Carolyn remembers her mommy and begins to cry softly. "I want Mommy."

In the lobby several older people smile and nod, a few bend down to kooch the children in high-pitched sing-song voices. One woman asks Chana if she knows anyone who might be available to clean in her daughter's new kosher restaurant. Chana says she will keep it in mind and has her own request: "We're trying to collect blood for Harriet Eisner. She's at Einstein Hospital and needs B-negative. If you know anyone who can help, please call me."

On the street people smile, wave, and speak. One woman tells Chana she found a store in the neighborhood to get "sensible shoes." Chana thanks her. The nursing home is around the corner and so, for all the preparation and bundling up, the group arrives in four minutes. Through the front door the social worker, a middle-aged woman with large glasses and traditional wig and hat, greets the children with genuine enthusiasm. She speaks to each by name and helps unbundle them and put their things on a couch in her office on one wall of which are eight photographs of previous visits—children and old people sharing a snack, a conversation, or a song—with a large heading: "Chana's Toddler Care and Us." This relationship appears to have a mutual benefit and a shared importance.

The children know the way to the recreation area and several rush down a corridor through swinging double doors, past a waiting area with a forlorn traffic jam of wheelchairs and immobilized people waiting, and into the room with a table set up for them. Nine ancient women in wheelchairs are pulled up to the table as the children swirl in: Jesse is sleeping with her head tilted back, Lillian laughs and claps as the children arrive, Aileen begins talking to Josh who smiles every few words and says "no" without deterring Aileen in the least, Esther takes a child's hand and pats it lovingly. Chana greets each old woman by name, going from one to the other, touching each on the arm or the hand, asking about family. Fanny, regal but emaciated, looks up at her through thick bifocals and flashes yellow teeth through a worried smile. Chana introduces herself to Ethel, and Alexandra says, "She's new."

"What's new?" responds Ethel. "I'm old."

"Never mind," says Alexandra. "I'm here two years. It's OK. What are you going to do?"

Everyone shares a laugh.

The nursing home and toddler care staffs serve a snack of apples and oranges, toast with marmalade, and juice to the old and young people gathered around the table. As they eat, the staffs sing a name song called "Here We Are Together" in which each name is sung in turn. Several clap in time or sing bits of the song. After snack everyone shares paper and markers to make pictures together for one of the children's birthdays. Aileen encourages Daniel to keep the markers neat and in order, saying, "Keep it nice and together and they won't get lost." Daniel smiles as he works furiously on the paper, oblivious to her well-meaning advice. Carolyn remembers her mommy again and Chana picks her up, explaining to general sympathy that she is having a rough day missing her mommy. "We'll see Mommy right after lunch," she says to Carolyn.

CONCLUSION

In their outstanding study of contemporary American culture, *Habits of the Heart*, Robert Bellah and his colleagues make a penetrating observation about work:

> With the coming of large-scale industrial society it became more difficult to
> see work as a contribution to the whole and easier to view it as a segmented,

self-interested activity. But though the idea of a calling has become attenuated and the largely private "job" and "career" have taken its place, something of the notion of calling lingers on, not necessarily opposed to, but in addition to job and career. In a few economically marginal, but symbolically significant instances, we can still see what a calling is.[5]

Bellah's example of an economically marginal but symbolically significant worker happens to be a ballet dancer, but that description perfectly fits many fine teachers, including the preschool teachers of this autobiographical project. These teachers continue to find in their work a vital link between private and public worlds, between personal fulfillment and social responsibility. They bring to their work a sense of commitment, of connectedness to other people and to shared traditions, and of collective good will. They also seem to reject the calculation and contingency that pervades so much of work today, embodying instead a sense of work closely tied to a sense of self, a view that work is not merely what one does, but who one is. And they accomplish all of this as an act of affirmation in a social and cultural surround that devalues their contribution and rewards them sparingly.

In contrast to the dominant pattern of our society which defines "personality, achievement, and the purpose of human life in ways that leave the individual suspended in glorious, but terrifying isolation" we see in these outstanding teachers people whose work is "morally inseparable" from their lives, and whose social commitments are coherent with their private pursuits.[6] These teachers seem to have found ways to talk of values in an environment that constrains that talk, and to be public and political in a world that diminishes both.

These teachers seek an authentic meeting of subjects—a meeting that acknowledges the humanity, intentions, agendas, maps, dreams, desires, hopes, fears, loves, and pains of each—and in that meeting they model what they themselves value. Because they are aware of this, they work to make explicit, at least to themselves, their own values, priorities, and stories, because they know that these things will impact teaching practice. Being aware of oneself as the instrument of one's teaching, and aware of the story that makes one's life sensible allows for greater change and growth as well as greater intentionality in teaching choices.

Robert Bellah noted that "Finding oneself means, among other things, finding the story or narrative in terms of which one's life makes sense".[7] It is possible that a kind of steady, empathetic scrutiny can help in this sense-making, and can even improve teaching. There is no reason whatsoever that this kind of work needs to be the exclusive province of university-based researchers. This method could be adapted to action research projects, peer review, and teacher-run development projects. Teacher autobiographies can provide the kind of detail from which one can fruitfully interpret practice, value, and belief in light of an unfolding story. For teacher educators, researchers, and especially for teachers themselves who are seeking understanding and meaning in their work, this enterprise may provide a means of stretching their own contexts. A successful autobiographical method has positive implications for allowing greater questioning, critique, and intentionality.

Alice Walker's comment about her co-biographical projects among black women in Mississippi is applicable in a way to teachers:

> Slowly I am getting these stories together. Not for the public, but for the ladies who wrote them. Will seeing each other's lives make any of the past clearer to them? I don't know. I hope so. I hope contradictions will show, but also the faith and grace of a people under continuous pressures. So much of the satisfying work of life begins as an experiment; having learned this, no experiment is ever quite a failure.[8]

NOTES

1. F. Bolin, *Vocational Choice and the Realities of Teaching*, unpublished program outline for the Institute on Teaching, Teachers College, Columbia University, July 1986.

2. Malcolm X and Alex Haley, *The Autobiography of Malcolm X* (New York: Grove Press, 1965).

3. J. P. Eakin, "Malcolm X and the Limits of Autobiography," in *Autobiography: Essays Theoretical and Critical*, ed. J. Olney (Princeton: Princeton University Press, 1980), p. 191.

4. David Denton, *Existentialism and Phenomenology in Education* (New York: Teachers College Press, 1974), p. 108.

5. Robert N. Bellah, R. Madsen, W. N. Sullivan, A. Swidler, and S. M. Tipton, *Habits of the Heart* (New York: Harper and Row, 1985), p. 66.

6. Ibid., p. 6, p. 66.

7. Ibid., p. 81.

8. Alice Walker, "But yet and still the cotton gin kept on working," *The Black Scholar* 1, 3–4 (1970): pp. 13–17.

KELVIN L. SEIFERT and LAURA E. ATKINSON

Chapter Four

Does Home Hinder
Professional Commitment?
The Case of Early Education

This article considers the effect of gender on the balance between home and
school life among teachers of young children and examines how that balance influences the nature of teachers' professional commitment to teaching. The study on which this article is based accomplishes these goals by
observing three highly experienced kindergarten teachers, one male and
two female, and by relating the observations to ideas about professionalism
from the literature on women and work and on professionalism in teaching.

The case implied in the title of this article has a double sense. On the
one hand, it refers to early education in general, as an example of teaching
in general. On the other hand, and more modestly, the case refers to the
variety within this particular field of teaching, the variety within early education. In the latter sense, the title might be more accurate if plural: "The
Cases of Early Education." As will be seen, the balance(s) worked out by
individuals were both similar and different, both one and many.

FRAMEWORK FOR THE STUDY

Recent research on teaching has produced important insights into how
teachers themselves view their own work and careers.[1] This approach has

stimulated new appreciation for how gender, and especially female gender, affects individuals' views of teaching. More critical views of the effects of gender on teaching in the past[2] have given way to more sympathetic and positive views of women as teachers generally, and as teachers of young children in particular.[3] This has happened even though the *facts* about women have not changed much in the last twenty years. Women still comprise the majority of teachers, especially in elementary and early childhood education. And for various reasons, they still show marked tendencies to interrupt or limit their teaching careers. The interruptions are especially noticeable in early childhood education and actually characterize even the small minority of males who teach this age-group as well.[4]

But recent research on women and teaching no longer interprets these interruptions as automatic evidence of lack of commitment to teaching. On the contrary, they may signify positive efforts to integrate home with school and the personal with the professional. When studied case by case, female teachers with interrupted careers often express strong, internalized commitment to teaching, even at times when they happen *not* to be employed[5] as teachers.

But does this way of construing interruptions apply to men as well as to women? Earlier analyses of teachers portrayed male teachers as feeling trapped and female ones as lacking commitment.[6] Newer analyses have really revised only the female part of this equation. Little attempt has been made to compare male and female teachers directly, using revised ideas of professionalism from the scholarship on women in education.

The current study addresses this ambiguity by comparing how the competing demands of home and school were resolved in the life of three highly experienced kindergarten teachers, one male and two female. Using classroom observations and in-depth interviews, the study investigates these teachers' commitment to working with young children over the course of their teaching careers. In particular, it explores how pressures and expectations from personal life affected work life, and vice versa. The relationships between home and school, in turn, helped reveal the kind of professional commitment held by these teachers; or more precisely, they showed what the teachers meant by the notion of "professional commitment." When and how much did these teachers show intrinsic, internalized commitment to teaching, as found by Sari Biklen? To what extent did they still consider themselves teachers, even when not working in a classroom?

While shedding light on these issues for teaching in general, the study also illustrates how they are apt to be resolved in one especially female-dominated teaching field, early childhood education. In addition to the more frequent career interruptions, it is a field characterized by an even "flatter" career structure than is the norm, and by even lower public status. Viewed this way, early education poses the same problems faced by women in other areas of teaching—only more so. It also poses career challenges for those few men to enter it, because such individuals contradict the usual gender expectations about male careers and about male motivations. For these reasons, early education appeared to be a good occupation for testing and exploring the idea of internalized commitment.

METHODS AND DATA SOURCES

The Teachers

The study used three early childhood teachers—Randy, Louise, and Janice—each initially chosen for the following qualities:

1) each was highly experienced (ten years or more in teaching specifically in early education);
2) each had experienced an interruption to his or her work (minimum interruption—one year);
3) each made an articulate informant about his or her personal and professional history and about the circumstances of early childhood teaching;
4) the three represented both sexes.

Three individuals who met these criteria were found through word-of-mouth nominations. They were typical of teachers in their school district (on qualities one and two) but had higher educational attainments than most teachers (quality three). It is not clear, in retrospect, whether their above average level of education reflected a greater than usual commitment to teaching; but it probably helped make them articulate and therefore relatively skilled as research informants.

In spite of the commonalities just mentioned, the three teachers were distinctive in several ways. *Randy,* age forty-five at the time of the study had taught in kindergarten and/or nursery classrooms for twelve years. This made him one of the most experienced males in early education in the community. Prior to teaching young children, Randy had taught high school social studies and history for seven years, "until I got bored with it." He interrupted his teaching twice, each time for one year: first to get retraining as an early education teacher and later to open a small sporting goods store. At the time of the study, Randy had recently separated from his wife, was living with his teenage son, and had frequent visits from his teenage daughter.

Louise was forty-eight years old and had taught kindergarten and/or nursery school for twenty-five years. Early in her career, she interrupted her teaching because of a divorce; but at the time of the study, she had been teaching continuously for more than a decade. As sole breadwinner, she had an obvious economic "commitment" to teaching, though the study did not investigate whether her economic needs were any more compelling than the other two teachers'. She had one child, a son about to graduate from high school at the time of the study.

Janice was thirty-five years old and the youngest and least experienced of the three teachers. She had taught kindergarten and/or nursery school for ten years altogether, a period interrupted recently to bear a child (her first), who was two years old at the time of the study. She was married to another teacher, another one of the few men in the community who had actually taught kindergarten and nursery school for several years. As of the time of the study, however, her spouse had shifted to teaching in the upper elementary grades and was also taking a year off from classroom teaching in order to serve as the (paid) president of the local teachers' association.

The Schools

The schools employing these three teachers belong to the same administrative district, but they differed among themselves in the types of neighborhoods they served. Louise's school served a middle-to upper-middle-class, settled residential area. Janice's school served the opposite end of the spectrum economically: a low-income, inner-city neighborhood with many bilingual children and recently immigrated families. Randy's school fell between these extremes; but it was not so much lower-middle class as "mixed" or transitional in composition, serving both middle- and lower-income families who lived in close proximity.

The differences in the neighborhoods may have affected each teacher's relationships with parents and therefore how the teachers combined home and school responsibilities. Parents at Louise's school were the teachers' social and economic equals, or even betters. The reverse was true of parents at Janice's school. Parents at the "high-class" school may therefore have felt more able and entitled to seek contact with Louise, even after school hours. Parents at the "low-class" school may have felt inhibited socially; but perhaps more importantly, some of them may also have lacked English language skills, or worked night shift hours that prevented communication.

As discussed further below, these possibilities are consistent with the ways that Louise and Janice in particular described how they balanced home and school. But they remain only possibilities; the study did not directly explore how parents felt about their relationships with these teachers. It focused instead on how the teachers felt about these relationships and on how teachers reconciled them with other, home-related activities and relationships.

The Observations and Interviews

The teachers were observed with a combination of participant observation, open-ended interviews, and occasional telephone conversations. These tasks were shared by the authors of the study. One or the other observer visited a teacher for one or two hours per week. Visits occurred over a six-month period and averaged one per week, although they happened more frequently during the first half of the study than during the second half. Early visits emphasized classroom observations, but interviews and conversations dominated the meetings increasingly as time went on, eventually constituting the bulk of the contacts with each of the teachers. The conversations dwelled on three topics: how the teachers became interested in early education, how their motivation to teach changed over the years, and how at the time of the study they organized their personal and professional lives.

Most of these interviews took place during the lunch hour at the teachers' schools; but occasionally they happened at a local restaurant and on one occasion in a teacher's home. Data for the study, then, consisted of field notes from school visits, transcripts and notes of interviews, and field notes from lunch conversations. In all, about three hundred pages of information were accumulated about the teachers, representing about one hundred hours of contact time with them. When an interview was not taped, notes from the interview were rewritten and elaborated within a few hours after the interview. Quotations in these cases were approximations of the teachers' words, rather than exact reproductions.

As notes and interviews accumulated, both authors coded and classified them so as to reveal evidence about the balance of home and school and about the consequent nature of the teachers' commitment to early education. The method of constant comparison was used in this part of the analysis in order to arrive at sensible, valid categories within the body of data itself[7]. After first classifying the results in this way independently, each author then collaborated with the other to achieve a stable consensus for interpreting the results. As this consensus emerged, the results were also compared to other published literature on teachers' commitment to teaching.

RESULTS: RELATIONS OF HOME AND SCHOOL

For all three teachers, home affected work, and vice versa. The effects were both day-to-day and long-term, but the long-term ones were more obvious and significant to the teachers themselves. On the other hand, daily influences were more obvious or visible to us as authors, perhaps because our observations were themselves "daily," and not actually longitudinal or long-term.

The Daily Preoccupations

For Randy, home sometimes encroached on the day's teaching. During the first weeks of the study, particularly, Randy seemed distracted or preoccupied during parts of some class sessions.

> Randy began the morning by paying close attention to the craft table. In doing so he ignored the majority of the children, who were having "free play" in various other parts of the room. The "free play" children were considerably more active physically, more interactive, and full of conversation, compared to the craft table children. Presumably Randy was making sure that the craft table activity went smoothly; but in doing so he missed out on most of the social events for that part of the morning. (Week 2, pp. 6–7)[8]

As the semester went on, though, Randy became more consistently responsive to the children.

> Today Randy took the kids outdoors for free play. The children had a good time swinging, climbing, and sliding on the playground equipment. Randy looked cheerful throughout this time--meaning that he smiled frequently at things the children did or said. Once I heard him laugh heartily at something a child said; but the wind made it hard to make out the exact words. (Week 8, p. 62)

As time went on, Randy seemed more "psychologically present" and interactive with the children. These changes occurred even though his opinion about the value of oral interaction remained high throughout the weeks of the research project: from time to time, during interviews, he affirmed the importance of talking actively with the children. Yet he embodied this ideal less perfectly at the beginning, and more fully toward the end.

Major changes outside work help account for the changes in Randy's behavior. First, just before the beginning of the study, Randy had divorced from his wife. This event forced him to refinance his house, and to lose daily contact with one of his children (his teenage daughter), who had previously supported his commitment to early childhood teaching—"and she used to even visit my class," he said. Second, his son had recently been arrested for minor theft; Randy had even taken two days off from teaching early in the study in order to go to court about this problem. And third, early in the time of the study, Randy's (aging) mother sold her house and moved into a retirement home. As the geographically closest child, Randy was heavily involved after school in making the arrangements for this move. "I'm caught in the middle, as they say," he said, meaning that he had responsibilities for relatives both older and younger than himself.

For Louise as well, life outside of school often influenced her approach to daily teaching. When she felt hard-pressed, her classes would be less planned and she would draw on her preexisting, large store of ideas for materials and spontaneous, unplanned activities. One Monday morning, for example, she confessed to feeling exceptionally tired. Her weekend had been taken up with family and professional events: an all-day workshop on Saturday and a family gathering on Sunday involving her elderly mother and large extended family (Week 5, p. 15). Her class that morning seemed about as open or free as usual, and Louise responded to the children in her usual manner. She later said, though, that the structured circle time at the end of the session, involving a song and discussion about feelings, had been completely impromptu. On other, less tired days, Louise showed a great deal of preparation—preparation that made her extremely effective in dealing with the children most of the time and that presumably made her more able to cope with the times when she felt tired or preoccupied.

Compared to Randy and Louise, Janice approached teaching in a generally more structured way, and she therefore often found it hard to do all of the planning and preparation that she thought was necessary. She continued to struggle to plan thoroughly, though, because she said, "I wouldn't be able to live with myself if I didn't do it right" (Week 5, p. 24). She frequently talked about feeling hardpressed for time, especially after the birth of her first child.

> Janice said that before having a child, her marriage "had been much more egalitarian, and we each went our own way." Now, though, she cannot plan anything for an evening "unless I know way in advance." She finds herself with the majority of child care responsibilities, and says she feels tied down as a result. She can no longer go to workshops or meetings in the evening even if she wants to. She also says she resents having to rush home after work and take all her work with her. (Week 11, pp. 46–47)

Janice would have liked to stay late after school to arrange the room, plan activities, and organize materials, as she had done earlier in her career, before she had children. (Week 26, pp. 99–100). Although she seemed to have maintained high standards for her program, it was at the cost of constant time pressure and a sense of urgency. In Janice's (implicit) opinion, too much spillover usually occurred between her home life and school life, and she had to work at minimizing it. She took pains to guard and allocate time carefully: as the study progressed, for example, she became more strict about when she was willing to be interviewed and more cautious about the information she disclosed. Implicit in her efforts was a recognition of the power of Janice's job to "take over" her personal life.

Louise allowed the line between personal life and her job to become quite blurred. When she lacked time during the week, she often suggested that parents of her students call her on the weekend. She did not mind being "a neutral person that parents can talk to about family problems" (Week 5, p. 19). She reported shopping for school food and supplies at the same time that she did her own shopping; she said that she prepared school activities at home and invited former students over for dinner; and at night she consulted with her classroom aide on the telephone about current problems and activities from class.

The People in Both Realms

Louise regarded—or at least referred to—the parents of some of her former students as her personal friends. She frequently attended meetings with them, belonged to the same associations, and sometimes ran workshops for parents and other educators on her own time. She complained about these demands but usually accepted them cheerfully, recognizing that in most cases, they were self-imposed.

> She said that it was "part of doing her job" properly to be involved in teacher-support groups, community associations and professional organizations that were furthering the development of good early childhood education. Presumably she was aware that such involvement made her job invade her personal life and sometimes leaves her exhausted. But if she was aware, she did not say so directly. (Week 12, pp. 56–57)

All three teachers described particularly close friends they found through work, who served as confidantes and advisers on various topics, both personal and professional. Randy's school-based relationships were not numerous, but they were lasting and significant. They consisted primarily of two individuals: a female teacher, mentioned further below, and Mr. Gardner, the school's resource (or special education) teacher. Evidence of contact with Mr. Gardner was not hard to find:

> Part way through group time, Mr. Gardner (Randy's close friend) came in and whispered something in Randy's ear. While the children waited, Randy replied quietly, "I was at Hamilton (high school) this morning. It was interesting—I'll tell you about it more later." (Week 4, p. 26) Randy (to KS during interview): Richard Gardner is probably the closest friend I have at school. Last year we tried taking one other staff member with us to lunch every week. But eventually we stopped because having the others got in the way of talking. (Week 9, p. 66)

The selective, intense pattern of Randy's relationships contrasted markedly with the two women, who each reported broader, more extensive networks. Randy's intensive pattern probably also helped create an impression that home and work did not overlap, at least in his own mind, and perhaps also in the minds of casual acquaintances not in his inner circle.

> Q: How much work do you take home with you? Randy: I like it that with teaching, you can do most of your work at school. Having an aide helps with this, too. I don't think much about school at home. Maybe if a child is having trouble. (Week 4, p. 26)

In spite of this belief, though, Randy's actions did not suggest such a clean separation—as will be seen later in his comments about the links between family members and his motivation to enter teaching.

Both Janice and Louise made close and important friends in the early childhood professional community. The community was "almost incestuous," according to Janice, because "each time you meet a new person, you find out that they have connections to all kinds of other people you know" (Week 8, p. 39). The network included teachers, university and community figures, and consultants with various school districts. Friendships with members of these groups were particularly important for Janice and Louise at the beginning of their teaching careers. Each of them had been fortunate enough to find support and information from colleagues in their first teaching jobs (Week 26, pp. 97–98). Both of them were not teaching in schools where they felt isolated from networks of support. Louise actively sought out like-minded people and groups on her own time. Janice, perhaps because she had small children and could not get out as much, complained of being isolated from the network.

> "You don't realize," (she said,) "how valuable it is until it's not there any more. I feel as if I'm running the whole thing on my own. I still want to do it right, but who else even cares?! No one else in the school really knows what I'm doing. I don't blame them. They don't have time. And I guess I don't care what they're doing in Grade 6." (Week 6, pp. 44–45)

Career Directions and Personal Directions: The Long Term

In the consciousness of the teachers, home and school influenced each other more over the long term than over the short term. For all three individuals, for example, levels of commitment to early education depended in various ways on who belonged to a teacher's family. Randy and Louise both believed that raising children of their own had helped to inspire their classroom teaching.

Q: Can you trace your interest in young children back in your life?

Randy: My wife was involved in early childhood education. We had discussions. My kids were two and four years old. I was fascinated by their learning. Versus in high school (teaching that Randy had done previously): there the kids were a bunch of faces. You didn't know if they were learning or what. (Week 9, p. 47)

As these comments imply, spouses also made a difference—though not always a positive one. In another interview, Randy put it this way:

Q: Did Fern (your wife) influence your decision to go into early childhood education?

Randy: Yes, she really did. And my kids were preschool age, and that stimulated my interest. Fern used to talk about her work when she came home.

Q: Does that mean that when you broke up, you questioned your commitment to early education?

Randy: Yes I did, but not consciously. And fortunately not permanently. During the last several years, Fern and I just never spoke to each other much about our work. I would invite her to visit my classroom, but she never came—always "too busy" or something. (Week 12, p. 138)

Janice too pointed out that her spouse encouraged her to enter early childhood education. She had met him part way through her year in teacher training; he had already been teaching in prekindergarten and kindergarten for several years. "When we went to the library, he'd always check out about fifty children's books that he thought I should know about. Then he'd read to me. He's the one who taught me to do 'voices'" (Week 26, pp. 97–98). [Janice was a wonderfully dramatic storyteller, with a range of vocal styles that kept her class enthralled.]

Her husband also first directed her attention to in-service workshops she could attend in early childhood education, which sparked her interest in innovative programming in the field. Subsequently his career went in other directions, so that what was initially a daily influence was probably now more indirect or general. Unlike Randy, she had not separated from her spouse. Perhaps for this reason, her reports about her husband's influence were more consistently positive than Randy's reports about his wife's influence.

Louise's comments about family influence had more of the double-edged quality of Randy's, but for different reasons. Louise had been a single parent for most of her life as a teacher. For her, therefore, "family influence" had more to do with her son and his development than with a spouse. Her son originally helped to inspire and motivate her involvement in early education.

> "I started taking courses in child development at the university because I wanted to do everything right—be a 'supermom'." (Week 3, p. 6) "I met people there who had great ideas and I got hooked. I wanted to teach kindergarten because I wanted to work with kids, to help them, in ways that didn't put more pressure on them, the way later school does." (Week 12, pp. 54–55)

Now that her son was graduating from high school, though, Louise felt less enthusiastic: "The kids aren't as cute any more," she said. Whether this feeling would eventually pass, as did Randy's reaction to his divorce, still remained to be seen at the time of the study. Whatever the eventual outcome, though, her reactions testified to the importance of personal relationships, not only in creating commitments to teaching but also in challenging those commitments.

Interruptions versus Commitment

Like many other teachers, personal circumstances also caused extended work interruptions for Randy, Janice, and Louise. But the interruptions had complex effects on the teachers' professional selves. In some ways all three of the teachers maintained a commitment to teaching anyway, as Biklen observed in her research. But to some extent, too, the commitment of these three teachers waxed and waned in response to events outside of themselves.

Janice and Louise, for example, each interrupted teaching to bear children. But the effect of the interruption differed for the two women. Janice emphasized repeatedly that "having children made no difference to my coming into this field"; but Louise emphasized that "my children made early education seem more urgent and important." After leaving teaching once to retrain in early education, Randy left teaching again for a year to start a small sporting goods store. At the time, each decision to leave implied "lack of interest"—first in high school teaching and then in early education. In retrospect, however, each departure looked less like lack of commitment to education and more like a test of continuing commitment. Randy was back teaching kindergarten again after one year in the retail sales business, even though (as he pointed out) the store prospered economically. "I missed the kids," he said simply.

These three teachers seemed to share an internalized commitment to teaching, but one that had to compete with other goals and commitments. The other commitments could be considered either "internal" or "external" to the individual teachers, depending on how they were viewed. From either perspective, though, they affected the teachers' priorities and therefore also the teachers' commitment to teaching.

CONCLUSIONS: WAYS OF FINDING THE BALANCE

These results suggest several conclusions about professionalism and the relation of home and work in teaching, at least in early childhood teaching. First, personal life and teaching can affect each other not only among women but among men as well. Janice, Louise, and Randy are not necessarily "typical" early childhood teachers, but their experiences do suggest the variety of relationships that such teachers may construct between home and school. Sometimes, as with Janice, the relationship amounts to seeking a "divorce" between the two realms; but even this separation takes effort. Among female teachers more generally, Dee Ann Spencer[9] has already shown the varied forms that spillovers between home and school can take. This study confirms that variety, but also suggests that spillovers are not confined to women.

Second, the results suggest that what is gender-related may be the nature and direction of spillovers and not their mere existence. For the male teacher in this study, influence worked most obviously from home to school. Randy's family affected his decision and commitment to teach, as well as his questioning of that decision and commitment. Events in his family sometimes also affected his daily behavior in class. But Randy reported comparatively little evidence that teaching spilled over in the other direction. Yet, such effects did occur in that direction: Randy did make friends with one teacher, and he married another. The latter event presumably provided an important reverse influence, from school to home. But most daily school activities and relationships appeared to encroach little on Randy's daily personal time.

For the two female teachers, though, influence worked more explicitly in both directions, both from school to home and vice versa. Like Randy, Janice and Louise also reported emotional support from family members— Janice from her spouse, and Louise from watching her son grow up. But both women also filled many evenings and weekends with people, materials, or activities related to their daily teaching. The line between home and school, and between friends and colleagues thus seemed more unclear for Janice and Louise—and particularly Louise—than for Randy.

This pattern confirms but also qualifies, previous research showing stress or "role overload" among women who combine thorough work commitment with other family responsibilities[10]. Like that previous research, this study found the women's lives very full of responsibilities and indeed verging on being overly full. But this study also found the man's life full of responsibilities and in its own way overly full as well. What differed for the two genders here was not the existence of overload, but its sources and signs.

Third, in addition to blurring gender differences about the relations of home and work, this study found evidence of the stable, internalized commitment to teaching that Biklen[11] previously described in successful elementary teachers. But the evidence was mixed. The three teachers' enthusiasm and commitment actually originated and developed from a mix of external circumstances and lasting personal motives; and as the external supports waxed and waned, so did the teachers' enjoyment of children, in spite of its underlying constancy. Randy, Janice, and Louise continued to care about teaching, literally for years, as Biklen found with her elementary teachers. But these three individuals also cared more when well supported by spouses, by children of a "relevant" (that is, young) age, and by sympathetic peers. When these external supports failed, finished, or left, commitment faltered but did not disappear.

Biklen's idea of internalized commitment may therefore be right, but also in need of qualification. It seems in particular that role overload may foster both a socially traditional and a revised form of commitment at the same time, at least in early childhood teaching. Role overload may trigger "old," traditional separations of work and family; but it may also stimulate a "new" internalized commitment—one freed from the need for continuous, physical presence in the workplace. In early education, women and men may live with these conflicting notions of professionalism at the same time.

What remains to be seen is how widely this type of commitment occurs in other teaching specialties or in other work dominated by women. Jennifer Nias, for example, found a range of commitments among British primary teachers. The nature of the commitments were found to be closely related to the self-selected reference groups of individual teachers.[12] A teacher's choice of important or valid models for teaching had much to do with the kind of commitment the teacher felt: committed models made for committed self-image as a professional. Or perhaps it was also the other way around: being committed led a teacher to locate committed models. Nias's study was not designed to clarify cause and effect; it simply showed that a considerable variety of commitments exists, both in level and in type.

If so, then the research question becomes this: assuming that internalized commitment does in fact exist in some teachers, how do these teachers acquire it, and how do they nurture and maintain it? Three preliminary answers suggest themselves, though both still need proper investigation. First, perhaps internalized commitment develops more among women than men, because women are more often socialized to care for others, especially the very young. To this extent, they are already "trained" in early education when they begin teaching.[13] At the same time, of course, not all women have this personalized "training" in their backgrounds, nor do all choose to apply that training to early education.

Second, perhaps internalized commitment develops more fully among teachers in high-status elite schools, like the ones Biklen originally studied. Conditions in elite schools may make internalized commitment both more possible and more worthwhile. Teachers may find it easier to feel psychologically connected to the students, working conditions may be attractive and favorable, staff may feel an interest in each other's personal lives, and job interruptions may be tolerated relatively well. These factors may make internalized commitment a sensible, *professional* attitude. In the more typical situation, however, working conditions will not be uniformly favorable, and constant uninterrupted presence in the workplace—a traditional sign of professionalism—may therefore take on greater importance.

Third, it may be that internalized commitment happens most often to occupations—such as elementary and early childhood teaching—that set high value on developing networks of attachment among individuals, both young and old. The occupational cultures of such fields would favor individuals who believe in social continuities, including their own personal continuity with the field itself. In such fields, work would lead to what Nel Noddings calls "fidelity" in teaching[14] with the proviso that the fidelity applies not only to relationships with students but also to self-imposed commitments to teaching itself.

On the other hand, internalized commitment may happen in such fields for more strictly economic reasons. Early childhood and elementary education also happen to suffer from low social status and low pay, both of which encourage high turnover. The result, at any one moment in time, is a relatively large number of individuals out of work, some of them with strong internalized commitment. Many of these strongly committed individuals would have stayed at work if economic conditions were better; their careers would look very "professional," in the old sense of being continuous and uninterrupted. Their situation would be the converse of what would happen in high status, high pay fields: there, some people might stay on the job even though they lack commitment, instead of being off the job even though they have it.

All of these considerations imply that internalized commitment is important and valuable, though it may not necessarily lead to professionalism for teachers, any more than steadfast employment might have been in the past. We still have much to learn about the meaning of interruptions. For example, what are the limits of internalized commitment? Randy, Louise, and Janice hinted at some of them in this study, but no doubt there are others. How long can a person really stay away from the classroom and remain firmly committed to teaching? Perhaps there is some outer limit of time (twenty years? forty years?). And do positive experiences at teaching strengthen internalized commitment? Do they give an immunity that sustains individuals through periods when they are not teaching? So far we do not know.

POLICY IMPLICATIONS: SUPPORTING INTERNALIZED COMMITMENT

In addition to suggesting these research questions, the observations about teachers' commitment, reported here, imply policies for making teaching more humane as a career. Teachers' balance of home and work show a need to make teaching more like what Madeleine Grumet calls an aesthetic experience, an activity bounded in time and space, voluntary, free of pressing external demands, and constituted by dialogue between the *artist* (teacher) and her audiences (students, colleagues, and parents)[15]. These conditions can be fostered by policies that encourage internalized commitment.

One of the most obvious policies is to create employment practices that tolerate interrupted careers. Leave of absence, for example, should not be difficult to arrange; such leave—as well as part-time work or the sharing of jobs should not jeopardize a teacher's long-term earning, priority in school and classroom placements, promotion prospects, and the like. Neither should an absence from teaching—whether partial, brief, or extended—should be regarded, in and of itself, as showing indifference to teaching; instead it should be treated as a normal course of life events, though certainly not the only normal course.

But there are other helpful policies as well. "Professional" development takes on a new meaning, for example, when significant numbers of staff feel internalized commitment to teaching without being physically present at school each school year. Under those conditions, truly *professional* development experiences need to give high priority to building contact, support, and community among teachers, including those who happen not to be teaching at a given time. All committed teachers should be welcome and eligible to attend workshops, in-service courses, or other professional activities—on the assumption that, whether currently teaching or not, all teachers need and deserve to develop themselves and will eventually share their learning with students, colleagues, and parents upon their return to work.

For best results, such professional development activities need to be devised and led by teachers themselves. They should not be "laid on" by administrators, or rewarded with externally controlled salary increases or promotions out of classroom work. The latter arrangements have been typical in the past, but they lead too easily to developing administrative dominance hierarchies and too easily lose contact with teachers' true expertise—namely sensitivity to others, young or old, and willingness to collaborate with them in projects mutually constructed.

Perhaps therefore one other policy implication of internalized commitment is both superficially simple, yet psychologically hard: teachers need to rethink what they mean by being professional and communicate that new definition to others. No longer should professionalism mean exclusive dedication to work: such a notion can also mean exclusivity or the excessive exclusion of nonwork parts of life. And no longer should professionalism mean something quite so separate from the personal: the two realms can grow together and perhaps usually do if viewed up close. Paradoxically, then, teachers should therefore both aspire and *not* aspire to *being professional*. Whether to pursue this goal will depend on what we mean by it, what we want to convey by the term *professionalism,* and what others need to hear or learn about it.

NOTES

1. Sharon Feiman-Nemser and Robert Floden, "The Cultures of Teaching," in *Handbook of Research on Teaching*, 3d ed., ed. Merlin Wittrock, (New York: Macmillan, 1986), pp. 505–526. Feiman-Nemser and Floden speak of teachers in general, though they recognize that a majority are women, and that a different, but overlapping majority teach the elementary grades. For a specific focus on early education as a career, see Jennifer Nias, "Reference Groups in Primary Teaching: Talking, Listening and Identity," in *Teachers' Lives and Careers*, eds. Stephen Ball and Ivor Goodson (London: Falmer, 1985), pp. 105–119. See also Sara Delamont, ed., *The Primary School Teacher* (London; Falmer, 1987).

2. Daniel Lortie, *Schoolteacher* (Chicago: University of Chicago Press, 1975).

3. For example, the essays by Madeleine Grumet, *Bitter Milk: Women and Teaching* (Amherst: University of Massachusetts Press, 1988). The list of references of supportive portraits of female teachers is growing and diverse, though perhaps never sufficient. Ironically, one area still neglected in the feminist literature on teaching is early childhood education as an occupational culture, analogous to Grumet's depictions of teaching in general. Early educators themselves usually claim distinctive qualities for this specialty of teaching (for example, it supposedly demands more nurturance); but the claims have been neither researched nor subjected to philosophical scrutiny. For a sample of what has been done, though, see Lillian Katz, "The Nature of Professions: Where is Early Childhood Education?" in *Current Topics in Early Childhood Education*, vol. 7, ed. Lillian Katz (Norwood, N.J.:

Ablex, 1987), pp. 1–17. For views from the British context, see Sandra Acker, "Primary School Teaching as an Occupation," and Andrew Pollard, "Primary School Teachers and their Colleagues," *The Primary School Teacher*, Delamont, ed. pp. 83–99 and 100–119.

4. Patterns of dropping in and out are documented in Michael Sedlak and S. Scholssman, "Who Will Teach? Historical Perspectives of the Changing Appeal of Teaching as a Profession," in *Review of Research in Education*, ed. Edmund Gordon (Washington D.C.: American Educational Research Association, 1987), pp. 93–132. Male patterns of employment in early education are discussed in Kelvin Seifert, "Men in Early Childhood Education," in *Professionalism in Early Childhood Education*, eds. Bernard Spodek, Olivia Saracho, and Donald Peters, (New York: Teachers' College Press, 1988), and in Kelvin Seifert, "The Culture of Early Education and the Preparation of Male Teachers," *Early Child Development and Care*, 10 (Fall 1988): pp. 35–50.

5. For the view that professional development reflects all realms of living and not just the realm of work, see Sarah Lawrence Lightfoot, "The Lives of Teachers," in *Handbook of Teaching and Policy*, eds. Lee Shulman and Gary Sykes (New York: Longman, 1983), pp. 241–260. For a portrait of the professionalism implicit in *not* dedicating oneself totally to work, see Sari Knopp Biklen, "Can Elementary Schoolteaching Be a Career? A Search for New Ways of Understanding Women's Work," *Issues in Education*, 3, no. 3 (Winter 1985): pp. 215–231. Biklen studied elementary education teachers—admittedly not quite the same as early childhood teachers, but a group that does share important circumstances and values with early childhood educators. Nias, using a British sample, finds that all teachers have strong commitments to teaching but that only some have what Biklen (and we, here) are calling "internalized commitment." See Nias, "Reference Groups in Primary Teaching".

6. Lortie, *Schoolteacher*. For newer viewpoint about male teachers in particular, see Seifert, "The Culture of Early Education." For samples of feminist revisions, both historical and contemporary, see Martin Lawn and Gerald Grace, eds. *Teachers: The Culture and Politics of Work* (London: Falmer Press, 1987); see also Grumet, *Bitter Milk*.

7. Judith Goetz and Margaret Lecompte, *Ethnography and Qualitative Design in Educational Research* (New York: Academic Press, 1984). See also S. Merriam, *Case Study Research in Education* (San Francisco: Jossey-Bass, 1988).

8. All quotations are from the field notes of the study, which are available on request. For each quotation, the page number cited is the consecutive page in the field notes for the particular case-study teacher cited. The "Week" number refers to the time of contact for that particular teacher. "Week 2" in this quotation, for example, occurred during the second week of contact with Randy, which was not the second week for the other two teachers.

9. Dee Ann Spencer, *Contemporary Women Teachers: Balancing Home and School* (New York: Longman, 1986).

10. Joseph Pleck, "Husband's Paid Work and Family Roles," *Research on the Interweave of Social Roles*, vol. 3 (Greenwich, Conn.: JAI Press, 1983).

11. Biklen, "Can Elementary Schoolteaching Be a Career?"

12. Nias, "Reference Groups in Primary School Teachers."

13. Seifert, "The Culture of Early Education."

14. Nel Noddings, "Fidelity in Teaching and Teacher Education," *Harvard Educational Review* 56, no. 4, (Summer, 1986): pp. 496–510. See also Nel Noddings, *Caring* (Berkeley and Los Angeles: University of California Press, 1984).

15. Grumet, "Where The Line Is Drawn," in *Bitter Milk*.

Part II

Within the Schools

BRONWYN DAVIES

Chapter Five

The Accomplishment of Genderedness in Pre-School Children[*]

INTRODUCTION

Gender is a central defining feature of people in our society. In order to interact comfortably we each need to know the gender of the person we are interacting with and we need, in return, to act in such a way that we do not lead others to misconstrue our own gender. Our taken-for-granted knowledge about gender is that maleness and femaleness are the only and mutually exclusive categories relevant to gender. Part of being a competent member of society derives from our capacity to attribute to others, and to aid others in attributing to ourselves, the 'correct' gender identity. The work that we do to cue others to our gender is also done for ourselves in the sense that we each have an emotional commitment to the gender we have been assigned.[1] This commitment is developed at a very early age. As Kessler and McKenna point out:

> Most of the evidence for the development of gender identity during a critical period comes from cases where the initial assignment was deemed in error and an attempt was made to 'correct' it by re-assigning the child and making the necessary physical changes. Almost all attempts of this sort made after the age of about three are unsuccessful, in that the individual either retains her/his original gender identity or becomes extremely confused and ambivalent.[2]

83

By about the age of 3, then, we have learned the rules associated with competent presentation of self as male or female, and it is difficult if not impossible to unlearn these rules and to learn the rules appropriate to the alternate gender. This difficulty is presumably exacerbated by the fact that part of the definition of maleness, in particular, is *'not-femaleness'*.

Thus gender is central to each person's identity and each child is faced with the task of discovering how maleness and femaleness is elaborated in the everyday world, and of accomplishing for themselves their 'gendered-ness'.[3] This accomplishment enables them to be perceived by others as 'normal', competent members of the social scenes in which they are engaged.

In what follows I will use children's responses to liberating stories to show the ways in which small children deal with the differences between the world as it is being socially constructed and understood by them, and the liberating messages which are *potentially* available in their play and in their stories.[4]

The central problem that children face in understanding and accepting non-traditional messages, is to know how a person (real or mythical) who acts *outside* of what is commonly understood as appropriate for their gender, can be *recognized* as expanding what is positively available to other like-gendered people. It is not enough that the model be there—i.e. that the non-conventional action be engaged in by a known person or known hero. It is essential that there is, as well, a conceptual framework which allows that person to be located not only as a positive member of his/her gender but to be seen to be behaving *appropriately* for that gender.

The study reported here is part of a larger study of pre-school children and gender. In this chapter I will analyze the responses of seven children with whom I worked individually and intensively over a period of several months. Each child chose the stories they wanted to hear from a selection of ten stories. Each story was read to the child individually and the reading and the surrounding talk were audio-recorded. They could hear each story as often as they liked. Following each story some of the children were invited, wherever this was possible, to recreate the story by making the characters out of plasticine and play-acting the story as they remembered it. For the purpose of this chapter I will discuss the responses of the seven children who chose *The Paper Bag Princess* and the six who chose *Oliver Button is a Sissy*.[5]

Since the first two of these stories are referred to in detail it is necessary to 'tell' each of the stories before proceeding with the data.

Oliver Button is a boy who likes to do 'girls' things'. His father finds this distressing. However, Oliver persists and his parents eventually decide to send him to dancing school. Oliver is teased mercilessly by the boys at his normal school but he keeps dancing. The boys write 'Oliver Button is a sissy' on the school wall. Oliver goes in a talent quest and dances well but does not come first. When he goes to school the next day the boys have crossed out 'sissy' and written 'star'.

The Paper Bag Princess is about the beautiful Princess Elizabeth who plans to marry Prince Ronald. She lives in her castle and has expensive princess clothes. A dragon smashes Elizabeth's castle, burns all her clothes and carries off Prince Ronald. Elizabeth decides to chase the dragon and save Ronald. She finds a paper bag to wear and sets off after the dragon. She comes to the dragon's cave and, despite the dragon's resistance, gains his attention by asking him if it is true that he is 'the smartest and fiercest dragon in the whole world'. He claims he is and so she is able to persuade him to go on demonstrating his fantastic powers until he is exhausted and falls into a deep sleep. She then walks over the dragon and opens the door of the dragon's cave where Ronald is imprisoned. But Prince Ronald doesn't like the way Elizabeth looks. He says 'Elizabeth, you are a mess! You smell like ashes, your hair is all tangled and you are wearing a dirty old paper bag. Come back when you are dressed like a real princess'. Elizabeth replies 'Ronald, your clothes are really pretty and your hair is very neat. You look like a real prince, but you are a bum'. Elizabeth and Ronald don't get married and Elizabeth skips off into the sunset.

The children were: Anika, aged 5 years; Rebecca, aged 5 years 4 months; Katy, aged 4 years 11 months; Sebastian, aged 4 years 10 months; Robbie, aged 5 years 4 months; Mark, aged 5 years; and Leo, aged 5 years 1 month.

Although the children's responses varied considerably, as I will show in what follows, a persistent theme in their talk involved getting their genderedness right. They vary in the extent to which they see male and female behaviours as overlapping or as mutually exclusive, but they are all concerned that one's boyness and girlness should be clearly displayed. The distress that Oliver Button's dad feels when Oliver Button engages in what his dad takes to be girl behaviours, is seen by the children as understandable 'because he thinks he's pretending to be a girl' or 'because everyone'll think he's a girl'. This sympathy is felt even by the children who think Oliver Button should be free to do what he likes to do. Four of the six children who chose *Oliver Button is a Sissy* thought he should not have continued with his dancing, or if he did, he *should be teased*. These children are clearly aware that Oliver Button is unhappy doing boy things and unhappy to be teased, but they do not question the teasing—Oliver Button should know, or should be told, that he is not 'getting it right'. In this way these children reveal their adherence to a central construct of children's culture, that of *reciprocity*, or the 'active reflecting back to the other of the other's self'.[6] In this case, the children believe that it is correct to call

Oliver Button a sissy because that is what he is. It is also interesting to note in this and later transcripts that I am providing the children through my questions and responses, with an interactional other who makes theoretically possible the extension of maleness and femaleness to include non-traditional behaviour. My requests that they explain and justify adherence to traditional stereotypes are met with the required explanations, not with a reassessment of the answer, even when such a reassessment is clearly being invited.

Robbie	(*Oliver Button is a Sissy*)
BD	So why doesn't Oliver Button like to play 'boys' games'?
R	Because he likes girls' things.
BD	Because he likes girls' things. Mm. (Reads about Oliver Button going to dancing school.)
	So all the others are little girls, aren't they? (Looking at picture.)
R	That's wrong.
BD	It's wrong, is it? So you wouldn't like Oliver to go? If you were Oliver and you hated all the boys' things and you wanted to do girl's things would you want to go to dancing school?
R	(Shakes head.)
BD	Even if you loved to dance you wouldn't want to go to dancing school?
R	No.
BD	(Reads about the boys teasing Oliver.)
	So what sort of boys are they?
R	Big, they . . .
BD	Big boys, and should they say that to Oliver Button?
R	Yes.
BD	They should? (surprised) . . . (Read about boys writing 'Oliver Button is a sissy' on the school wall.) How does Oliver feel?
R	Sad.
BD	He's very sad, isn't he? So should the boys have written that on the wall?
R	(Nods).
BD	They should? (surprised) Why should they have written that on the wall?
R	Because he, because he is a sissy doing tap dancing.
BD	(Reads about Oliver practising his dancing.) So why do you suppose he keeps going even though everybody keeps giving him a hard time?
R	Because he just wants to.

BD	He just wants to and should you keep doing what you want to do even though everybody keeps giving you a hard time?
R	(Nods).
BD	Uh huh. (Reads story.) So his dad doesn't mind any more, does he, that he's a tap dancer. Why do you suppose that is?
R	Because he was good on stage.
BD	Uh huh. So if you keep doing something that you're not supposed to do if you're a boy and you get to be good at it then it's quite all right?
R	(Nods).
BD	Uh huh.

Robbie believes it is wrong for Oliver to go to the dancing school. What seems logical to me—that if you hate 'boys' things' and love dancing, you should dance—does not follow at all for Robbie unless you are able to develop a high level of competence at dancing. But correct genderedness for himself is far more important than what he might like or dislike. Similarly for Katy and for Sebastian, Oliver was behaving inappropriately—he should have done what he was told and played with the boys. Sebastian explains that he personally would do as his Dad says because his Dad can show him how to be a boy. The story of Oliver Button creates an obvious discomfort for many of the children who listen to it. For boys, it seems, gender is not fixed, it is not immutable, and there are clear risks in engaging in girl behaviour, even to the extent in some children's minds that you could become a girl. Maleness in our society is defined in a large part in terms of one's capacity not to behave like a girl and is thus construed by some boys as something that has to be ongoingly achieved. Females, in contrast, are not seen as at risk of becoming males. Some non-traditional female behaviours can be engaged in with impunity, though this may not change one's thinking about what females generally do, as is shown in the following transcript, nor, as is shown in a later transcript, does it change one's capacity to engage in behaviours labelled exclusively male.

Anika	(*The Paper Bag Princess*)
BD	If you were Princess Elizabeth would you be chasing the dragon? Would you be that brave?
A	(Nods).
BD	If I was Princess Elizabeth would I be that brave do you think?
A	(Shakes head).
BD	No? What about if mummy were Princess Elizabeth, would she be that brave?
A	(Shakes head).
BD	No? Who do you know that would be that brave?

A	Daddy.
BD	Daddy would be that brave, would he?
A	(Nods).
BD	And who else.
A	David (brother).
BD	Anybody else that you know?
A	(Shakes head).

Thus Anika, along with her father and brother, can be brave like Princess Elizabeth while other females are still limited to the traditional stereotypes.

The delight for adults in *The Paper Bag Princess* lies in Elizabeth's capacity to turn the tables on Ronald and skip happily off into the sunset. But for children this is a puzzling and not altogether satisfactory ending. It takes several readings of the story to get them used to the ending, but generally the girls still preferred Elizabeth at the beginning rather than at the end of the story. In the following talk around the plasticine reconstruction of *The Paper Bag Princess,* I explore the ending with Anika, discovering to my surprise that not only does she not share my definition of the ending, but nor does she share my definition of Ronald. As with the older children of my earlier study, these 4 and 5-year-old children showed a belief in the existential or plastic quality of people—if Ronald is nice tomorrow, even though he was 'a bum' today, it will be alright to marry him.[7] Thus the traditional ending of getting married and living happily ever after is not out of keeping with Anika's idea of who Elizabeth and Ronald are.

Anika	(*The Paper Bag Princess.* Plasticine reconstruction)
BD	And so then what happens? Are you putting some mess on her face?
A	Mmmm, that was soot.
BD	Right, and so Prince Ronald tells her that she 'looks really like a pig' (using Anika's words.)
A	Mmmm.
BD	And then what does she say?
A	Oh, Prince Ronald, you are a bum!
BD	Right, and then what happens?
A	They don't get married after all.
BD	And what's happening in this very last picture here?
A	The paper bag princess is going off into the sunset. . . .
BD	What do you think she'll do after she skips off into the sunset?
A	Go home.
BD	To her burnt down castle?
A	No.
BD	Where will she go?
A	Um, to rent a house.

BD	Uh huh.
A	Until someone's built a house for her.
BD	Until she's got a new castle?
A	Mmm.
BD	And what will be the first thing that she does when she gets back to her rented house?
A	Clean up the place.
BD	Clean up what? The new flat? Or where the castle got burnt down?
A	Mmm, where the castle got burnt down.
BD	And what about cleaning herself up? Will that be important?
A	Yes.
BD	And will she buy new clothes?
A	Yes.
BD	Tell me what sort of new clothes she'll buy.
A	Princess ones.
BD	Princess ones? Like right back at the beginning? (surprised tone of voice)
A	Mmmm.
BD	(Points) Like that?
A	Mmmm.
BD	Un huh, and will she grow her hair all pretty again?
A	Yes.
BD	And what will happen when she sees Prince Ronald in a few days after she's got all dressed up and Prince Ronald comes to visit her?
A	I don't know.
BD	What would you like her to say?
A	Hello.
BD	Mmm? (surprised)
A	Hello.
BD	Hello, and what will he say? What would happen here? Here's Prince Ronald, he's come to visit. She's all dressed up and pretty again and she says, 'Hello Prince Ronald'. Ronald says, 'Hello Elizabeth. How are you?' What does she say?
A	'Good'.
BD	She says, 'I'm good'. And he says, 'Well, you look like a real princess now!' And what does she say?
A	I don't remember.
BD	Remember? We're making this up!
A	I know.
BD	Um, what if she says, um, 'Yes, I do look like a real princess now'. And he says, 'Well then we can get married'. And what does she say?
A	'Yes, we will get married'.

BD   So, she doesn't think he's a bum anymore? (surprised tone of voice)
A   (Shakes head).
BD   Why doesn't she think he's a bum anymore?
A   I don't know.
BD   Don't know?
A   No.
BD   She just thinks he's being nice now, does she?
A   Yes.
BD   Right. OK, shall we do another story?
A   Yes.

The salience in *The Paper Bag Princess* for Anika lies, therefore, not in Elizabeth's capacity to walk away. She says elsewhere that she really likes the story because Elizabeth calls Ronald a bum, just as she calls her brother a bum if he is mean to her. But just as she gets over her fights with David, so she presumes must Elizabeth get over her fight with Ronald.

In the following transcript, Anika carefully elaborates her beliefs that males and females should be free to step outside traditional gender roles. She does this by creating a *third gender* which she labels 'tomboy'. Anika knows a girl who is called a 'tomboy' and who is accepted as such. She extends this knowledge to create a category to which males and females can belong though is careful to explain elsewhere that she is not a tomboy. Her description of the personal difficulties she encounters in engaging in male behaviour is fascinating and illustrates that the use of the third gender category is in part a device for maintaining a clear definition of the other two gender categories.

Anika   (*Oliver Button is a Sissy*)
BD   (Reads: 'Oliver Button was called a sissy. He didn't like to do the things that boys are supposed to do') What are boys supposed to do?
A   Be very rough.
BD   And what's, what's Oliver doing?
A   He's being like a girl.
BD   Is he? Why is that like a girl?
A   Because he's picking flowers.
BD   Uh huh.
A   And that's sort of, that's mainly girls'.
BD   And is that an all right thing for boys to do?
A   Mmmm. But it's just not a boy's thing.
BD   Right.
A   So I think he should be called a tomboy.

BD   Right.
A   Not a sissy.
BD   Right.
A   A tomboy.

(Discussion as to whether her brother does what Oliver Button does.)

BD   So sometimes he'll do those things but mostly he doesn't.
A   Except he really *doesn't* skip. He *never* skips.
BD   Right. Righto, would you like it if he did?
A   (Nods.)
BD   Yep.
A   But I can't skip.
BD   Right. But if he could skip he might teach you how, mightn't he?
A   He *can* skip.
BD   Can he?
A   Yep, but he just doesn't like to do it.
BD   (Reads—'Oliver, said his dad, don't be such a sissy!') Why did he say that?
A   Because he's pretending he's a girl.
BD   Right. (Reads 'Go out and play baseball or football or basket ball, *any* kind of ball!') Why did his dad say that?
A   'Cause he's doing girls' things.
BD   Mmm, and does it, does that matter? Is that a problem?
A   Yeah.
BD   Do you think his dad thinks it's a problem?
A   (Nods).
BD   Why do you think his dad thinks that?
A   Cause he, I think his dad um thinks he wants to be a tomboy.
BD   Do you think his dad might be unhappy if he wants to be a tomboy?
A   Mmm, cause he just wants a boy called Oliver Button.
BD   (Reads about Oliver Button going to dancing school.) And what would you think if David got some tap shoes and had dancing lessons. Would you like that, or would you hate it?
A   No, I think, I'd laugh at him.
BD   Would you? Why would you do that?
A   Because it's a tomboy thing.
BD   Is it?
A   And David's got no friends that are tomboys.
BD   Would it be all right if he had friends who are tomboys?
A   Mmmm.
BD   So why would you laugh at him?
A   Because it's sort of a girl's thing.

BD   Right, and you would feel funny about him doing a girl's thing?

A   Mmm, I feel, you know, funny.

BD   Feel.

A   Feel funny.

BD   Yeah.

A   And when people, when people, when the wrong kind of human being does that, I get a (pause) tickle in my brain.

BD   Do you? When.

A   Mmmm.

BD   If a boy does a girl thing you get a tickling feeling in your brain?

A   Mmmm.

BD   And what about if a girl does a boy thing?

A   I get (pause) the same thing.

BD   It makes you feel really funny?

A   Mmm, and it makes me laugh.

BD   Does it?

A   Mmm, and it's like a little man is in my brain, tickling my brain.

BD   Does it feel horrible or funny?

A   Funny.

BD   Funny.

A   Like, it's like a piece of string like this tickling from side to side. (Motions as if drawing string back and forth through her brain.)

BD   And that tickling makes you laugh?

A   Mmmm.

BD   Does it make you feel unhappy at all?

A   No.

BD   So, if you were to do a boy thing and that made you laugh, but you *really* wanted to do it and it started making you tickle and laugh would you keep on doing it?

A   Oh, no.

BD   No? Is the tickling enough to make you stop?

A   Yeah, because I'd only do it when I was practising and no girl or boy is around, no one because they might laugh at me.

BD   And if you were just practising it alone, and um say like what, what would be a boy thing that you'd really like to do?

A   (Pause) Um, fly a racing, fly an aeroplane.

BD   And if you were flying that aeroplane and you were practising it all by yourself where nobody could watch you, um, would you get tickling in your brain then?

A   Yeah.

BD   You would, but you wouldn't care?

A   No.

BD   If your mum or your dad was watching you would that matter?

A   Ooh, if I got a ticklish thing I wouldn't laugh.

BD   You wouldn't.

A   Because they might hear me.

BD   So you'd just go on playing the plane, flying the plane, if they were there but you wouldn't if there were other boys or girls there?

A   Mmm. I mean if there were boys and girls there I still wouldn't laugh because you know I, you know (pause). Let's just get on with the story.

BD   Right, OK. It's hard to explain isn't it?

A   Mmm, very.

For Anika the correct behaviour for girls and boys is relatively flexible. Activities are not solely the province of one or the other—they are just what that group 'mainly' does. It is not a problem, in fact it can be quite pleasant, if people step outside of their gender appropriate behaviours, as her brother does, occasionally. However, some behaviours such as tap dancing, are problematic and lead to 'a tickle in the brain'. This can be overcome by a group of people taking up the behaviour in question so they are all doing it together, or by practising the skill alone, presumably so that one can be accepted as Oliver Button eventually is through being good at it.

This should not be taken to indicate that acquiescence to the traditional roles is easy or straightforward. Rebecca revealed quite unexpectedly for instance in the plasticine play following the reading of Oliver Button that she felt very negatively towards the boys who had pressured Oliver Button towards 'normal' behaviour even though she had stated that acquiescence was an appropriate response.

Rebecca   (*Oliver Button—plasticine reconstruction*)
(R constructs Oliver and BD constructs the boys. They play out the story to the point where the boys are teasing Oliver.)

BD   He feels sad doesn't he?

R   (Giggles).

BD   He tries not to cry and then, what's he doing? What are you making him do? Jump on the boys, is that what he should have done? (R makes Oliver jump on the boys and angrily pounds them into little bits.)

While Rebecca could not put her anger toward the boys into words, she could demonstrate it. Mark is able to go one step further than Rebecca. He is quite clear in his mind that the socializing power of the boys must be actively counteracted, although he did not know how this might be done. When the tape was finished he said at first that he might talk to them.

When encouraged to think of what he would say he said he could think of
nothing. In a second reading of the story he said it would be more effective
to throw sticks at them though adults would say it was better to just ask
them not to. Mark is accompanied by a 3-year-old girl, Kim, in this particular episode.

Mark and Kim	(*Oliver Button is a Sissy*)
BD	Is he nearly going to cry?
M	Yes.
BD	He doesn't like being called a sissy does he?
M	(Shakes head).
BD	Would you call somebody a sissy if they went to dancing lessons? (Interruption).
BD	Right. If those big boys were your friends Kim, and they wanted to tease Oliver would you tease him too and call him a sissy?
K	(Nods).
BD	You would? Um, and if you saw him looking sad like that how would you feel?
K	I'd still tease him.
BD	You'd still tease him, and why would you do that? (Silence). If those big boys were your friends . . . and what about you Mark if those big boys were your friends and they were teasing Oliver would you tease him too?
M	No.
BD	What would you do?
M	I would, I would stop them.
BD	Would you? What would you say to them?
M	I dunno.
BD	You don't know. You'd just manage to stop them somehow?
M	Mmmm.
BD	(Reads 'Almost every day the boys teased Oliver Button') Mmm, how does he look?
M	Sad.
BD	(Reads about how Oliver went to dancing school and practised and practised.) Is that the right thing for him to do keep on going to the school?
M and K	Yes (Simultaneously).
BD	Why was it the right thing to do?
M	Because he couldn't dance himself.
BD	Because he couldn't what?

M	Because he couldn't dance himself.
BD	Because he couldn't dance he had to go to Miss Leah to learn how?
M	Yes.
BD	And if you'd been Oliver Button would you have kept going to the dancing school, Mark?
M	Um, yes.
BD	Even though the boys teased you?
M	Mmmm.
BD	What about you Kim? Would you keep going to the school even though the boys teased you?
K	(Shakes head).

But Mark was an exception. The other children either thought it correct to adhere (and to ensure that others adhered) to traditional roles. Where they thought it correct to be able to be liberated from traditional roles, the power of what was taken to be normative strongly influence what they chose to do.

So what do these episodes tell us about what facilitates the transition from being bound within traditional gender roles to being able to both see and act outside of them? Anika describes the possibility of occasionally stepping outside. She alludes, on several occasions, to the liberating effect that friends can have if they choose, to allow more consistent stepping outside simply by being friends or by engaging in the behaviour with you. Success at the non-traditional behaviour is fairly consistently seen as a means of legitimating that behaviour. Generally, however, the power of what is taken to be normal for a girl or a boy was taken to be unquestionable. It was acceptable for Oliver Button's dad to 'just want a boy called Oliver Button' even though this made life hard for Oliver Button. Similarly, parents were included with peers in the class of people in front of whom non-traditional behaviours could not be practised.

In analyzing the children's responses to *The Paper Bag Princess* I have found an intriguing difference between those who understand the story as it is intended, and those who do not. Of the girls Anika and Rebecca and Katy all identify with the princess. They see her as nice, beautiful etc. All three understand her plan. All three see Ronald as not very nice, though Katy believes he is reasonable and that Elizabeth should have done as he asked, cleaned herself up and then they could have got married.

Of the boys Sebastian and Robbie have little interest in the character of Elizabeth though are able to understand her plan. They both appreciate that she is cross and angry. Both identify with the clever prince. To see Ronald as clever is a considerable accomplishment. In order to create and sustain Ronald as a hero these boys had to attend to minute details in the picture, to successfully accomplish male genderedness, as they understood it, for Ronald. Neither Sebastian nor Robbie sees any problem in Elizabeth's rejection of Ronald, Sebastian because he presumes Ronald will find someone else and Robbie because he believed that Ronald didn't like Elizabeth in the first place. Leo and Mark both see Prince Ronald as not nice, though Leo would like to be like him. Both are aware of Elizabeth's plan to save Ronald. Both are aware of her dirtiness. Thus three of the four boys identify with Ronald and turn him into the central character. Only Mark sees Ronald as unacceptable and identifies with the dragon (who is, after all, 'the smartest and fiercest dragon in the whole world').

Apart from this strong and predictable trend that the girls identify with the princess and the boys with the prince, other differences one might have predicted are not there. For example the amount of detail perceived in the individual characters and in the relationshp between the characters varies within gender as much as between gender. Both Anika and Robbie give a great deal of insightful comment on the characters and relationship (albeit from the perspective of the character they identify with). However it is possible to gain a more subtle insight into the individual children's understanding of the story, if the children are divided not according to gender, but according to whether they understand that Elizabeth is the hero and that Ronald is not at all nice. Anika, Rebecca, Mark and Leo are focussed on Elizabeth as the hero and on her plan to save Ronald. In contrast Katy, Sebastian and Robbie turn Ronald into a nice person or even the hero. For these three, Elizabeth's action is seen in terms of re-establishing her coupled state (getting her prince back) and all three think Ronald is reasonable in his request that Elizabeth clean herself up. Interestingly, the four who understand the story as it is intended with Elizabeth as hero have mothers who engage in paid work outside the home and two of them have fathers who have taken a substantial share of nurturing and domestic activity. The three children who are unable to appreciate Elizabeth as hero have full-time mothers. There seems therefore to be an interesting connection between having a mother in paid work and the capacity to imagine women as active agents in the world, as powerful people, and to see men as other than central in action outside the home. The essential *liberating* message of the story is available to these children as a way of conceptualizing the world, while the others must distort the story in order to understand it. This is not to say that the other children fully understood the story. Two of the children of working mothers saw Princess Elizabeth as 'nice', which is not an appropriate description for Elizabeth and is also an imposition of stereotypical constructions of gender on the story.[8] And as noted earlier Anika quite readily went on to bring about a traditional 'happy ending' when prompted in that direction.

The link between having a mother who works and the capacity to accept Oliver Button's right to dance is not so clear. Sebastian, Robbie and Katy, whose mothers do not work, all thought that Oliver should do boy things and Sebastian and Katy believe he should do as his father tells him whether he likes it or not. Anika, Rebecca and Mark, whose mothers do work, thought Oliver should continue to dance (as did Robbie) but Anika and Rebecca were ambivalent about whether they would tease him or not, even though they quite clearly believed he should be free to do as he wanted. Mark is the clearest about Oliver's rights and refers to his own experience of 'girl's' things to justify this. He says 'I do lots of things that girls do and lots of things that boys do. Like my dad bought me a She Ra, and I like skipping and stuff and also I'd like to get the castle that She Ra lives in and stuff like that . . . I feel happy doing girl things, and after all I do go to dance.'

This link between the capacity to understand (at least partially) the liberating message of the stories and having a mother who works outside the home has emerged in other research. Urburg has shown that girls are 'less sex-typed in their concepts than boys, *particularly girls whose mothers worked also.*[9] As well, Zuckerman and Sayre have shown that 'the sons of the full-time home-makers (i.e. mothers) tend to refuse to consider opposite sex career choices, which suggests that the role-model of the home-maker mother has a negative impact on boys' perceptions of women or women's role options'.[10] This pattern has an interesting correlation, too, with the work of Lunneborg who found that having a working mother was the most salient feature in the backgrounds of women with non-traditional careers.[11] Kessler, Ashendon, Connell and Dowsett also point to the increase in the number of married women who work as the most significant development in families in relation to changes in adolescents' conception of sex-roles.[12]

CONCLUSION

What I have shown through children's responses to liberating stories is that the accomplishment of genderedness is a central and complex task necessary in the elaboration of oneself as a normal and competent member of society. Some children are locked into traditional conceptions of gender while others are able to move partially towards a more liberated view of gender, where their social environment includes women who are active agents in the world, where there are men who have undertaken a significant proportion of the nurturing and traditionally female roles, *and* where they have been free to practice non-traditional behaviours in an environment where this is taken to be a normal thing to do.

I have shown that it is not enough to believe that one might be or ought to be liberated from traditional roles nor is it enough to engage in isolated interactions with liberated others, particularly if those liberated others are merely assigned to a third gender catagory thus removing any necessity to generalize from their non-traditional behaviour about what males or females are capable of doing. It is necessary to know *how* one might be liberated *and* to have the interactional and conceptual others to turn liberated ideals into possible realities. Just as some of the children could not hear or see that Elizabeth was a hero and Ronald a fool, so the people with whom a child interacts must be able to hear and see the child's actions as normal for their gender, in order for the child to proceed comfortably with those actions.

Teachers working with children must be aware of the fact that currently our society is divided into male and female categories and that children are required to accomplish not only their distinct maleness or femaleness, but if they are male they have also to achieve their not-femaleness and vice versa. The categories are taken in our society to be mutually exclusive—one cannot be both, and one cannot be roughly one or the other. It is therefore inappropriate to merely assert that it is alright for boys to do what girls do and for girls to do what boys do. For children that must be a fairly empty statement and in fact the assertion itself still maintains as given the distinction between 'girls things' and 'boys things'. What a boy *is* and what a girl *is* must be extended in such a way that liberated behaviours are seen as 'normal' behaviours which will not lead to a misreading of the gender of the actor. The extension must be both conceptual and interactional. As Evans has shown, it is all too easy for teachers to espouse liberated ideals without actually translating these into their interactions with the children.[13]

Children must be encouraged to find ways of clearly signalling their maleness and their femaleness without limiting or constricting their potential. Most children will need a great deal of support and reassurance in this extension of themselves into liberated forms of activity, though the more they are surrounded by books which depict liberated behaviours as normal and by people who engage in liberated behaviours as if that is normal, the more secure they will feel in stepping outside of the traditional bounds and the less anxious they will feel that such stepping out compromises the accomplishment of their genderedness.

NOTES

*Reprinted from Andrew Pollard, ed., *Children and Their Primary Schools*, Falner Press, 1987.

1. S. Kessler and W. McKenna, *Gender: An Ethnomethodological Approach* (Chicago: University of Chicago Press, 1985).

2. Ibid., p. 10.

3. S. Thompson, "Gender labels and early sex role development," *Child Development* 46 (1975).

4. J. Zipes, "The potential of liberating fairy tales for children," *New Literary History* (1982).

5. R. N. Munsch and M. Martchenko, *The Paper Bag Princess* (Toronto: Annick Press Ltd., 1980); T. DePaolo, *Oliver Button is a Sissy* (London: Methuen, 1981).

6. B. Davies, *Life in the Classroom and Playground: The Accounts of Primary School Children* (London: Routledge and Kegan Paul, 1982), p. 76.

7. Ibid., p. 77.

8. D. Ullian, "Why girls are good: A constructivist view," *American Journal of Orthopsychiatry* 54 (1984).

9. K. Urburg, "The development of the concepts of masculinity and feminity in young children," *Sex Roles* 8 (1982): p. 668.

10. D. Zuckerman and D. Sayre, "Cultural sex-role expectations and children's sex role concepts," *Sex Roles* 8 (1982): pp. 860–861.

11. P. Lunneborg, "Role model influences of non-traditional professional women," *Journal of Vocational Behaviour* 20 (1982).

12. S. Kessler, D. Ashendon, B. Connell, and G. Dowsett, *Ockers and Disco-maniacs* (Stanmore, England: Inner City Education Centre, 1982).

13. T. Evans, "Being and becoming: Teachers' perceptions of sex-roles and actions towards their male and female pupils," *British Journal of Sociology of Education* 3 (1982).

ELIZABETH BLUE SWADENER

Chapter Six

Race, Gender, and Exceptionality: Peer Interactions in Two Child Care Centers

Children's awareness, attitudes, and interaction patterns related to race, gender, language, class, and developmental differences have lifelong implications and have been the subject of research in several disciplines. Many socially critical values, perceptions, biases, and behavioral roles are first demonstrated and internalized by preschool children—typically through their play, formal and informal curricular experiences, and interactions with adults and peers in their homes, neighborhoods, and, increasingly, child care or preschool environments. The impact of mainstreaming preschool children with special developmental needs, as required by Public Law 99–457, has also been the subject of research, much of which has focused on cross-ability peer interactions and attitudes in preschool and elementary settings.

In recent years, strategies for multicultural education, human relations, and antibias approaches have been applied to progressively younger preschool children. Often these applications have taken an additive and superficial approach, focusing on holidays, foods and customs of "other people, other places" and becoming essentially a *tourist curriculum* rather than being implemented in any sort of pervasive developmental framework for encouraging self-esteem, empathy, or increasing social sensitivity and responsibility. A needed, yet infrequent expectation for quality early childhood caregivers and teachers is multicultural competence and sensitivity.

Thus research evidence from preschool settings where teachers have consciously attempted to promote acceptance of diversity and positive peer interactions can be important in charting a course of recommendations for education that is multicultural applied to young learners.

Several approaches to multicultural education have been identified and described by Christine Sleeter and Carl Grant.[1] These include: (1) teaching the culturally different, (2) single group studies, (3) human relations, (4) multicultural education, and (5) education that is multicultural and social reconstructionist. Of these five approaches, human relations is the model most frequently applied to early chidhood settings. The goals of this approach include helping children communicate with, accept, and get along with people who are different from themselves, reducing or eliminating stereotypes, and helping children develop a healthy self-esteem and identity, often including an *individual differences* approach. A major focus in the human relations approach, as well as in other approaches to multicultural education, is on the importance of teachers and caregivers using nonstereotypic materials with children. The single group approach in early childhood settings is far less frequent though it can be seen in Afrocentric[2] and some bilingual child care and early education programs.

The chief weakness of the human relations approach is that it seems to suggest that people should get along, communicate, and appreciate each other within the existing stratified social system. Issues such as poverty, institutional racism and sexism, handicapism, and other examples of the lack of equity in American society are not fully addressed in the human relations literature nor in their early childhood applications.

Education that is multicultural goes beyond more typical forms of multicultural education to include issues of race, class, gender, age, and exceptionality. A recent publication, *Anti-Bias Curriculum: Tools for Empowering Young Chidren,*[3] presents one of the first curricula to apply education that is multicultural to toddler through kindergarten settings. In applying an antibias or social reconstructionist perspective to early childhood programs, several potentially challenging issues are apparent. The first concerns preschool children's assumed lack of *developmental readiness* or cognitive capacity to deal with complex cultural content. The risk of providing children with only a caricature of diverse cultures is a very real concern. The importance of first enhancing young children's sense of self, power to make authentic choices, and opportunities to interact with diverse peers cannot be underestimated in any multicultural recommendations for caregivers, teachers, and parents working with young children. Children in bi- or multilingual, mainstreamed, and other diverse settings have many natural opportunities to learn firsthand about individual differences and many aspects of cultural and human diversity.

The development of racial identity and attitudes is also of great importance to early childhood programs attempting to promote education that is multicultural. By ages three to four, most children are aware of color and racial differences[4] as well as of gender differences, and by age four race or color becomes effectively laden though the child may lack a highly developed understanding of race.[5] Racial identification appears to develop similarly to gender identification with girls tending to use gender for identification more than race.[6]

Social interaction is particularly important to preschool children with developmental delays and disabilities. It is often argued that play can be a time for learning and for observing models of appropriate behavior. Research findings are mixed in terms of the interaction patterns described. Some earlier findings, for example, described mainstreamed children as rejected or less well accepted than normally developing children.[7] Other studies have reported quite different findings, including no significant difference in peer status accorded handicapped and nonhandicapped peers.[8]

Studies that look at the development of social skills over time report increasing levels of both cross-ability interaction and positive attitudes toward these interactions as time in the integrated setting and opportunity interaction increases.[9] Other studies in the early childhood mainstreaming literature examine the interrelationships of the types of activities and play and role of the teacher as facilitator of mainstreamed interaction during different parts of a preschool day. Findings generally suggest the importance of adults in facilitating positive peer interactions as well as availability of appropriate activities.[10]

CASE STUDY FINDINGS

Settings and Methodology

The following sections present data from a yearlong ethnographic case study of two child care centers located in an urban midwestern community. The study focused on the older groups of children at both Children's Place and The Willows Early Childhood Program. These children ranged in age from 3.9 to 5.5 at the beginning of the study. Both child care centers offered full-day programs and were mainstreamed (that is, served children with both developmental disabilities and delays). The use of two centers provided a method of constant comparison in terms of programs that expressed a commitment to education that is multicultural yet differed in several relevant ways.

These differences incuded staffing—in terms of the racial and gender diversity of staff, in the degree of cultural/racial diversity of children in the two centers, and in the ways in which the mainstreaming components of the program was supported (for example, the special needs resource teacher and team-teaching models). Although not a major focus of the study, there were also perceived class/economic differences in the two centers, with Children's Place serving many single parent, graduate and undergraduate student, and working-class families. The Willows Center, in contrast, served a number of academic, medical, and other white collar professionals, several of whom worked in the same building or in a nearby hospital.

Participant observations were conducted at the two child care centers for six to eight hours each week throughout the year with both informal and semistructured interviews with children and their teachers conducted at regular intervals throughout the period of study. Observations were conducted primarily during the morning and included most of the center's scheduled activities including free choice activity times, snack and lunch time, teacher-guided small and large groups, outside play, schedule transitions, and some field trips and other special activities.

Field notes were discussed initially with teachers immediately or shortly after most observations in order to clarify what was observed and add additional contextual information. As data were transcribed and analyzed and further issues identified, observations were more focused on these issues with data coded accordingly. Following the data collection period, interpreted summaries of field notes were shared with teachers. Since names had been changed, teachers were asked to identify the children described and to give feedback to the researchers regarding the accuracy of the initial interpretations.

The data presented in this article focus on children's peer interactions and conversations during indoor and outdoor free play, or *activity times*. Data were also collected on the formal and informal (hidden) curricula vis-à-vis human diversity; these findings are reported elsewhere and are beyond the scope of the present article.

Children's Place Day Care Center

Children's Place is a full-day program located in an older three-story house with the first two floors used by the children and the third comprised of offices and meeting space for staff. Children's Place had 43 children, ages two to six, enrolled during most of the year. At the beginning of the study there were 22 boys and 21 girls. Children were grouped by age into 5 small groups; this study focused on the children in the 2 older groups. At the beginning of the study there were 2 male staff; in March, a third male teacher was hired to work primarily with the younger children. In addition to a gender-balanced staff, Children's Place also had a racially diverse staff, with one Nigerian teacher, an African-American special needs resource teacher, and several African-American volunteers.

During the period of the case study, 25 percent of the children enrolled at Children's Place were from countries other than the United States, and most of these children were learning English as a second language. Approximately 6 percent of the children were African-American, Hispanic or Native American, and the remainder were European-American.

Children's Place had two mainstreamed children in the older group. Marita had Down's Syndrome and Umaru was considered "autistic-like and hyperactive" with language and social delays. Both children took part in most of the regular activities at the center and had a special resource teacher working with them most of the time they were at Children's Place. Both spent half their day in the local public school's early childhood special needs program.

The Willows Center Early Childhood Program

The Willows Center is a mainstreamed, full-day program located on the first floor of a larger research and rehabilitation facility; approximately 40 percent of the children enrolled during the period of study had a developmental disability or delay. Thus the staff makeup at this center included a number of special education teachers, as well as support staff (such as speech and physical therapists) and trainees.

This study focused on the room with the oldest children. At the beginning of the year this classroom had 14 four- and five-year-old children; 10 boys and 4 girls. This changed to 9 boys and 5 girls in November. Four children in this room were described as having special needs. One child had cerebral palsy; another had brain damage-related developmental delays and began the school year with very little verbal language and with behavior problems; another child was considered "socially constricted" with some large motor delays; and another child received speech therapy. In this group, there were 2 children from European countries who had learned English as a second language; the other children were European-American in heritage.

Two staff were the regular team teachers in this classroom. One colead teacher was trained in early childhood special education; and the other was an experienced preschool and kindergarten teacher. Both were European-American. A Hispanic research assistant working on a microcomputer project was the only male staff member in this classroom on a regular basis although several of the children's fathers were often seen at the center.

Race, Language, and Gender in Peer Interactions

Throughout the period of study, gender was observed to be a stronger criterion for playmate and friendship choice than was children's racial or ethnic background. Several strong cross-racial friendships were observed throughout the year at Children's Place. Children at this center also had a variety of daily cross-racial interactions with their mainstreamed peers who were African-American and Nigerian. Shared language, however, appeared to contribute to several friendships or peer playmate choices.

One dyad of particular relevance to cross-racial peer interactions consisted of two girls, Marissa and Alison, who were best friends. In the nine months of weekly observations, these girls played together virtually exclusively during 32 of 36 free play observations. They typically sat together at snack and project times and frequently played together during free choice times engaging in a variety of dramatic play themes (for example, teenagers, sisters, animal families, and rocket pilots), often involving just these two girls. They often *mirrored* or collaborated on each other's art projects, including taking turns drawing themselves as twins—once both girls drew themselves as fair skinned with long, blonde hair and blue eyes (like Alison), and another time they drew themselves as brown skinned with short curly hair (like Marissa).

The role of shared first language in peer playmate choices could be illustrated by another dyad at Children's Place consisting of two boys, Tomas and Carlitos, often joined by Brandon (who was European-American). Thomas was Puerto Rican and Carlitos was Mexican-American. These two boys were not as exclusive in their play as were Marissa and Alison. Carlitos also had frequent interactions with Nikki, a Native American girl, who was in the younger group.

Another *shared heritage* friendship and play group that was frequently observed at Children's Place consisted of three girls from Israel, frequently joined by Fahria, who was from Turkey. The three girls from Israel often switched from English to Hebrew when playing together. Similar to Marissa and Alison, these girls sought each other out during free choice and outdoor times. Naomi, Masha, and Rebeccah were most frequently seen playing with each other on the playground, at the art table during free choice times, and sitting together at lunch.

Gender segregated interactions at Children's Place appeared to be consistently related to the type of activity or setting of the interaction. For example, children sat next to same gender peers at snack 72 percent of the time, and at table activities 65 percent of the time. When there was more freedom of movement (for example, during unstructured activities such as small and large block play) this was not typically the case. At Children's Place cross-gender play and cooperation was observed more frequently in block play, dramatic play, woodworking, science area, and to a lesser degree in the games and small manipulative area. During these free choice activities, cross-gender play was observed about 50 percent of the time.

On the playground children were observed to play with same-gender peers approximately 75 percent of the time. The exception to this was observed in the children who had formed best friendships across gender. These children also played together on the playground, though they were more likely to participate in gender-segregated activities outside than inside.

A partial interpretation of the observed increase in gender cleavage outside can be found by examining the themes and types of dramatic and large motor play engaged in by the children on the playground. The most frequently observed play themes among boys, for example, consisted of "superhero" chasing games—particularly involving male staff and volunteers at Children's Place—riding tricycles and scooters and playing on the tire swing. Boys also frequently played together on the climber, making airplane or space ship sound effects or role-playing animals such as cougars and jaguars.

Girls often continued family dramatic play themes outside (for instance, assigning family roles to each other or pretending to be teenagers or big sisters). They also frequented the tire swing and playhouse when the boys were in another area of the playground—typically on the bike and scooter path or climber. Both boys and girls played—and played together—in the sandbox and on the large wooden platform of the climbing structure. A wide variety of dramatic play themes were developed and carried out in these adjacent areas of the playground at Children's Place.

The most consistent cross-gender friendship observed at Children's Place was that of Eric and Brigitte. Eric was new in September and was quickly befriended by Brigitte. Although they did not always sit together during snack and other table activities, Eric and Brigitte were observed playing together on every observation of the oldest group during *project times*, which took place in small manipulatives, large blocks, woodworking, science, and dramatic play areas of the center. Eric and Brigitte also played together during the free choice time that followed project time.

By late April, however, these two good friends were playing together less frequently—particularly on the playground. Eric was now playing more during free choice times with the older boys, and Brigitte was playing more with the girls. When asked whether Eric was her "good friend," Brigitte replies, "Not any more! You know why? 'Cause he pretended to shot Rebeccah, and I don't like guns!"

The oldest group at Children's Place included three girls who were leaders and often initiated play themes with boys as well as with other girls. One of these girls, Trina, also engaged in some dramatic play with boys on the playground—particularly wild animal role play followed in frequency by superhero play. A favorite theme of virtually all the older children, particularly the boys, was animal-related role play (cougars, Siberian tigers, cheetahs, and various species of whales and sharks).

Turning to The Willows Center Early Childhood Program, an observer entering the oldest children's room might initially be struck by the ratio of boys to girls. When observations began in September the ratio of boys to girls was 11:4, which changed to 10:5 later in the fall. This ratio appeared to be more central to the *classroom dynamic* earlier in the year than later, in winter and spring observations. By later in the year, increased cross-gender cooperative play was observed along with more obvious female leadership in the classroom. A wide variety of behavior and interaction patterns were exhibited by both the boys and girls in this room with boys exhibiting a slightly wider range of roles and behaviors in classroom and playground play.

Particularly during the fall at the Willows Center gender cleavage was evident for most of the children, varying with the type of activity and similar to Children's Place. Specifically, children played with same-sex peers in the gym and on the playground during approximately 80 percent of the interactions observed. Free choice activities (small manipulatives, blocks, and dramatic play) also were the occasion for much gender-segregated play. In contrast to Children's Place, somewhat more cross-gender play was observed in the skills and science area, in the art area, at the computer, and at snack and lunch times.

Although there was a predominance of same-gender play groups during choice time activities, the observed effects of many of the weekly theme-related dramatic play props developed by teachers deserves comment. For example, during eight observations, a group of four to five boys engaged in *nurturant* dramatic play themes, such as taking care of baby dolls or role-playing parental roles. On two other occasions when a beauty and barber shop was set up, a number of boys dressed up, put on makeup, and competed for the *best* costume jewelry.

The same group of boys who engaged most frequently in *nurturant* play themes also actively included Jimmy, one of their mainstreamed peers, during five of the eight dramatic play interactions observed. Jimmy liked babies and doll play, and other boys frequently included him when these props were available in the dramatic play area.

The girls were observed to play together exclusively in a variety of choice activities, particularly on the playground and in the gym. Girls were also frequently heard to describe other girls in their classroom as *best friends*. These friendships changed very little over the course of the school year. One such relationship was between two girls, one of whom had cerebral palsy. By early winter, both girls made consistent reference to each other as *best friends* and were frequently observed moving from one activity to another together.

Two cross-gender friendships were observed at the Willows Center. One was between Ruth and John. This friendship appeared to be stronger in the fall semester than later in the year and was similar to the cross-gender best friendship at Children's Place. During the fall Ruth and John's most frequent shared activities were working together at the computer, doing skills or small manipulative activities together, and, less frequently, engaging in dramatic play.

The only other strong cross-gender friendship observed at the Willows Center was between Jimmy and Kathryn. Their interactions will be described in more detail in the following section focusing on cross-ability interactions. Kathryn frequently let Jimmy, a mainstreamed peer, play on or near her cot during afternoon rest time and also frequently played chasing games with him outside during spring and summer. They also sat by each other at snack or during table projects such as cooking.

Three girls (Ruth, Elizabeth, and Kathryn) emerged as leaders. Ruth was frequently observed either entering or attempting to enter play with boys. Two of the boys (Josh and John) usually accepted her into their activities—at the computer, dramatic play, or table choices. Other boys were typically less willing to have her join in their projects as the following dialogue illustrates.

This interaction took place during a small group project in the block area—building a maze for the gerbil. On this occasion, the boys were working together on a fairly intricate construction and Ruth was attempting to work with them.

Ruth: "Can I help?
Peter: "No!"
Ruth: "You guys . . . I CAN play with you!"
Diego: "No! We don't need your help now."
Ruth: "Yes I can."
Josh: "Yes. She CAN play!"
Diego: "No, 'cause we don't have the hardest part done yet."
Ruth: "I can play—see, here are some of my blocks, and I think I'll build right here . . ."
Josh: "Let her play . . . she can bring her blocks over here by us . . . C'mon!"

Just as at Children's Place, some of the most obvious gender cleavage was observed on the playground and during other large motor activities, followed in frequency by dramatic play and block area interactions. In these settings when cross-gender play did occur, it typically consisted of girls trying to join in with boys' activities. This was particularly true at Willows. At least four consistent cross-gender friendships were observed at the two centers. Still, much gender segregated activity was observed—particularly during outside play and many of the dramatic play interactions observed.

The teachers observed used nonsexist language and also encouraged boys and girls to take on many roles in play—including trying out new activities and role playing nontraditional gender roles. The gender-balanced staff at Children's Place provided frequent opportunities for stereotypes to be directly confronted and discussed by teachers (for example, whether men could have long hair, have a pierced ear, or be toddler teachers, or whether women could carry heavy objects, repair things, or be "the boss"). The staff makeup at Children's Place also provided opportunities for children to observe men in nurturing caregiving roles and women in leadership roles. Intentional confrontation of gender-related hidden curriculum was incorporated by some of the feminist and antiracist everyday teaching practices of both the female and male staff observed—particularly at Children's Place.

The typical child-initiated dramatic play themes were different for male and female play groups much of the time. Male peers tended to play animal and superhero themes, and female peers tended to develop dramatic play around family (including animal families, such as kittens) and career themes. During units emphasizing caregiving roles (infant nursery, hospital, veterinary clinic), boys at Willows Center frequently engaged in nurturant role play. Two boys at Children's Place were frequently observed switching between male and female play groups during project and free play times.

Female leaders were observed at both Children's Place and Willows Center, with more girls in leadership roles at Children's Place. This may have been due, in part, to the more balanced ratio of girls and boys at this center. Children's dialogue reflected an attempt to use less sexist terms, particularly later in the school year—even if this meant inventing new words ("Of course girls can be chefs—they're 'cheffas'!'").

At the Willows Center, more cross-gender cooperation was observed during creative arts, small manipulative, computer, and more structured small group activities. These instances of cross-gender play were not limited to girls joining in activities of boys; more cooperative play was observed during these activities. Initiation of activities and conversations was also seen as more evenly balanced between girls and boys during these activities, which was in contrast to the obvious leadership role many of the boys had in dramatic play, blocks, and during many large motor activities.

Both gender segregation and some cross-gender cooperation were observed in the dramatic play area and appeared to be correlated with the theme of play and props available each week. For example, during "infant nursery," "art gallery," and "hospital" units, there was fairly equal participation and cooperation between boys and girls. In "restaurant," "fire-fighters," and "underwater world" themes, however, more gender segregated play was observed. One ironic comment was made by Kathryn, who had stopped role playing the fire chief and became receptionist at the "fire station" set up in the dramatic play corner. Her reason, when she was asked why she was no longer the fire chief, was that "We went to the real fire station and there were no women!"

Cross-ability Interactions and Mainstreaming Support

This section will summarize free play observations and interviews with children that pertained to interactions between children at both centers and their mainstreamed peers. Two children were mainstreamed in the four-year-old group at Children's Place. Both children attended a public school program half days and spent the remainder of their day at Children's Place. Both Marita and Umaru were supported by a resource teacher (different teachers for morning and afternoon) during most of the time they spent at the center. Marita attended mornings and Umaru, afternoons. Since most observations were conducted during the morning, the following analysis will focus on Marita.

Marita (who is African-American) had Down's Syndrome; at the beginning of the year she was nonverbal and was beginning to learn sign language. Due to her level of disability, she required virtually constant support from a resource or regular teacher. In analyzing field notes related to children's interactions with Marita, the role of the resource teachers was apparent. Although the special needs resource teachers interacted frequently with the other children, when Marita was inside her resource teacher's role included speaking for Marita (e.g., interpreting her behavior, feelings, and needs to other children). Marita's resource teachers were also frequently observed preventing and redirecting inappropriate behavior and modifying activities as necessary to enhance her participation.

Thus in describing Marita's interactions with peers and the types of activities that appeared to foster the greatest amount of cross-ability interaction, there will necessarily be some description of the resource teacher's interactions with the other children. An obvious advantage of this level of one-to-one support for Marita was that she participated in virtually all the activities available to her group. She was not frequently excluded from her peers' activities, and she was encouraged by all the teachers to try out a variety of experiences and activities.

The children were in frequent interaction with Marita. Overall, the relationship of her peers to Marita could be described as "accepting." In general, activities that fostered the most interactions between Marita and her peers were project times—particularly simple table activities and large motor activities. The fewest cross-ability interactions were observed during indoor free choice and large group activities, when children tended to seek out special friends to play with or sit next to (as described in the previous section) and often excluded Marita.

Since Marita was virtually nonverbal, resource teachers and regular staff were teaching her to use sign language. The other children appeared to enjoy learning to use signs as well as helping Marita learn to sign. Several children stated that what they liked to do best with Marita was "help her learn to talk" or "help her learn sign language."

Marita needed the least one-to-one support when participating in large motor activities such as games indoors or during playground free play. Her sense of balance was excellent, and Marita particularly enjoyed playing on the tire swing with the other children. During such interactions, she would swing with two or three other children—usually other girls, who also appeared to enjoy these interactions.

An example of how a motor activity was modified slightly to better include Marita's participation was observed as children in Marita's small group were taking turns tossing bean bags into a stand-up clown with holes in it. Her resource teacher helped Marita throw hers, and when she got one in, all the children cheered for her. Later the same group played a step-taking game, "What time is it?" Marita and her resource teacher took their turn together, holding up a number of fingers for the number of steps. Again Marita's peers appeared to enjoy her participation. Several of them incorporated signing or holding up fingers when it was their turn to be the leader.

At times, however, Marita's outbursts and physical behaviors did upset the other children. The following dialogue during free play in the block room was representative of children's differing feelings about Marita. In this case, children had been building an airport together in the small back room when Marita entered with Anne, her resource teacher. Randy blurted out, "Oh no, Marita's here!" When Marita sat down virtually on top of Rebeccah's construction, Rebeccah responded, "Marita did this—but I can fix it. That's OK, Marita!"

In summary, both Marita and Umaru enjoyed frequent interaction with their peers at Children's Place. Marita's interactions were typically with her resource teacher and a small group of children. Umaru was seen as being more independent and played alone and without a resource teacher during many of the afternoon observations. Interactions between the children at Children's Place and their mainstreamed peers were, for the most part, quite positive, accepting, and helpful. Children seemed to enjoy learning and teaching sign language and helping their mainstreamed friends.

Four children in the room observed at the Willows Center were considered to have special needs. Susan had cerebral palsy, affecting primarily her legs and one arm (she wore leg braces); Jimmy had several developmental delays, particularly in language and cognition; Steve had large motor delays; and Ruth had some speech difficulties and regularly received speech therapy. Jimmy and Susan will be the focus of the following discussion.

Children at the Willows Center were in frequent interaction with their mainstreamed peers, and a number of close cross-ability friendships grew throughout the year and were discussed briefly in the previous section. Although the two regular team teachers in this classroom consisted of one early childhood and one special education teacher, both teachers shared in overall classroom responsibilities fairly equally. The attempt was being made for the Willows Center to avoid a pull-out program for its special needs children, with speech therapy, sign language lessons, and other special supports being provided in the regular mainstreamed classroom.

Jimmy progressed from having virtually no speech early in the school year to learning sign language and then greatly increased his vocabulary by June. In terms of interactions with peers, it appeared that both Jimmy and his peers experienced a year of changes and growth together. Jimmy grew in terms of his social adjustment, communication abilities, and overall cognitive functioning; and his peers, in their acceptance and increasing friendship with Jimmy.

Several themes were obvious in the repeated observations of Jimmy and his peers. These included the use of humor—increasingly laughing with (versus laughing at) Jimmy, learning from Jimmy—particularly learning sign language and taking pride in his other accomplishments.

Several of the boys welcomed Jimmy into their dramatic play themes—typically in the block or adjacent dramatic play areas at choice time. On another occasion four boys, including Jimmy, were playing in the infant nursery and were washing dolls in the water table. Jimmy was very involved in washing a doll in the water table and saying "babeee, babeee," while three other boys found places to put their dolls to bed. Josh then helped Jimmy find a bed for his doll, saying "Here's a bed for your baby." Then Jimmy started to take another doll out of the dramatic play corner and Josh told a student teacher about this. After she explained to Josh that "there's a baby for everyone," Josh took Jimmy's hand and said, "It's OK, it's OK!"

This sort of supportive, though at times protective, interaction was frequent between Josh and Jimmy as well as between several of the other children and Jimmy. Another classroom interaction pattern involving Jimmy was the less positive tendency of some of the boys to "lead Jimmy on" or encourage him to make sounds, run around, or engage in other behaviors generally considered inappropriate in their classroom. The most frequent example of this involved other boys encouraging Jimmy to make motorcycle or car noises. They would sometimes make the sound or show him a toy car, then "tell on him" when he started making noises. This sort of play was not discouraged on the playground and was most frequent outside.

Susan wore leg braces, which she explained to her peers both verbally and through a photo essay done by Susan and her mother describing "How my braces are made." Susan definitely progressed in terms of social integration in the group during the year. During observations in the fall, particularly during free choice activities, Susan often played alone or on the periphery of other children's play. She seldom initiated or attempted to join in dramatic play or table activities with other children, and often spent time at the computer or alone at the art or skills tables.

This began to change, however, by late November. Part of this appeared to be associated with her growing best friendship with Elizabeth, who was very vocal and a leader in the classroom. Susan also played, off and on, with other special needs children in her room. Susan got along very well with Steve, and frequently played with him at the computer or at table activities. With Jimmy, Susan tended to play with blocks or on the periphery during dramatic play. By spring Susan played more actively in dramatic play, climbed up to do the activities on the classroom loft, and asserted herself much more with the boys.

Overall there were very consistent and positive interactions between handicapped and nonhandicapped peers at the Willows Center. Some of the most striking observations of relationships were of Jimmy and several of the children in his room. Potential contributors to the growth of the mainstreamed children included different factors for each child. For Jimmy the increased instruction in sign language and coteaching of sign language to his peers (with a teacher), coupled with friendships with valued or popular children were seen as contributing to his improvements from fall to spring. For Susan the year-long growth from being on the sidelines to greatly increased and varied interactions with peers of both genders was attributed, in part, to her strong friendship—both at the center and at home—with Elizabeth.

When children did have questions about their mainstreamed peers, the answers given were consistently matter-of-fact and honest. For example, two young children in Marita's group at Children's Place grappled with whether she was a "baby," and were told, in age-appropriate terms, that her rate of development in some ways was just different from theirs. Children at both centers were also given straightforward explanations for why certain peers could not talk or were just learning to talk or why a child with cerebral palsy might need leg braces. In this case, at Willows Center it was Susan who explained her braces to her peers. All of these approaches were seen as most consistent with the human relations approach to multicultural education.

CONCLUSIONS AND IMPLICATIONS FOR PRACTICE

This case study took a parallelist perspective on issues of race, ethnicity, gender, and exceptionality in a typical setting for early childhood socialization—the day care center. The attempt was made throughout the study and in the preceding descriptive data highlights to avoid a reductionistic or uni-dimensional analysis. Multiple voices and social forces are present in the child care setting just as they are in the larger community and society. The role of the children themselves, given virtually constant opportunities to interact with diverse peers and with diverse caregivers in the formation of early attitudes, friendships, identities, and understandings was a central focus of the study.

The facilitating or potentially empowering role of teachers and care-givers, importance of selection of materials, dramatic play props and weekly themes, and inclusion of mainstreamed peers in as many activities and valued roles as possible were all discussed in previous sections. Although this article did not discuss the planned or spontaneous *diversity curriculum* in these centers per se, much of the implicit curriculum, whether reflected in the staff's diversity or lack of gender balance or in the increase in gender-segregated play during large motor activities, can contribute to a more eco-logical account of how children come to understand and deal with diversity.

One of the most encouraging human findings of this study was the degree to which children accepted and valued, particularly at the Willows, their mainstreamed peers. From day-to-day interactions to their responses during semistructured and sociometric interviews, children appeared to have a basic understanding of their handicapped peers' strengths and limitations. This supports the contention that mainstreaming in early childhood programs can enhance both mainstreamed children's socialization and skill learning, and the extent to which they are accepted and valued by their peers.

Teachers—both preschool and special education teachers—were seen as playing a key role in encouraging children's acceptance of and interactions with mainstreamed peers. Teachers were obviously committed to suc-cessful mainstreaming in their day-care centers. Appropriate special needs support appeared to contribute to teachers' positive attitudes toward main-streaming. Additionally, teachers modeled their enjoyment of interactions with special needs children, answered children's questions openly and hon-estly, and encouraged children with disabilities to be "teacher assistants" on several occasions (e.g., in teaching sign language). This valuing and appreciation of all children set an inclusive and accepting context in which young children could learn similar attitudes. Neither program used a pull-out model of special services with handicapped children. Removing special needs children from regular activities or doing so at inappropriate times was viewed as something to be avoided whenever possible.

Early childhood programs that are serious about implementing educa-tion that is multicultural are encouraged to look at their enrollment prac-tices as well as their staff, environment goals, and curriculum. Providing a setting in which both men and women are seen as caregivers and leaders is more likely to counter stereotypes than even the most consistently used anti-sexist activities and books. A pluralistic group of children, as well as a racially and, when possible, linguistically balanced staff, provided for frequent sharing of *authentic* cultural knowledge. Just as exposure to mainstreamed peers does much to debunk myths and sterotypes, interactions with racially and linguistically diverse peers remains one of the best strategies for moving closer to education that is multicultural in early childhood settings.

Whether a *pure* interpretation of education that is multicultural is possible in early childhood settings, the two programs observed did appear to create milieus in which human diversity was openly acknowledged, discussed, and appreciated. In other ways the stereotypes prevailed. With few exceptions, boys were generally the leaders in large motor, blocks, and much dramatic play with more assertive girls joining into boys' activities, but rarely was it the other way around. Girls typically emulated nurturing teacher behavior with some notable exceptions, including several boys who frequently took on nurturant roles. Gender segregation was apparent in all small manipulative and computer activities and in some creative arts activities. Yet the consistent use of nonsexist language and attitudes by teachers did appear to have some encouraging effects, as discussed above. Most progress was made at Children's Place—the center with a more gender-balanced staff and enrollment. At the Willows, several boys frequently took on nurturing roles. These findings point to the critical role of caregivers in any antibias or multicultural, nonsexist environment we may attempt to create for preschool children.

In summary, teachers' consistent interventions to correct or redirect sex-stereotypic language or stereotypic assumptions[11] was seen as having an impact on children's language, roles in play, and activity preferences to at least a limited degree. Consistent use of nonsexist language, a gender-balanced staff at Children's Place, and encouragement at both centers of children taking on a variety of roles and challenges appeared to have a cumulative effect on the children throughout the year. The settings that appeared least conducive to cross-gender cooperative play were the playground and indoor large motor activity areas.

In terms of the models of multicultural education described earlier, both centers were seen as implementing a human relations approach, with particular emphasis on accepting individual differences and creating a nonsexist environment. Other promising approaches, including Afrocentric and early language/cultural immersion programs, await documentation and further discussion.

NOTES

1. Christine E. Sleeter and Carl A. Grant, "An Analysis of Multicultural Education in the United States, *Harvard Educational Review* 57 (November 1987): 421–444.

2. Janice E. Hale-Benson, *Black Children: Their Roots, Culture and Learning Styles,* rev. ed. (Baltimore: Johns Hopkins University Press, 1986; Jawanza Kunjufu, *Developing Positive Self-Images and Discipline in Black Children* (Chicago: African-American Images, 1984).

3. Louise Derman-Sparks, *Anti-Bias Curriculum: Tools for Empowering Young Children* (Washington, D.C.: National Association for the Education of Young Children, 1989).

4. Roland C. Crooks, "The Effects of an Interracial Preschool Program Upon Racial Preference, Knowledge of Racial Differences and Racial Identity," *Journal of Social Issues* 26 (Autumn 1970): 137–143; Gwendolyn M. Green, "African-American Four-Year-Olds' Self Esteem: A Field Study of a Southern Rural Head Start Program" (Ed. D. diss., Pennsylvania State University, 1989); E. G. Johnson, "The Development of Color Knowledge in Preschool Children," *Child Development* 48 (March 1977): 308–311.

5. Alice S. Honig, "Sex Role Socialization in Early Childhood," *Child Development* 48 (1983): 57–69; Martha Van Parys, "Preschoolers in Society: Use of the Social Roles of Sex, Age and Race for Self and Others by Black and White Children," paper presented at the Biennial Meeting of the International Society for the Study of Behavioral Development, Toronto, 1981; Malcolm Watson and Kurt Fisher, "Development of Social Roles in Elicited and Spontaneous Behavior During the Preschool Years." *Developmental Psychology* 16 (September 1980): 483–494.

6. Alvis V. Adair and J. Savage, "Sex and Race as Determinants of Preferences, Attitudes and Self Identification Among Black Preschool Children," *Journal of Social and Behavioral Sciences* 20 (1974): 94–101; Katrine G. Kirn, "Racial Identification and Preference in Young Children as a Function of Race and Sex of the Experimenter and Child" (Ph.D. diss., University of Florida, 1973).

7. P. J. Gerber, "Awareness of Handicapping Conditions and Sociometric Status in an Integrated Preschool Setting," *Mental Retardation* 15 (1977): 24–25; Richard P. Iana, Dorothy Ayers, Howard Heller, James McGettigan, and Valsida Walker, "Sociometric Status of Retarded Children in an Integrated Program," *Exceptional Children* 40 (January 1974): 267–271.

8. Kathleen H. Dunlop, Zolinda Stoneman, and Mary L. Cantrell, "Social Interaction of Exceptional and Other Children in a Mainstreamed Preschool Classroom," *Exceptional Children* 47 (October 1980): 132–141; Patricia Kennedy and

Robert Bruininks, "Social Status of Hearing Impaired Children in Regular Classrooms," *Exceptional Children* 40 (February 1974): 336–342; N. L. Peterson and J. D. Haralick, "Integration of Handicapped and Nonhandicapped Preschoolers: An Analysis of Play Behavior and Social Interactions," *Education and Training of the Mentally Retarded* 12 (October 1977): 235–245.

9. B. Gentry, "Does Mainstreaming Insure Integration?" (ERIC Document No. ANED 231108); Nancy Hazen and Betty Black, "Social Acceptance: Strategies Children Use and How Teachers Can Help Children Learn Them," *Young Children* 39 (September 1984): 26–60.

10. F. L. Kohl and P. J. Beckman, "A Comparison of Handicapped and Nonhandicapped Preschoolers' Interactions Across Classroom Activities," *Journal for the Division of Early Childhood* 8 (1984): 49–56; Elizabeth B. Swadener, "Implementing Education that is Multicultural in Early Childhood Settings: A Case Study of Two Day Care Programs," *Urban Review* 20 (Spring 1988): 8–27; Francisco Villarruel, W. Patrick Dickson, and Carole A. Martin, "Using a Microcomputer to Create Social Interactions Among Handicapped and Nonhandicapped Children in a Mainstreamed Preschool," paper presented at the Annual Meeting of the American Association of Mental Deficiency, Denver, Colorado, May 1986.

11. Kathleen Weiler, *Women Teaching for Change: Gender, Class and Power* (South Hadley, Mass.: Bergin and Garvey, 1988); William Ayers, *The Good Preschool Teacher: Six Teachers Reflect on their Lives* (New York: Teachers College Press, 1989).

MARIAJOSÉ ROMERO

Chapter Seven

Work and Play in the Nursery School*

Early childhood educators commonly believe that play is a fundamental element of children's life worlds. Play has been incorporated into nursery and kindergarten curricula because it is seen as the *work* of children, as the process through which they learn and develop, understand themselves and others, and "become at home in the world."[1] This view has been reinforced by a substantial body of research illustrating the contributions of play to cognitive, social, emotional, and physical development.[2] The current literature in early childhood education attests to this emphasis on play in that teacher strategies that enhance its educational value are extensively discussed.[3]

Academic, achievement-oriented early childhood programs, however, do not include play as a learning activity.[4] The early childhood curriculum debate, in addition, has focused on the effectiveness of academic, teacher-directed versus developmental, child-centered curricula.[5] This debate, characterizing the history of the early childhood curriculum, constitutes a tension between the "learning through work" and "learning through play" models of instruction.[6] Advocates of the latter claim that an early academic emphasis may be detrimental for children's performance and motivation and that providing opportunities for play during the early years may help children to cope with the increasing pressures of modern life.[7]

Nancy King's studies suggest that kindergartners and teachers do not agree in their definitions of play: The former view play as voluntary and free of adult supervision and control with the implication that work characterizes most classroom experiences; the latter seem to equate play with pleasure and creativity and describe classroom activities under the label of play.[8] In addition, King identifies an important socializing effect of schooling: Fifth graders in her study had already internalized the institutional definitions of work and play, associating play with positive personal feelings, attitudes, and experiences and classifying more classroom activities under this label than did kindergartners.[9] Finally, King argues that play has a paradoxical status in schooling because its incorporation into the curriculum has not altered school's work orientation, which has in turn undermined the capacity of play to "embody the autonomous personal expressions of the players."[10] She ascertains, moreover, that this paradoxical status is the source of most of the tensions and negotiations in the classroom.[11] In her view, play in schools contradictorily serves both as student resistance and as means of teachers to maintain classroom control.

King's studies help raise pertinent questions as regards the role of play in early childhood education. First, we must explore the extent to which children's understanding of classroom life reflects adults' emphasis on play. Indeed it is too often assumed that children view play as the main business of preschooling.[12] But as King remarks, adults' perspectives may not necessarily match young children's beliefs. The presence of play artifacts, in addition, does not guarantee that play will in fact occur in the classroom.[13] The little research available suggests that children learn to separate work from play only in those nurseries in which time is differentially allocated to "required play" as distinct from "free play."[14] In short, inquiring into children's perspectives allows us to examine what meanings preschooling has for them, whether they become aware of tacit classroom rules, and whether these tacit rules contradict intended pedagogic and educational aims.[15]

Second, actual classroom dynamics in preschools and their socializing effects also ought to be explored. Preschooling appears to lay the foundations for appropriate performance in formal schooling by imparting not only prerequisite skills but also behaviors and attitudes necessary to later academic success. According to Gracey,[16] adopting the student role constitutes the major outcome of preschooling; for Michael Apple and King, this experience helps children to internalize the social definitions of the school institution.[17] Tensions and conflicts also seem to characterize classroom interaction. According to Corsaro, learning the student role is based on becoming a member of the peer culture, which, in turn, emerges from children's identification with one another as well as their differentiation from the opposition to adults.[18] Only by examining actual classroom dynamics and their socializing effects can we assess the extent to which intended pedagogic and educative aims are realized in classroom life.

Finally, these questions need to be addressed in the light of broader structural issues: what do the pedagogic discourse on play and the reality of preschool classrooms mean vis-à-vis the role of education and schooling in the functioning of society and its institutions? Several theorists on the hidden curriculum of schools link the socializing function of education to the preservation of capitalist economies.[19] It has been argued, moreover, that the advent of capitalism brought with it the separation of work and play and the privilege of work.[20] Work and play, however, have been substantially transformed throughout capitalist advancement. While work has lost the sense of a craft, of control over one's actions as a result of the institutionalization of technical and bureaucratic control in the work place,[21] the growth of the leisure industry has turned play into a commodity for consumption and has thus withdrawn play from its opposition to material production and utilitarian concerns.[22] Yet play, Francis Hearn contends, has been deprived of its political potential because, having become an escape or momentary release from the hardships of work, play has failed to challenge the established order. If a major role of education is the student's technical and social training for the world of work, then it is crucial to understand how work and play are structured in school life and how their organization and meanings may influence children's socialization.[23]

It is not my intention to dismiss play completely as an educational tool but rather to refine our understanding of the internal dynamics of preschool classrooms and their socializing consequences. In spite of a number of critical sociological and anthropological studies of early childhood education,[24] research in this area and on play in particular largely follows a psychological framework that takes children's perspectives for granted.[25] Students, however, are not passive recipients of school norms and values but actively mediate and transform them in everyday classroom interaction.[26] Thus research on work and play in preschools demands not only that these categories be comprehended from teachers' points of view; it also requires that both children's notions and their resistance to the adult organization of classroom life be systematically examined.

This study explored the extent to which the distinction between work and play illustrated by King in kindergartens also emerged as a dominant theme of children's socialization at earlier stages of preschooling. The study focused on the ways in which nursery teachers and children defined school work and play and used these labels to characterize the nursery experience. This study also examined how the institutional organization of classroom life was resisted by children on a day-to-day basis.[27] The article offers the researcher's interpretation of classroom dynamics in terms of the opposition to the adult organization of activities that children labeled as work and play.

THE STUDY

The study was conducted in a predominantly white, middle-class, private nursery school associated with a Presbyterian church and located in a northeastern urban center of the United States. Best described as an educationally oriented early childhood institution, the Nursery School[28] offered a day care and a nursery program that stressed the development of the whole child and the individual. The curriculum centered on school and reading readiness, emphasizing those socioemotional skills that would help children cope with the more structured, academic, and task-oriented environment of kindergarten. Accordingly play was seen as a means for children to learn to relate to others and to develop self-confidence, self-esteem, autonomy, and independence.

Ethnographic procedures were used for data collection. Observations of the four-year-old nursery group were carried out once or twice a week between September and December 1986 and for three weeks during early 1987. I conducted a total of 26 four-hour observation sessions. There were 21 children in the group, 10 boys and 11 girls, most of whom had attended the Nursery School for at least two years. Most of their parents were professionals and lived in single family dwellings, and none of them was unemployed or on welfare at the time of the study.[29]

The two teachers from this group were formally interviewed to clarify their philosophy and goals for the classroom and their notions of work and play. In two of these interviews, both teachers were present and attention was paid to ensure that the opinions of each were adequately discussed. Each teacher was also interviewed individually and asked to classify classroom activities as play or work and to explain their selections.

The eleven children interviewed, six girls and five boys, were drawn from those who were attending the Nursery School at the time of the study and who were not enrolled in the Rehabilitation Program.[30] The procedure followed was similar to that employed by King. Each child was observed during an entire morning, and his or her activities were recorded. Narrative accounts describing these activities were written, and the child was interviewed the next day about particular activities he or she had performed. Three sets of questions were addressed: First, children were asked why they came to the Nursery School and whether they had played or worked the previous day; they were also asked to give examples of the work and play done the previous day. Second, they were presented with a list of activities they had carried out. Once it was clear that children remembered a particular activity, they were asked to classify it as either work or play. These lists were sampled from narrative accounts so as to represent academic, nonacademic, required, voluntary, planned, unplanned, individual, and group activities. Most activities in this set of questions appeared in nearly all the individual lists. Finally, children were asked to determine the relative importance of play and work for them and for teachers. Answers were written in interview formats and further questions were asked when responses needed clarification.

TEACHERS' PERSPECTIVE ON WORK AND PLAY

Teachers believed that children did not work in the Nursery School because work, as separate from play, was the exclusive domain of elementary schooling. In their view, school work involved tasks that had a clear academic content (such as reading, math, and science) and made use of paper and pencil.

The Nursery School experience comprised, instead, play and "structured activities," teachers claimed. They often stressed that the four-year-old nursery group represented "the last year when kids can be really able to play." Accordingly teachers applied this label to nearly all the classroom activities, yet almost always with a qualifier. "It's learning play, another part of the structured morning." These activities encompassed both optional and unsupervised ones (playing in the housekeeping corner, block building, running around in the classroom, drawing, and using academic and nonacademic manipulatives) and most assigned and supervised tasks (academic and nonacademic large group talks, games and stories, aerobics, and some projects).

"Structured activities" were defined as planned and designed tasks that were "something in between work and play." Structured activities were academic without being work, teachers maintained, since the term *academic,* broadly understood, also referred to social, cognitive, and motor skills contributing to school readiness. In their view, school work differed from structured activities in that the former was strictly assigned and evaluated whereas the latter allowed children to get involved and to participate, to learn, and to develop at their own pace, "without [teachers] standing over them and beating it into them," "without being put on the spot."

Teachers expressed, nevertheless, that for some children some nursery school experiences could be work. This included activities with clear academic content (such as numbered dittoes) that were defined, required, and controlled by teachers (such as cleaning up and lining up) and optional and unsupervised activities (such as exercising with the gym equipment or playing with the snake alphabet). They argued, however, that preschoolers were not workers and did not separate the notions of work and play.

It was at first difficult to identify patterns explaining teachers' use of the labels work and play. The type of activities and materials themselves seemed to be relevant since elementary school work was equated with academic, paper-and-pencil tasks. But these attributes were not present in all the activities that teachers viewed as work. The social context of activities also appeared significant. Teachers characterized "real play" not only as being devoid of adult supervision and control but also as associated with choice. But they distinguished between different types of choices: while some assigned and controlled activities were play because children were free to use the end product in any way they wanted, others were not play because children had to conform to the adult definition and organization of tasks. Yet all these instances were not work because children could decide whether or not to participate actively. In short both work and play encompassed required and supervised as well as voluntary and self-directed activities.

It became evident that teachers' criteria for differentiating work from play were based on the psychological context of activities—that is, personal attitudes, preferences, and feelings toward a particular activity, largely regardless of whether the activity was mandatory or voluntary, supervised or self-directed.

Teachers characterized play in the Nursery School as those activities in which children not only became actively involved but also manifested interest and willingness to perform. In their view, play was mostly initiated by children. Teachers characterized play as being creative, fun, pleasing, and rather easy. Play was completely devoid of any pressure or stress either because it did not demand the completion of an end product to be evaluated or because it was not authoritatively imposed and evaluated.

In principle teachers maintained that all forms of play resulted in learning, a characteristic they believed to be overlooked in commonsense views of play. But their classification of activities suggests a subtle distinction between "learning play" and "just play." Indeed teachers labeled most structured activities as learning play, stressing the concepts and skills being mastered. They described as "just play" and without any learning component only those child-initiated and self-directed activities that transgressed classroom norms and that were, therefore, often interrupted by teachers.

Nursery School work was seen, in turn, as including not only academic, paper-and-pencil tasks but also those teacher-structured and required activities that implied the manual elaboration of a product to be evaluated. More importantly, work for teachers involved activities imposed on children against their will, interests, and preferences as well as obligatory and optional tasks that were difficult, uncreative, boring, and even tedious—tasks that often became exceedingly stressful given the pressures of their mandatory, evaluated, or arduous nature. In short teachers' notions of work are best described by the following remark: "I hate to use the term "work," because they [children] are going to have to spend the rest of their lives working."

Work and play were not clearly separate categories for teachers. On the basis of their personal standards, they discerned various kinds of work and play and often compared activities in order to explain the label ascribed. Looking at books after snack, for instance, "was play but not in the same way as playing a game," because it was not "an active play situation"; doing aerobics in the gym was play in that it was fun, yet it also resembled work since it could be difficult, but "not in the same sense as a ditto." From their perspective, moreover, work could become play and vice versa.

That most classroom activities were classified as play seemed to be consistent with the Nursery School focus on children's socioemotional development and with the view of play as the vehicle for bringing about self-confidence, autonomy, independence, and ability to relate to others. But it was precisely here, in the perception of the aims of the nursery experience vis-à-vis formal schooling, that the latent distinction between work and play became evident and the function of play clarified: play in the nursery school became a preparation for later work.

> [Julie:] The major philosophy of the School . . . is that four year old children really need to play and they are not given enough time to play. It's been a big discussion . . . that there's been this push for kids to learn all their academics and all this early reading and what is happening is that . . . they're not having enough time to play and therefore . . . their emotional and social growth is being withheld. . . . [They] have been pressured and when they're found in the structured situation of primary school, they're not coping well because they didn't have enough time to play and get all this other stuff out of their system when they should have.

CHILDREN'S NOTIONS OF WORK AND PLAY

Contrary to teachers' beliefs, both work and play appeared as salient notions whereby children structured their nursery experiences. All activities in their lists were categorized under one of these labels, and none of them was described as being both work and play. Children, moreover, characterized more classroom activities as work than as play.

The analysis of children's responses suggests that work and play were not associated with a specific activity, material, space, or time. Both categories included individual and collective activities with varying academic content and degree of skills and concentration required. Work and play also did not differ in terms of the psychological context of experiences. Activities in each category did not appear to exhibit any distinguishing pattern as regards the pleasure, involvement, concentration, effort, or willingness displayed by children who seemed, instead, equally to enjoy and to become involved in both work and play. Furthermore, children described most of the work activities as fun, and many of them explicitly said: "Fun is work and play."

It was only in the social context of activities—that is, in the type of interaction between teachers and children—that these two categories exhibited distinguishing patterns. With few exceptions, two salient features of work were that it was required and directed by teachers. Children thus appeared to equate work with having to conform to teachers' specifications of the tasks to be done as well as the materials, time, and space to be used. Activities labeled as play, in contrast, were voluntary and self-directed. Children thus seemed to identify play by their control of classroom events and resources. That is, they themselves decided the type of activities to be performed and the ways in which materials, time, and space were used. The relevance of the social context in children's notions of work and play is further illustrated by the fact that the same activity was labeled as play if children had chosen it for themselves, whereas it was classified as work if teachers had assigned it. Looking at books after snack, tracing dittoes, and doing number exercises, for instance, were described as play when children undertook these activities on their own. But they were considered as work when teachers requested children to perform them.

In general, teachers were not involved in most of the activities labeled as play, except when children's behavior contradicted classroom norms. Interestingly enough, children also said they were playing on those few occasions in which adults were present. In those instances, however, teachers did not adopt a directive and supervisory role but rather became active playmates; children still maintained control over the course of events.

Activities described as play exhibited a substantial variability since they were self-directed: the specific form of play largely depended on the individuals involved. Activities described as work were, in contrast, somewhat uniform with all the children, following teachers' instructions, carrying out nearly the same actions, and using materials in similar ways. Some of the activities described as work, however, were not accomplished in such a homogeneous way; children could sometimes decide how to perform the task within the specifications provided by teachers. In spite of the choices allowed and of the diverse complexity of these tasks, children classified nearly all the assigned and supervised activities as work.

On the whole, teachers and children differed radically in the criteria used to separate work from play as well as in their descriptions of the nursery experience. They expressed, moreover, divergent interests regarding work and play. While children disagreed on which of these activities was their main concern, they unanimously held that work was the main focus of teachers, who in turn were rather ambivalent on these questions. Teachers hesitated to affirm that play was the most important activity for them, although they believed work to be exclusive to elementary schooling and regarded play as crucial for learning and development. Because of their contribution to school readiness, teachers deemed projects to be the most important classroom activities, tasks that children classified as work. Teachers claimed, however, that play was the dominant interest of children although, as already noted, they stressed their doubts as to whether children perceived these categories and used these labels.

The foregoing pages show that children's perspectives cannot be taken for granted but ought to be examined in their own right. This enables us to understand how children perceive intended educative aims, as well as what notions they form about schools throughout their preschool years. Although these ideas reflect to some degree the level of cognitive development, they also emerge from children's participation in the social structure of the classroom. In this respect, examining children's perspectives also helps us gain insight into a powerful force shaping classroom dynamics: the peer culture, which may not necessarily be aligned with that of adults in the institution. The evidence presented here attests to children's active role in making sense of their nursery experience. Indeed, theorists on the hidden curriculum have argued that students do not passively acquiesce to the norms and values of schools but, through their cultural production, actively resist and transform them in everyday interaction.[31] In the light of the incompatible notions of work and play and the arising opposition of interests, the following question emerges: what was the children's reaction to the adult organization of the classroom?

CHILDREN'S INCIPIENT RESISTANCE[32]

Play in the Nursery School was contained within the institutional framework of adult-defined norms. From the beginning of the school year, teachers introduced children to the rather long, intricate code of rules circumscribing play. While some of these norms were clearly aimed at preventing accidents (for example, blocks must not be brandished in the air), others were intended to preserve a calm and quiet atmosphere and to ensure work performance (for example, "There's no running and no thunder-catching in the room, otherwise they don't do anything in the whole morning").[33]

Children's incipient resistance to the norms of play was reflected in the repeated transgressions of the institutional code. Despite the norm that

"Everybody can play with everybody," playmate selection was characterized by exclusion instead of integration: most of the negotiation during play
dealt with the conflict resulting from the rejection of potential playmates
rather than with the aggregation of peers of play, regardless of the particular individuals involved.

In a similar manner the ownership of materials elicited a great deal of
conflict, in spite of the norm of sharing. Children often took possession of
play materials and prevented others from using materials even after they
had left the game. Play, moreover, frequently evolved into running around,
crawling on the rug, hiding beneath the tables, yelling and screaming, and
occasional pillow fights. The teachers' unceasing reminders—"use your inside voices," "you've forgotten the rules about the blocks," "no thunder-
catching in the room"—momentarily halted the infringement of classroom
norms. Yet children often resumed their own definitions of play shortly after teachers were out of sight.

The enforcement of play norms did not occur without substantial conflict
for teachers. Indeed they were aware that the sanction of the institutional
code constricted play, thereby contradicting their concern for children's
well-being. Thus teachers allowed such imaginative play as monsters and
superheroes—but only in the gym—once its contribution to self-esteem had
been stressed in the educational literature. They were also apprehensive that
the institutional code could repress central ingredients of play: "No jumping,
no running, no screaming, no yelling, no guns, it sounds like no fun at all!"

The incipient resistance to the imposition of school work appeared to
be varied and elaborate. Children played a substantial role in setting the
pace of work performance, frequently delaying the initiation and completion of work. As the year progressed, they became increasingly less responsive and ready to follow teacher signals and instructions. They were slow to
start cleaning up the room or to get ready for lining up, large group, and
games in the gym. On those occasions when teachers were not overseeing
the group, children took the opportunity to avoid the cleanup altogether and
sat on the rug and played.

The performance of work was also slackened by an incipient subversion
of work routines. This can be seen as the children's attempt to oppose the
imposition of work and transform its institutional organization by incorporating play elements into tasks. The subversion of work routines took different forms first, children disrupted the smooth unfolding of work by
apparently complying with classroom norms. During cleanup time, for instance, some children helped to tidy up the room just for a little while; then
they rushed off to sit on the rug and quietly waited for large group to start,
while teachers and the remaining peers continued putting toys away. Likewise children selected to clean up those materials that allowed them to play

the most, that they liked the best, or that their friends were already tidying up while teachers insisted: "It's not time to play, it's time to clean up." Similarly, as soon as lights went off calling for cleanup time, some children rushed to the toilet while others started painting on the easel or tracing dittoes, all activities that teachers were unlikely to interrupt. Still others simply wandered around the room, telling everybody else to begin the cleanup.

Second, children frequently interrupted the progression of work. Such disruption as volunteering irrelevant information, talking, laughing, sitting improperly, and covering their ears or remaining silent when called on was immediately repressed by teachers since it overtly transgressed classroom norms. But a different type of disruption seemed to conceal this infringement by its apparent concern with work performance. For instance, children frequently said after attendance was called: "You called Laura twice" or "You forgot to call Joanne." Teachers would then check the attendance list and count students. When children insisted that someone had not been called, teachers asked them to count everybody in the group in order to ensure that nobody had been missed. Similarly after saying the days of the week, children said: "We forgot to say Tuesday," or any other day. The resulting argument was commonly closed when teachers remarked: "Let's repeat the days of the week to make sure that we don't forget any day."

Last, children also appeared to subvert the unfolding of work routines by "showing too much excitement" during work. They broke into yells, claps, and laughter after being told to line up in order to go to the playground, gym, or films. Children, moreover, very often initiated the cleanup, screaming: "It's cleanup time, it's cleanup time," while teachers urged: "I heard nobody say you should scream," "Instead of screaming why don't you help clean up."

Interestingly enough, teachers were aware of children's incipient resistance when it overtly transgressed classroom norms: "At large group . . . a good portion of the kids don't listen, it's like they do everything possible not to listen." But they seemed unaware of the children's emerging resistance when it was masked by an apparent compliance with classroom norms or by an ostensible concern with work. Referring, for instance, to children's interruption after saying the days of the week, one teacher said.

> I think it's just their awareness of a structured situation, I guess, of their expectations to meet my expectations. I don't know exactly under what that goes [play, work], I think that falls more under listening and communication skills.

In short, children did not passively accept adult organization of classroom life. They seemed, on the contrary, to actively challenge and attempt to redefine the organization of work and play in ways that incorporated their needs and interests in play. Thus play in the classroom becomes a form of resistance in that it conveys students' interests and meanings, allowing them to envision alternatives to the dominant social order.[34]

The increasing lack of responsiveness to adult instructions seemed not to derive from children's developmental characteristics. By the end of the period of study, teachers maintained that children had substantially progressed in school readiness skills so as to be able to perform activities on their own. The increasing resistance was in contrast to their behavior during the first weeks of school when children promptly responded to instructions and signals, rapidly completing work tasks within a calm and organized atmosphere.

Children seemed, furthermore, to possess a rather keen understanding of classroom norms. They were frequently observed enforcing rules not only with their peers but also in their symbolic play. They checked, moreover, to see if teachers were around, using those occasions during which adults were not overseeing the group to evade the rules, which suggests the children grasped the norms and were to some extent aware of their transgression.

But in the light of young children's cognitive and social development, their attempts at opposing and transforming the adult organization of their environment must be interpreted with caution, as William Corsaro points out.[35] Indeed, Jean Piaget characterizes preoperational language and thought as egocentric—that is, as a "cognitive state in which the cognizer sees the world from a single point of view, his own but without knowledge of the existence of viewpoints or perspectives and *a fortiori*, without awareness that he is prisoner of his own [viewpoint]."[36] He remarks, moreover, that due to this egocentrism children fail to coordinate their actions through cooperation with peers.[37] Preschoolers' potential to challenge the adult configuration of their environment, however, cannot be completely dismissed. According to Piaget, the intensified social contact with peers contributes to establishing a relativism of perspectives as well as cooperation and reciprocity in personal relationships.[38] The increased exposure to diverse and conflicting viewpoints, Piaget adds, not only helps children to become aware of the individual and social aspects of their thought and to reassess their own viewpoints but also enables them to articulate their actions with others. Corsaro's research suggests, furthermore, that preschoolers already have clear notions of the relevance and restrictiveness of the adult world as compared to their own world.[39] In this view these notions lie at the root of children's strategies to evade institutional rules—secondary adjustments— through which children not only cooperate actively among themselves but also draw upon existing routines to satisfy their personal ends.

It is my impression that children in this study did to some extent share an awareness of their incipient resistance and approached it as play, although I have little evidence to support this claim. Children were never observed discussing classroom norms and their resistance among themselves, except for enunciating a specific rule in front of a mischievous peer. Neither did they discuss these issues or the purposes of their oppositional behavior during the interviews. It may well be, as Corsaro remarks, that due to cognitive developmental factors preschoolers' knowledge of their behavior is for the most part spatially and temporally bound and, therefore, shared primarily when it is produced during peer interaction.[40] As a consequence, he adds, preschoolers are not able to deal with this knowledge on a more abstract level and to reflect upon their behavior in ways that allow them to talk about it with others. Moreover, whenever children volunteered information on and examples of their play, they tended to focus on those activities on which they had spent a considerable amount of time the previous day and seldom referred to instances of resistance. The four children who were explicitly asked about examples of the oppositional behavior classified all these instances as play.[41] It may be argued that children viewed their resistances as play since the shared the same structural characteristics—that is, being voluntary and self-directed—as those activities labeled as play. This interpretation is tentative, however, because the patterns of resistance described above only became evident in the later analysis of fieldnotes and were not subject to indefinite triangulation with children.

The fact that children do not passively conform to teachers' arrangements of classroom life can be seen as an incipient resistance that may be significant for their socialization in nursery schools. This opposition helps children build a sense of group identity and distance their world from that of adults.[42] Children also learn modes of opposition that may prove useful in later schooling. Moreover this incipient resistance substantially alters classroom dynamics since the smooth unfolding of routines depends upon children's acceptance of the adult organization of their environment—an acceptance that in turn must be won and maintained by teachers.

DISCUSSION

This study suggests that the separation of work and play permeates the early stages of preschooling. The study also shows that the role of play in early childhood education must be critically examined vis-à-vis children's understandings of classroom life and actual classroom dynamics. As King argues, children's perspectives on work and play are not captured in adults' beliefs. Teachers resembled elementary school students in that both drew upon the *psychological context* of activities in order to distinguish between work and play. In contrast, the children in this study seemed to differentiate these categories in experiences as work. Moreover, they did not passively acquiesce in the adult organization of work and play but seemed instead to transform it in ways that satisfied their interests in play. Children's resistance thus involves teachers in particular forms of imposition and negotiation about the appropriate classroom behavior and activities.[43]

It has been argued that play has an ambiguous status in formal schooling.[44] This study indicates, in contrast, that both work and play in the Nursery School were ascribed a conflicting status, which appeared to stem in part from the rather informal character of this early childhood setting. For teachers, the nursery experience was not part of formal schooling because in their view the Nursery School was not devoted to the performance of work nor were young children workers. This perspective seems to agree with popular notions of early childhood education, based on "the false assumption that children are free of institutional pressures during the early years."[45] which hold that play is the real business of preschooling. The nursery experience, however, was not only expected to prepare pupils for elementary school but was also built on the institutional model of the school. In fact, the organization and use of time, space, activities, and materials were patterned after the model of a worksite—the school—and were reflected as such in the schedule, the grouping of children, the compartmentalization of topics, and the general planning. Thus the Nursery School, although it did not embrace the achievement of work, also did not entirely detach itself from that purpose.

The contradictory status attributed to work and play also appeared to emerge from the theoretical and ideological orientation of the Nursery School. The rather progressivist emphasis on the *whole child* and her or his development toward self-confidence and autonomy together with the view of play as the paramount channel for learning were somewhat reflected in the organization of the classroom and in the curriculum. Play in the Nursery School existed, however, only within adult-defined frameworks and consisted for the most part of routinized tasks; it was dichotomized in various ways—for example, in the distinction between *learning play* and *just play;* it existed in a context structured as a workplace yet apparently not fully devoted to work; and it was perceived by teachers as a means for children to become *good workers* in later schooling. Thus the ascribed status of play was as ambiguous in the Nursery School as in kindergarten, revealing in both contexts the contradiction between the rhetoric and the reality of schooling: the apparent needs of children coalesce with the work orientation and organization of schools.[46]

The ways in which children and teachers defined the purpose of the Nursery School appeared to reflect the contradictory status of work and play. While children viewed play, work, and learning as the major pursuit of the Nursery School, teachers were reluctant to express the goals in terms of these categories, mentioning instead learning and development. This contradictory status was also latent in teachers' description of classroom activities as "structured activities" and "learning play." Children, on the other hand, drew a clear distinction between work and play and classified activities accordingly. Teachers almost never employed the label *work* in the classroom. But this omission did not mask the separation of work and play for children—a separation that was implied every time a teacher said, "It's not time to play, it's time to clean up." Classroom dynamics also revealed teachers' hierarchy of activities. As Rachel Sharp and Anthony Green[47] illustrate, progressive teachers do not perceive the outcomes of children's choices neutrally in spite of their child-centered ideology. Thus children in this study clearly understood that work was the concern of teachers, who in turn lacked a definite stand on this point, uncovering the contradictory status of work and play.

Most classroom tensions and negotiations were rooted precisely in the contradictory status attributed to work and play.[48] In spite of its brief impact, children's resistance substantially shaped the course of events in that it demanded that teachers devote time, attention, and energy to changing classroom organization and routines. But the resisting potential of play may be limited by the egocentric character of social cognition during early childhood. This political potential also remains largely unrealized since young children's opposition does not attempt to redistribute power in the classroom but rather to achieve momentary self-expression as well as release from work. Play as resistance may, on the contrary, help strengthen teachers' authority by giving them opportunities to display their control over the classroom.[49] Furthermore, while children are active agents of their socialization, they hold unequal power to define the classroom situation vis-à-vis adults.[50] Thus the political potential of play is limited since teachers largely control children's access to play. In the final analysis, play as resistance contradictorily encourages the maintenance of the institutional order.

CONCLUSIONS

This study suggests that this particular nursery school introduces children to the definitions and organization of school work and play through patterning their experiences of being workers. That is, they learn to distinguish systematically between these categories and to relegate them to distinct times and spaces; they gain an understanding of the meanings, interests, and work orientation of the institution; and they learn both to accept work and play routines and to resist and transform them.

As Apple[51] points out, students not only mediate and transform institutional messages, norms, and values but actively shape classroom dynamics. It is unclear, nevertheless, how preschoolers' particular interpretations of classroom life may affect their learning, development, and well-being in nurseries and kindergartens. This study indicates that we need to recognize children's perspectives and peer culture as powerful forces shaping classroom dynamics and therefore influencing the extent to which intended educative aims are realized in everyday classroom life. Our lines of inquiry need to be broadened to encompass issues having considerable practical implications: are the kinds of institutional arrangements and classroom experiences devised for young children compatible with stated pedagogic and educative aims? To what extent do these arrangements and experiences foster and limit children's learning, development, and well-being through play? What kinds of peer culture and classroom dynamics emerge within different institutional arrangements? Are pedagogic discourses of play meaningful for teachers vis-à-vis the concrete demands of the classroom and the institution? This research suggests that pedagogic discourses on play appear to be in conflict with the demands of a preschool arrangement patterned after the institutional model of the school and having an ambiguous work orientation. In this context, the central status of play is no longer clear in classroom practice. This ambiguous status shapes, in turn, the tensions and negotiations that occur in the classroom. Due to their overtly psychological emphasis on the individual child, pedagogic discourses on play fail to consider how the peer culture together with institutional demands affect the dynamics of the classroom, thereby reducing the operational significance of pedagogic theory for teachers' classroom practice.[52]

The results described here have two major implications for the current debate between the *learning-through-play* and *learning-through-work* models of instruction in early childhood education. On the one hand, children's perspectives must inform the assessment of the goals and effectiveness of early childhood programs. Indeed understanding children's points of view may enable curriculum planners and early childhood educators to determine the extent to which children's notions about preschooling reflect a pedagogic emphasis on play; such an understanding may also help to identify and transform those classroom practices that potentially contradict intended educative aims. On the other hand, actual classroom dynamics ought to be taken into account in the planning and evaluation of early childhood curricula. It is only when we examine the complex demands and constraints confronted by teachers and the messages embedded in the patterns and regularities of classroom life that we can meaningfully discuss the educational value of *learning-through-play* versus *learning-through-work* models of instruction.

On the whole, this research evidences the need for critical studies of socialization in early childhood institutions, an area that has received relatively little attention in the educational literature. Indeed, the impact of schooling on young children demands a more systematic inquiry, even more so in the light of the rapid expansion of early childhood services and the trend toward an earlier institutionalization of children.[53]

NOTES

*Portions of this paper were presented at the Annual Convention of the American Educational Studies Association, Chicago, November 1987. The author wishes to thank Lois Weis and Maxine Seller for their criticisms and contributions to the research reported here.

1. Barbara Day, "Contemporary Early Childhood Education Programs and Related Controversial Issues," in *Aspects of Early Childhood Education*, ed. Dale Range et al. (New York: Academic, 1980); Otto Weiniger, "Play and Early Childhood," in *In Celebration of Play: An Integrated Approach to Play and Child Development*, ed. Paul Wilkinson (New York: St. Martin's, 1980), pp. 43–62.

2. See Debra Pepler, "Play in Schools and Schooled in Play: A Psychological Perspective," in *School Play: A Source Book*, ed. James Block and Nancy King (New York: Garland, 1987), pp. 75–107.

3. See for instance Bernard Spodek et al., *Foundations of Early Childhood Education* (Englewood Cliffs, N.J.: Prentice Hall, 1987); Trevor Kerry and Janice Tollit, *Teaching Infants* (Oxford, Eng.: Basil Blackwell, 1987); Eli Am, "Play in the Preschool: Some Aspects of the Role of the Adults," *International Journal of Early Childhood* 18, no. 2 (1986).

4. Spodek, *Foundations of Early Childhood Education*.

5. Cynthia Wagner, ed., *A Resource Guide to Public School Early Childhood Programs* (Alexandria, Va: Association for Supervision and Curriculum Development, 1988).

6. Clem Adelman, "The Playhouse and the Sand Tray," in *Defining the Curriculum: Histories and Ethnographies*, ed. Ivor Goodson and S. Bale (Philadelphia: Falmer Press, 1984), pp. 77–88.

7. Joan Isenberg and Nancy Quisenberry, "Play: A Necessity for All Children," *Childhood Education* 64 (February 1988): 138–145; David Elkind, *Miseducation: Preschoolers at Risk* (New York: Alfred A. Knopf, 1987).

8. Nancy King, "Play: The Kindergartners' Perspective," *The Elementary School Journal* 80 (November 1979): 81–87.

9. Nancy King, "Play in the Workplace," in *Ideology and Practice in Schooling*, ed. Michael Apple and Lois Weis (Philadelphia: Temple University Press, 1983), p. 279.

10. Ibid.

11. Nancy King, "Children's Play as a Form of Resistance in the Classroom," *Journal of Education* 164 (Fall 1982): 320–329.

12. See for instance David Fernie, "Becoming a Student: Messages from the First Settings," *Theory into Practice* 27 (Winter 1988): 3–10.

13. Adelman, "The Playhouse."

14. Valery Polakow Suransky, *The Erosion of Childhood* (Chicago: University of Chicago Press, 1982).

15. Stuart Reifel, "Children's Thinking About Their Early Education Experiences," *Theory into Practice* 27 (Winter 1988): 62–66.

16. H.L. Gracey, "Learning the Student Role; Kindergarten as Academic Boot Camp," in *The Sociology of Education. A Sourcebook*, ed. H. R. Stub (Homewood, Ill: Dorsey Press, 1975).

17. Michael Apple and Nancy King, "What Do Schools Teach?" *Curriculum Inquiry* 6, no. 4 (1977): 341–358.

18. William Corsaro, "Peer Culture in the Preschool," *Theory into Practice* 27 (Winter 1988): 19–24; William Corsaro, *Friendship and Peer Culture in the Early Years* (Norwood, N.J.: Ablex, 1985).

19. See for instance Samuel Bowles and Herbert Gintis, *Schooling in Capitalist America* (New York: Basic Books, 1976).

20. Francis Hearn, "Toward a Critical Theory of Play," *Telos* 68–70 (Winter 1976–1977): 146–160.

21. Michael Apple, "Curricular Form and the Logic of Technical Control," in *Ideology and Practice in Schooling*, ed. Apple and Weis, pp. 143–165.

22. Hearn, "Toward a Critical Theory."

23. See for instance, Dennis Carlson, "Updating Individualism and the Work Ethic: Corporate Logic in the Classroom," *Curriculum Inquiry* 12 (Summer 1982): 125–160.

24. See for instance William A. Corsaro, "Routines in the peer Culture of American and Italian Nursery School Children," *Sociology of Education* 61 (January 1988): 1–14; Sally Lubeck, "Nested Contexts," in *Class, Race and Gender in American Education*, ed. Lois Weis (Albany: State University of New York Press, 1988); Block and King, *School Play;* Sally Lubeck, *Sandbox Society* (London: Falmer Press, 1986); Suransky, *The Erosion of Childhood*.

25. For a review of this literature, see Rimmer van der Kooij and Henriette Meyjes, "Research on Children's Play," *Prospects* 16, no. 1 (1986); see also Marianne Bloch, "Becoming Scientific and Professional: An Historical Perspective of

the Aims and Effects of Early Childhood Education,'' in *The Formation of School Subjects,* ed. Tom Popkewitz (London: Falmer Press, 1987), pp. 25–62.

26. Michael Apple, ''The Other Side of the Hidden Curriculum: Correspondence Theories and the Labor Process,'' *Interchange* 11 (Fall 1980–1981): 5–22; Michael Apple, ''What Correspondence Theories of the Hidden Curriculum Miss,'' *The Review of Education* 5 (Spring 1979): 101–112.

27. The study on which this paper is based also examined teachers' strategies for classroom control. The issue is not addressed here due to space limitations.

28. The names of the children, teachers, and the school are fictitious.

29. This information was obtained during interviews with teachers. No data on parents' education, occupation, and income were gathered.

30. The Rehabilitation Program served physically handicapped and learning disabled children attending the Nursery School. They were not interviewed following a request of the administration.

31. Apple, ''The Other Side of the Hidden Curriculum''; Apple, ''What Correspondence Theories of the Hidden Curriculum Miss.''

32. This section is based on classroom observations throughout the entire period of study. Narrative accounts were analyzed by looking at classroom activities according to children's systems of classification since their distinction between work and play followed criteria beyond their personal standards.

33. Thunder-catching was a game in which one child at a time chased peers around the classroom and the child caught ran in turn after his or her peers. Commonly initiated by a small group, this game spread fast around the room, involving more children chasing peers while all screamed and laughed. This game was often played during the free activity period, when children could choose their own activities provided that they did the required project at some point during the time frame.

34. King, ''Children's Play as a Form of Resistance.''

35. Corsaro, *Friendship and Peer Culture in the Early Years.*

36. Piaget (1954) as quoted by John H. Flavell, *The Developmental Psychology of Jean Piaget* (London: Van Nostrand, 1963), p. 60. John H. Flavell, *Cognitive Development* (Englewood Cliffs, N.J.: Prentice-Hall, 1985) remarks that the assumption of egocentrism in young children's communication has been questioned: Recent research suggests that preschoolers adapt their speech to the listener's characteristics and needs.

37. Jean Piaget, *The Moral Judgment of the Child* (London: Routledge and Kegan Paul, 1972).

MariaJosé Romero

38. Herbert Ginsburg and Sylvia Opper, *Piaget's Theory of Intellectual Development*, 2n ed. (Englewood Cliffs, N.J.: Prentice-Hall, 1979).

39. Corsaro, *Friendship and Peer Culture in the Early Years.*

40. Ibid.

41. In the following fieldnote, for instance, it seems clear that Christian is intentionally avoiding the cleanup by choosing an alternative activity, which he later described as play.

(9:45) When Julie says, "It's clean-up time," Christian goes to the easel and starts painting. Kristel is making a picture on the other side of the easel. Julie calls again for clean-up time but she does not turn off the lights as usual. Both Christian and Kristel continue painting. Several children approach them, saying: "Hey, it's clean-up time," and both Christian and Kristel reply: "We're doing something, we'll clean up when we're done." Their peers insist, "It's clean-up time," yet Christian and Kristel reply, "We'll clean up when we finish." This exchange, unnoticed by Julie who is supervising the clean-up in the block corner, is repeated several times until 9:53, when Christian leaves the easel, washes his hands and sits on the blue rug for Large Group. [Fieldnotes, names are fictitious]

42. Corsaro, *Friendship and Peer Culture in the Early Years.*

43. King, "Children's Play as a Form of Resistance."

44. King, "Play in the Workplace."

45. Suransky, *The Erosion of Childhood*, p. 174.

46. King, "Children's Play as a Form of Resistance."

47. Rachel Sharp and Anthony Green, *Education and Social Control: A Study in Progressive Primary Education* (London: Routledge and Kegan Paul, 1975).

48. King, "Children's Play as a Form of Resistance."

49. These are also King's points.

50. Apple and King, "What Do Schools Teach?"

51. Apple, "The Other Side of the Hidden Curriculum"; Apple, "What Correspondence Theories of the Hidden Curriculum Miss."

52. See Sharp and Green, *Education and Social Control.*

53. Wagner, *A Resource Guide.*

ANTHONY D. PELLEGRINI

Chapter Eight

Children's Rough-and-Tumble Play: Issues in Categorization and Function[*]

In this article I will describe what elementary school children, particularly boys do on the school playground during recess. Despite the fact that the recess period occupies a significant portion of the elementary school day (significant when compared to time spent on math and reading lessons), next to nothing is known about what children do during this period. Even less is known about the educational/developmental significance of the behavior children exhibit during recess. The paucity of research in this area does not, however, mean that recess has escaped controversy. In a suburb of Washington, D.C., for example, parents and school board members are engaged in a struggle over the elimination of recess. The school board, reflecting a time-on-task, back-to-basics orientation, wants to eliminate recess so that children can spend more time on "instruction." Parents, on the other hand, see recess as an important socializing experience. As noted above, there is virtually no data from which either side in this controversy can draw.

In this article, I will describe the results of an on-going examination of one aspect of elementary school children's recess behavior. We will first discuss a specific and frequently occurring playground behavior—rough-and-tumble play (R & T). Next, we will explicate relations between R & T and dimensions of children's social competence, such as popularity and social problem solving. Following Zigler and others, we suggest that children's social competence is an important dimension of schooling, along with more traditional achievement measures.[1]

R & T has a controversial history in child development and early education. It is considered a form of aggression by some researchers and playful and adaptive by others.[2] I will describe R & T vis-à-vis aggression, along behavioral, structural and ecological dimensions. Second, I will describe possible functions of R & T for elementary school children. My thesis is that R & T serves different functions for different children. This functional argument, following Hinde,[3] is based on a design feature argument (namely, that behavioral and structural dimensions of R & T, social affiliation, and social cognition are similar). For example, R & T and social games both involve alternating roles, chasing, and sustained social intercourse. Regarding social cognition, R & T and perspective taking both involve the ability to take different perspectives. I will suggest then that playground periods provide children, particularly boys, with opportunities to learn and practice useful social skills. As these social skills are an important dimension of elementary school children's development, recess periods should be considered to have *educational value*.

WHAT IS R & T?

First, definitions of play are typically confounded with other behavioral categories. For example, children's social play is often confounded with social interaction per se. Second, as will be illustrated below, some definitions of R & T are often confounded with aggression. Third, definitions of play are difficult at best or impossible at worst. This may be due to the fact that no single characteristic or category is a necessary and sufficient condition for play.[4] Consequently R & T will be defined polythetically according to a number of behavioral, structural, and functional dimensions.

The term R & T was first used in behavioral science by Harlow to describe the playful, quasi-agonistic behaviors of rhesus monkeys.[5] Since that time a group of human ethologists, led by Blurton Jones[6] and P. K. Smith[7] have provided extensive behavioral/structural descriptions of the category. In these studies, generally of preschool children, R & T emerged as a empirical distinct factor composed of the following behaviors: run, chase, jump, flee, wrestle, and openhand beat. In short, R & T resembles playfighting and chase-flee behaviors. Structurally, R & T involves children engaging in reciprocal role taking.[8] For example, in chase children typically alternate between the chaser and chased, and in playfighting, between the aggressor and the victim roles. Regarding the functional or consequential criterion, children remain together at the conclusion of R & T bouts, often engaging in other forms of social play like cooperative games.[9] Ecologically, R & T tends to occur out of doors on soft, grassy surfaces.[10] Like other forms of play, R & T follows an inverted U-development function, accounting for 5 percent of preschoolers' free play behavior, increasing to around 10–13 percent at age seven and declining to about 5 percent again for eleven-year-olds.[11] Boys engage in R & T more frequently than girls.[12]

As noted above, R & T is a controversial category because of its frequent confusion with aggression. Indeed Brian Sutton-Smith has shown how adults, including child and educational psychologists, often confuse the two categories.[13] Close examination, however, illustrates clear distinctions between R & T and aggression. Behaviorally, aggression is composed of the following behaviors, which are independent of R & T in most children: fixate frown, hit (closed-hand), push, take and grab. These behaviors, unlike play, are stable through childhood.[14] Structurally aggression is characterized by unilateral, not reciprocal, roles: Aggressors remain aggressors, and victims, victims. Further, victims try to separate themselves from aggressors after an aggressive behavior. Ecologically, aggression tends to occur in the context of property disputes.[15] Unlike R & T, no specific playground location seems to elicit aggression.[16] As with R & T, boys are more likely than girls to exhibit aggressive behaviors. In short, R & T is fun for children while aggression is not.

Another, separate reason for the controversial nature of R & T lies in the different types of children who engage in it. Research suggests that sociometrically defined popular and rejected elementary school children engage in R & T with near equal frequency.[17] Closer analyses, however, suggest that R & T is qualitatively different and serves different functions for these two groups of children.[18]

To explore further the categorical meaning and functions of R & T for sociometrically defined popular and rejected children, behavioral observational and interview techniques were utilized with a group of elementary school children.[19] The R & T and aggression behavioral subcategories were factor analyzed. The behaviors within each category are: R & T—tease, hit, and kick, poke, pounce, sneak up, carry child, play fight, pile on, chase, hold, and push; aggression—hit with closed hand or kick and insult. For the popular children, aggressive behaviors did not have significant loadings. This is consistent with the extant research suggesting that popular children's behavior is not typified by aggression.[20] Their R & T was characterized by two factors: one consisting of playful provocation (poking and teasing) and the other consisting of rough-house play (kick at, play, push, fight, and chase). The first factor may represent children's efforts to elicit a playful response from playmates, for these behaviors typically elicit a similar response. The second factor represents a more physical but nonaggressive dimension of R & T. In short, these analyses suggest that for popular children R & T is a playful and physical category.

The factor analysis for the rejected children tells a very different story. Aggression (in the form of hit and kick) was proximate to behaviors that are typically considered playful (such as pounce, play fight, chase, and hit). This factor could be labeled aggressive play in that aggression and play co-occurred. Thus R & T and aggression seem to be interrelated for rejected children.

An alternate interpretation for the co-occurrence of R & T and aggression for rejected children was that their hold and push behaviors were *not* play but really forms of aggression. That observers of behavior in this study were blind to children's sociometric status and popular children's pushing behavior co-occurred with more typically playful behaviors, e.g., chase, minimizes the possibility of R & T not really being playful.

These factor analysis results, however, differ somewhat from the one other factor analysis study of school-age children's R & T and aggression. Neill in his study of 12- to 13-year-old English boys, found that R & T and aggression co-occurred.[21] The reasons for the difference between the Pellegrini[22] results and those of Neill could have at least two explanations. First, the Pellegrini sample were substantially younger ($M = 7.5$ years of age). Consistent with Neill's findings, the animal literature suggests that rough play turns into aggression as animals move into adolescence. Another explanation may have been due to another sample difference. In the Pellegrini study, separate analyses were conducted for popular and rejected boys *and* girls; this was not the case in Neill's study where boys, presumably of different sociometric status, were not differentiated. Consequently the aggressive behavior of the rejected boys in Neill's study may have introduced an aggressive component into the factor pattern of the other, nonaggressive, children. These equivocal results obviously should be addressed in future research. Specifically, factor analyses of popular and rejected boys across the adolescent period are needed to resolve this issue.

To further investigate the meaning of the category R & T for rejected and popular children, these same children were interviewed individually regarding their perceptions of R & T and aggression. To this end, the same children who were observed were shown videotapes of 10 separate episodes that were either R & T or aggression.[23] At the conclusion of each episode, children were asked, "Was this playfighting or real fighting? Why do you think so?" Children's responses were audiotaped. Individual responses were put into one of 13 exhaustive and mutually exclusive categories; 10 of these categories were similar to those developed by P. K. Smith in Sheffield, England. Again there are striking differences between the two types of children. Popular children generally have more differentiated definitions of both aggression and R & T; for R & T and aggressive events separately, popular children listed 12 separate attributes while rejected children listed 5 attributes for R & T and 3 for aggression.

These interview data provided insight into the factor analyses results. It may be that the interrelation of R & T and aggression for rejected children is a result of a cognitive deficit that distorts the accurate perception of social information. In ambiguous social provocation situations, like R & T, rejected children may attribute aggressive intent while popular children may correctly interpret the act as playful. Such an interpretation is consistent with K. Dodge's social information processing theory of aggression.[24]

An alternate, sociobiological explanation to this social skills deficit explanation for the differential co-occurrence of R & T and aggression for popular and rejected children has recently been put forth by Peter K. Smith. He suggests that rejected children may *intentionally* use both R & T and aggressive strategies to intimidate, deceive, and manipulate their peers.[25] For example, rejected children may begin using playful behaviors to deceive their peers into thinking that the interactions are cooperative and playful. Then they may use aggressive behaviors to exploit their peers. More will be said about R & T to aggression transitions later.

To conclude this section, we can state that R & T and aggression may be distinct categories *only* for popular children; they seem to be interrelated for rejected children. This finding, in addition to the conflation of R & T and aggression is probably responsible for R & T being considered antisocial social behavior.

FUNCTIONS OF R & T

That specific groups of children assign different meaning to R & T behaviors has implications for possible functions of R & T. Indeed category membership and function are inextricably interrelated. This point was made by E. Sapir[26] in his classic 1925 work on phonemes. Sapir showed that two sounds, though identical in form, may serve different functions for different groups. the factor analyses reported above illustrated this point. In this section, possible functions of R & T for elementary school children will be examined. Function is defined as the beneficial consequence of a behavior or set of behaviors. The benefits may be immediate or delayed, general or specific.[27] As noted above, the function of R & T will be established by an argument by design.[28] The behavioral and structural characteristics of R & T are present in aspects of social affiliation (for example, cooperative games) and social cognition (for example, social problem solving).

Functional examinations of play have generally been concerned with motor, cognitive, or social skills training.[29] We will address only the possibility of play serving a social skills training function. Functional analyses of R & T were accomplished with the traditional tool employed by students of R & T: motivational analyses and regression models applied to cross-sectional and longitudinal data sets. The motivation for a behavior gives us insight into its function.[30] M. Tinbergen and P. K. Smith noted that motivation for a behavior can be established by examining the temporal association between the behaviors of interest.[31] In the case of R & T, we can examine the extent to which it serves an antisocial aggressive function by examining the probability of aggressive acts immediately following R & T bouts. This can be accomplished by sequential lag analytical procedures.[32] Pellegrini examined the probability of R & T being followed by aggression for popular and rejected elementary school children.[33] The probability of R & T moving into aggression was .0006 for popular children and .28 for rejected children. The transitional probability of R & T escalating to aggression was beyond the chance level for the rejected, but not for the popular, children. It seems then that R & T serves an aggressive function for rejected, but not for popular, children. As noted above, this finding can be interpreted according to a social skills deficit model put forth most convincingly by Dodge and his colleagues.[34] Alternately, it may be that rejected children *purposefully* turn R & T into aggression to deceive their peers. Following Fagen, these intentional escalations represent *cheating* at play as a means by which future benefits can be extracted from peers.[35] Clearly we need to know more about the actual processes by which R & T moves into aggression to learn what benefits children accrue from such *cheating*.

Another, related question is the extent to which R & T serves a prosocial function. The animal and human play literature suggests that it may serve social affiliation and social cognition functions. This function hypothesis is based on similarity in design features of R & T and aspects of social affiliation and social cognition. More specifically, we hypothesize that R & T would be followed by a specific class of social affiliation behaviors—games with rules—because of the similarities in design features of the two. R & T and games both involve vigorous movements (for example, both chase and tag involve running). Further, both involve reciprocal role taking; victim/aggressor and chaser/chased roles are reciprocated. At a more distal level, there is also reason to think that R & T and games are related: During the elementary school years, the frequency with which children engage in R & T decreases as the frequency of cooperative games increases. While similarities in design features between play and games are sufficient for a hypothesized relation between the two, they are not sufficient to assume a relationship; behavior, though structurally similar, may serve different functions.[36] The proximal relations between R & T and games were tested by examining separately the transitional probabilities of cooperative games immediately following R & T for popular and rejected children.[37] Again, this was tested with a two-state sequential lag analysis mode. The transition was beyond the chance level for popular but not for rejected children. Thus R & T is affiliative for popular children but not for rejected children.

The social affiliative function of R & T was also tested with the same group of students, using a longitudinal design.[38] This hypothesized distal relation was based on the notion that R & T should also have a delayed effect on social skill development. Of interest were the specific aspects of R & T in year one that predicted the occurrence of games with rules in year two. To this end, individual R & T behaviors were used as predictor variables, rather than the molar category R & T, because R & T is composed of a number of very different, though interrelated, behaviors. Different behaviors within R & T, such as playfighting and chase, may serve very different functions, such as dominance exhibition and social affiliation functions respectively.[39] For rejected children, no dimension of R & T in year one predicted games with rules in year two. This was probably the result of their R & T moving into aggression and not games. For popular children, chase and hit-at predicted games. The behavioral similarity between these two R & T behaviors and similar behaviors used in games, such as tag, is probably responsible for this relation.

Based on an argument by design, one would also expect R & T to be related to specific aspects of children's social cognitive status (that is, social problem solving). Regarding the relation between R & T and social problem-solving flexibility, the flexibility hypothesis of play states that R & T should predict flexibility through generalization and subroutinization.[40] In the play context, because of its safe, nonexploitative nature, children experiment with different social roles. Consequently individual social routines and strategies get broken down, recombined, and generalized. Cross-sectional research supports this hypothesis.[41] For popular children there was a positive, significant contemporaneous relation between R & T and social problem-solving flexibility, as measured by G. Spivak and M. Shure,[42] while there was a negative, nonsignificant relation for rejected children. Though the mechanisms for this relation remain elusive, role reversal has been given preferred, but unverified, status.[43] As such, the relation between R & T and social problem solving for popular children may have been due to their exchanging R & T roles—such as offender/defender. Such exchange is one way of preventing playmates' boredom and thus ensures sustained play.[44] Further, role reversals provide children, usually those in submissive roles, with opportunities to rest during R & T. These rest periods may be another strategy to ensure sustained play. Using these varied strategies to sustain play is similar to what children were asked to do on social problem-solving tasks: provide a variety of ways to initiate and sustain play.

The nonsignificant relation between rejected children's R & T and social problem-solving flexibility is also of theoretical importance. As noted above, rejected and popular children engage in R & T with near equal frequency; rejected children, however, exhibit aggressive behavior more frequently. Recent sociobiological theory suggests that children's use of aggression and R & T may be deliberate and reflect flexible behavioral repertoire to secure resources.[45] For example, rejected children may, deceptively, begin a social interaction under the guise of play and then use an aggressive strategy to exploit the situation. Sociobiologists see this as one of many social strategies used to gain resources. That rejected children's R & T was negatively correlated with a varied social problem-solving repertoire does not support this sociobiological position.[46] It would, however, be useful to examine the extent to which such deceptive strategies are related to resource allocation.

The results for the functional role of R & T in popular and rejected children can best be explained by the concept of reciprocal altruism.[47] The theory states that cooperation, not exploitation, in groups is an evolutionary adaptive strategy between children who meet repeatedly. In cooperative contexts like play, children have opportunities to try out new and different behaviors and roles because they do not worry about being exploited for aggressive ends. These cooperative groups tend to be composed of children of similar dominance and friendship status.[48] As a result of being in these equal and cooperative contexts, children have the opportunities to experiment with new and different social roles. In asymmetrical groups, there is danger that the more dominant children will exploit the play episodes to their own aggressive or dominance exhibition ends. This model seems to account for the extant data since R & T tends to occur among children of near equal friendship and dominance status and is characterized by cooperation and role reciprocation and not by exploitation and unilateral dominance displays.

LIMITATIONS

The literature, while providing interesting initial insights, is limited. Most notably, both Smith and Pellegrini confound children's gender and sociometric status. In light of the robustness of the reported gender differences for engagement in R & T, this certainly is problematical.[49] It may be that R & T serves a developmental function for boys but not for girls.

Another limitation of the work is that the social processes that lead rejected and popular children's R & T to proceed into aggression and cooperative games, respectively, have not been empirically verified. Future research on the principle of reciprocal altruism should first examine the symmetry of R & T lay groups for popular and rejected boys. Then the extent to which R & T is reciprocal for each group should be examined; after all, reciprocal role taking is the mechanism thought to be responsible for facilitating children's social flexibility. Third, the extent to which popular boys' social rule orientation is responsible for the R & T to games transition should be examined. Do they generate more social rules and norm statements than do rejected children? Are these statements followed immediately by games?

And it is probably the case that there is more than one way for children to learn or practice these social skills.[50] This notion of equifinality suggests that this is a problem in explaining outcome measures for organisms in open systems.[51] Girls, for example, do not engage in R & T at the same rate as do boys yet girls also have social skills. The equifinality argument becomes more convincing when we consider that R & T occurs in limited environments.[52] In short, R & T may not be an optimal and unique strategy for children's learning of social skills. It may be that R & T serves that function for boys not girls. In future research, we should separate R & T from other forms of social play.

Lastly, researchers in the area of children's play must be cautious of the "play ethos";[53] that is, the notion that play is all good. We should proceed with caution. Indeed, some of the problems in this area, particularly as they are applied to education, are the results of oversimplifying complex problems, like the role of play in development and education.

IMPLICATIONS

This body of research has important implications for children in schools, despite the limitations. In this section, I will outline some of those implications, drawn from the research cited above. The implications, however, should be tempered by the limitations of the research.

The first implication is that R & T does not escalate into aggression for most children. The research shows that aggression is a very rare phenomenon on preschool and elementary school playgrounds.[54] The likelihood of R & T escalating into aggression for popular children is 6 in 10,000. Why then does R & T have such a bad reputation among adults? Like aggressive and rejected children, adults, particularly principals, teachers, and playground supervisors do not differentiate R & T from aggression. This may be, as Sutton-Smith[55] points out, a form of sexism wherein female school personnel discourage this typically male behavior. Thus a necessary first step is to educate the educators on the R & T/aggression distinction.

The success of this educational phase, in my experience, is closely related to the second implication, that R & T and other forms of playground behavior predict more traditional dimensions of school behaviors. Indeed pilot data suggest that specific dimensions of kindergartners' playground behavior (including R & T) account for more of the variance in their grade one achievement than do their kindergarten Metropolitan Readiness Test scores.[56] This is the language that educators seem most willing to attend to.

The third implication is more universal and relates to the need for outdoor freeplay and recess periods. A number of school systems are considering the elimination of recess so that children can receive more *instructional* time. Experimental work by P. K. Smith[57] in Sheffield shows that children seem to *need* vigorous play periods and that those *confined* to indoor environments for longer periods of time exhibit high levels and longer durations of vigorous play than do those confined for shorter periods of time. Further, children's attention to seat work increased as a function of their level of vigorous play.

Another dimension of the need for recess relates to what is currently stressed in school. A long-standing criticism of school is that children's social-affective needs have been ignored while aspects of children's cognition have been stressed. It seems to me that the role of schools is to educate good citizens. Good citizens should be friendly and cooperative as well as literate and numerate. Indeed would school be considered successful if we had uniform literacy and numeracy but high levels of juvenile delinquency? Recess period provides opportunities for children to learn and practice skills necessary for good citizenship.

NOTES

*A version of this paper was presented at the Presidential Forum, University of Pennsylvania. Preparation of this paper was facilitated by a grant from the Harry Frank Guggenheim Foundation. The author acknowledges the comments of the anonymous reviewers.

1. Edward Zigler and Penelope Trickett, "I.Q., Social Competence, and Evaluation of Early Childhood Interview Programs," *American Psychologist* 33 (1978): 789.

2. G. Ladd, "Social Networks of Popular, Average, and Rejected Children in School Settings," *Merrill-Palmer Quarterly* 29 (1983): 283 G. Ladd, J. Price, and C. Hart, "Predicting Preschoolers' Peer Status from Their Playground Behav-

ior," *Child Development* 59 (1988): 986; A. Pellegrini, "Rough-and-Tumble Play: Developmental and Educational Significance," *Educational Psychologist* 22 (1987): 22; B. Sutton-Smith, "War Toys and Childhood Aggression," *Play and Culture* 12 (1988): 57–69.

3. R. Hinde, *Individuals, Relationships, and Culture* (New York: Cambridge University Press, 1987)

4. P. Martin and T. Caro, "On the Functions of Play and Its role in Behavioral Development," in *Advances in the Study of Behavior, vol.* 15, ed. J. Rosenblatt, C. Beer, M. C. Busnel, and P. Slater (New York: Academic, 1985), pp. 59–103.

5. H. Harlow, "The Heterosexual Affection System in Monkeys," *American Psychologist* 17 (1962): 1; H. Harlow and M. Harlow, "Social Deprivation in Monkeys," *Scientific American* 207 (1962): 136.

6. N. Blurton Jones, "Categories of Child to Child Interaction," in *Ethological Studies of Child Behavior,* ed. N. Blurton Jones (Cambridge, Eng.: Cambridge University Press, 1972), pp. 97–129; N. Blurton Jones, "Rough-and-Tumble Play among Nursery School Children," in *Play—Its Roles in Development and Evolution,* ed. J. Bruner, A. Jolly, and K. Sylva (New York: Basic Books, 1976), pp. 352–363.

7. P. K. Smith and K. Connolly, *The Ecology of Preschool Behavior* (Cambridge, Eng.: Cambridge University Press, 1980).

8. R. Fagen, *Animal Play Behavior* (New York: Oxford University Press, 1981); A. Humphreys and P. K. Smith, "Rough-and-Tumble in Preschool on a Playground," in *Play in Animals and Humans,* ed. P. K. Smith (London: Blackwell, 1984), pp. 291–370.

9. A. D. Pellegrini, "Elementary School Children's Rough-and-Tumble Play and Social Competence," *Developmental Psychology* 24 (1988): 802–806.

10. Humphreys and Smith, "Rough-and-Tumble"; A. D. Pellegrini, "Elementary School Children's Rough-and-Tumble Play," *Early Childhood Research Quarterly* 4 (1989): 245–260.

11. Humphreys and Smith, "Rough-and-Tumble."

12. Pellegrini, "Elementary School Children's Rough-and-Tumble Play"; B. Whiting and C. Edwards, "A Cross-Cultural Analysis of Sex-Differences in the Behavior of Children Age Three through 11," *Journal of Social Psychology* 91 (1973): 171–188.

13. Smith, "War Toys."

14. D. Olweus, "Stability and Aggressive Reaction Patterns in Males: A Review," *Psychological Bulletin* 86 (1979): 852–875.

15. Humphreys and Smith, "Rough-and-Tumble"; B. Sutton-Smith, J. Gerstmyer, and A. Meckley, *Western Folklore* (in press).

16. Pellegrini, "Elementary School Children's Rough-and-Tumble Play."

17. J. Cole and J. Kupersmidt, "A Behavioral Analysis of Emerging Social Status in Boys' Groups," *Child Development* 54 (1983): 1400–1416; Pellegrini, "Elementary School Children's Rough-and-Tumble Play.

18. Pellegrini, "Elementary School Children's Rough-and-Tumble Play"; A. D. Pellegrini, "What is a Category? The Case of Rough-and-Tumble Play," *Ethology & Sociobiology* 10 (1989): 331–341.

19. Pellegrini, "What Is a Category?"

20. Cole and Kupersmidt, "A Behavioral Analysis."

21. S. Neill, "Aggressive and Non-aggressive Fighting in Twelve-to-Thirteen Year Old Pre-Adolescent Boys," *Journal of Child Psychology and Psychiatry* 17 (1976): 213–220.

22. Pellegrini, "What Is a Category?"

23. Ibid.

24. K. Dodge, G. Pettit, McClaskey, and M. Brown, "Social Competence in Children," *Monographs of the Society for Research in Child Development* 51 (1986).

25. P. K. Smith, "The Role of Rough-and-Tumble Play in the Development of Social Competence: Theoretical Perspectives and Empirical Evidence," in *Social Competence in Developmental Perspective*, ed. B. Schneider (in press).

26. E. Sapir, "Sound Patterns in Language," *Language* 1 (1975): 37–51.

27. Martin and Caro, "On the Functions of Play."

28. Hinde, *Individuals, Relationships.*

29. Martin and Caro, "On the Functions of Play."

30. Blurton Jones, "Categories of Child to Child Interaction."

31. M. Tinbergen, "Comparative Studies of the Behavior of Gulls (*Laridae*): A Progress Report," *Behavior* 15 (1959): 1–70; P. K. Smith "Ethological Methods," in *New Perspectives in Child Development*, ed. B. Foss (London: Penguin, 1976): 85–137.

32. R. Bakeman and J. Gottman, *Observing Interaction: An Introduction to Sequential Analysis* (New York: Cambridge University Press, 1986).

33. Pellegrini, "Elementary School Children's Rough-and-Tumble Play."

34. Dodge, et al., "Social Competence."

35. Fagen, *Animal Play Behavior.*

36. Martin and Caro, "On the Functions of Play."

37. Pellegrini, "Elementary School Children's Rough-and-Tumble Play and Social Competence."

38. Pellegrini, "Elementary School Children's Rough-and-Tumble Play."

39. M. Boulton and P. K. Smith, "Issues in the Study of Children's Rough-and-Tumble Play," in *The Ecological Context of Children's Play,* ed. M. Bloch and A. D. Pellegrini (Norwood, N.J.: Ablex, 1989), pp. 57–83.

40. R. Fagen, "Play and Behavioral Flexibility," in *Play in Animals and Humans,* ed. Smith, pp. 159–174.

41. Pellegrini, "Elementary School Children's Rough-and-Tumble Play and Social Competence."

42. G. Spivak and M. Shure, *Social Adjustment of Young Children* (San Francisco: Jossey-Bass, 1979).

43. Fagen, "Play and Behavioral Flexibility."

44. O. Aldis, *Play Fighting* (New York: Academic, 1975).

45. R. Cairns, "An Evolutionary and Developmental Perspective on Aggressive Patterns," in *Altruism and Aggression,* eds. C. Zahn-Waxler, E. Cummings, and R. Iannotti (New York: Cambridge University Press, 1986), pp. 58–87; Smith, "The Role of Rough-and-Tumble Play."

46. Pellegrini, "Elementary School Children's Rough-and-Tumble Play and Social Competence."

47. R. Axelrod and W. Hamilton, "The Evolution of Cooperation," *Science* 211 (1981): 1390–1396; Fagen, "Play and Behavioral Flexibility."

48. A. Humphreys and P. K. Smith, "Rough-and-Tumble Play, Friendship and Dominance in School Children: Evidence for Continuity and Change with Age," *Child Development* 58 (1987): pp. 201–212; Fagen, "Play and Behavioral Flexibility."

49. Whiting and Edwards, "A Cross-Cultural Analysis."

50. G. Sackett, A. Sameroff, R. Cairns, and S. Suomi, "Continuity in Behavioral Development: Theoretical and Empirical Issues," in *Behavioral Development,* eds. K. Immelmann, G. Barlow, L. Petrinovich, and M. Main (New York: Cambridge University Press, 1981), pp. 23–57; Smith, "The Role of Rough-and-Tumble Play."

51. Martin and Caro, "On the Functions of Play."

52. Ibid.

53. P. K. Smith, "Children Play and Its Role in Early Development: A Reevaluation of the 'Play Ethos,'" in *Psychological Bases for Early Education,* ed. Anthony D. Pellegrini (Chichester, Eng.: Wiley, 1988), pp. 207–226.

54. Pellegrini, "Elementary School Children's Rough-and-Tumble Play and Social Competence"; Pellegrini, "Elementary School Children's Rough-and-Tumble Play"; Sutton-Smith, Gerstmeyer, and Meckley, *Western Folklore;* Pellegrini, "What Is a Category?"

55. Sutton-Smith et al., *Western Folklore.*

56. A. D. Pellegrini and C. D. Glickman, "It's the Same Old Song: Testing, Young Children, and Social Competence," *Young Children* (in press).

57. P. K. Smith, and T. Hagan, "Effects of Deprivation on Exercise Play in Nursery School Children," *Animal Behaviour* 28 (1980): 922–928.

CAROL ANN HODGES

Chapter Nine

Instruction and Assessment
of Emergent Literacy

According to a recent test publisher's advertisement, "an up-to-date education can't be measured by an out-of-date test." Intended as an inducement for schools to order the company's latest testing program, the ad also raises an important issue with respect to the assessment of early literacy in today's kindergarten classrooms. The question is not only whether current standardized achievement tests *can* be used to measure early literacy but also whether they *should* be used to measure the type of instruction required in kindergarten classrooms.

In *Critical Issues in Curriculum: Eighty-Seventh Yearbook of the National Society for the Study of Education*, George Madaus writes that

> testing is fast usurping the role of the curriculum as the mechanism of defining what schooling is about in this country. It is testing, not the "official" stated curriculum, that is increasingly determining what is taught, how it is taught, what is learned, and how it is learned.[1]

A number of early childhood educators agree with Madaus. Position papers from the National Association for the Education of Young Children, the Association for Childhood Education International, and the Early Childhood Literacy Development Committee of the International Reading Association report that the pressure to achieve high scores on standardized tests has resulted in changes in the content of kindergarten programs.[2] Moreover, these changes, often in the form of increased demands for traditional *academic* content, do not attend to the child's social, emotional, and intellectual development. In fact the methods, materials, and tests used in today's kindergarten classroom frequently represent an escalation to what were previously first-grade expectations.

Thus it appears that tests no longer merely measure the results of instruction but often determine that instruction's content. We need to ask what kind of assessment tools and strategies are developmentally appropriate for kindergarten children and are also useful for teachers engaged in making decisions about an instructional program that many early childhood researchers deem as *best practice* in encouraging literacy in the kindergarten classroom.

CONVENTIONAL READING READINESS PROGRAMS AND THE EMERGENT LITERACY PERSPECTIVE

Many current reading and writing programs in kindergarten do reflect this escalation of curriculum.[3] Lorrie Shepard and Mary Lee Smith report that academic demands are considerably higher than 20 years ago and continue to rise, partly as a result of the role that testing plays in driving the curriculum.[4] In addition, they suggest that because kindergarten attendance has become more nearly universal, first-grade teachers often expect that all children will have mastered certain social and academic skills by the time they enter first grade. Parents also impose demands when they judge teachers' effectiveness by their success in teaching children to read while ignoring any other evidence of success. Other variables that have contributed to the escalation of the kindergarten curriculum include the practices of raising the entrance age, *red-shirting*, as well as retention for a year.

Classroom observations and analyses of current materials show that, in kindergartens characterized by this escalating academic curriculum, beginning reading instruction generally follows a reading readiness or phonics workbook format. Instruction then emphasizes isolated drill on such skills as auditory and visual discrimination, auditory and visual memory, letter names and sounds, word recognition, and manuscript handwriting[5]—practices that many early childhood educators argue are developmentally inappropriate.[6]

In their book, *Emergent Literacy: Writing and Reading*, William Teale and Elizabeth Sulzby[7] outline the reading readiness concept as follows:

- Reading instruction cannot begin until children have mastered a set of basic skills. What happens before formal instruction is largely irrelevant.

- Skills are to be mastered in a hierarchical sequence. All children pass through the scope and sequence of readiness and reading skills in a similar manner.
- Instruction focuses on these formal aspects of reading while ignoring the functional uses of reading in real-life contexts.
- Writing (except for handwriting practice) is to be delayed until children learn to read.
- Children's progress through the scope and sequence of skills should be carefully monitored by periodic testing.

Thus for those who espouse the reading readiness approach, the period of time before children begin formal reading instruction in school is not characterized as *real* reading or writing but as a forerunner to it. Thus it is said that only after children master a hierarchical scope and sequence of readiness subskills through direct instruction can the *real* reading and writing begin.

These reading readiness programs seldom contain opportunities for children to listen to stories, to read along with the teacher, or to write for real purposes such as sending messages to one another or to the teacher. Young children are not given the opportunity to build upon and develop the emergent literacy abilities that they bring to school—the very opportunities that should make the transition to school learning much easier. Child development research recommends that learning experiences for children must be active in nature. Thus literacy learning should be a process in which children reconstruct the rules of literacy through participation in meaningful acts of reading and writing.[8] Teaching materials that separate literacy learning from meaningful communication and that define literacy as simply the recognition of words or the learning of the sounds that letters make are erroneous and confusing.

The emergent literacy perspective has recently begun to challenge the concept of reading readiness described above. This perspective, based on current research in the areas of reading, writing, listening, and speaking, casts serious doubts on the underlying assumptions of reading readiness. On the basis of school and home ethnographic studies, case studies, and structured interviews of children from a variety of ethnic and social backgrounds, educational theorists and researchers as well as scholars from the fields of linguistics and psychology have begun to think about literacy in a new way. This current research supports the idea that literacy is acquired through a "thinking, social, participatory, interactive process as youngsters engage in rich literate experiences,"[9] rather than in the part-to-whole, basic skills, building-block manner characteristic of the reading readiness approach. Studies of early readers and writers[10] suggest that in becoming literate young children are actually learning about

- functions and uses of literacy,
- attitudes toward literacy,
- conventions of written language,
- decoding and encoding strategies, and
- comprehending and composing strategies.

These studies and others provide evidence that children have learned much about the acts of reading and writing before they come to school. And what is most important, they have attained these perceptions and abilities in naturalistic ways based on the need to communicate with others and prior to formal reading or writing instruction.

Teale and Sulzby[11] suggest that what is called *reading readiness* is more appropriately termed *literacy development*, because reading and writing develop concurrently and are interrelated. They conclude

- that literacy development begins before children start formal instruction as they use reading and writing in informal settings in their home and community from birth onward;
- that, since children pass through the stages in their literacy development at different ages and in a variety of ways, attempts to provide instruction through a hierarchical scope and sequence must take this developmental process into consideration;
- that the *functions* of literacy are as important as the *forms* of literacy because literacy occurs in real life contexts in order to accomplish something;
- that children learn written language through an active engagement with other children and adults and can profit significantly from the modeling of literacy by their parents and other adults.

Thus for those who espouse an emergent literacy viewpoint, children's early writing and reading behaviors are not considered as prerequisites to *real* learning but are themselves integral parts of a language process that is emerging from the child as a result of environmental stimulation.

Elfrieda Hiebert describes several kindergarten programs in which curriculum and instruction are derived from emergent literacy research.[12] These programs attest to the effectiveness of involving young children with literacy in a variety of ways and building on the numerous literacy experiences that children bring to school. As teachers read aloud daily, children become acquainted with many types of children's books. Children also join the teacher in reading books with rhyme, rhythm, and predictable patterns. Later they read the same books to themselves or their friends in the classroom. Print is introduced naturally throughout the day as the opportunities arise. Children sign in as they come to school, they read the "daily news," and as they write letters, notes, menus, and lists. They also write or dictate, illustrate, and publish their own books. The teaching of reading and writing skills occurs when teachers observe that children are developmentally ready and have a functional need for such skills. Furthermore, this attention to skills occurs within the context of a whole story.

The accumulated research in child development and in the areas of early reading and writing would seem to support this emergent literacy perspective, which is derived from an understanding of the roots of language acquisition, incorporates the successful informal teaching methods of the home, and reflects the "best practice" in early childhood reading/writing instruction.[13] Are there assessment tools available that will evaluate this emergent literacy perspective?

ASSESSING EARLY LITERACY—CURRENT PRACTICE

Tests are increasingly becoming a part of the kindergarten child's life.[14] Many school districts now give tests before kindergarten and first grade to screen out *unready* children.[15] Constance Kamii reports that concern about the appropriateness of formal testing of young children has led to a call for a moratorium on the use of achievement tests in grades K–2.[16]

Because assessment information is used for such diverse purposes as a teacher's daily instructional decisions as well as for districtwide policy decisions, however, it is probably not possible to eliminate all forms of assessment. Teachers must be able to assess accurately the skills and knowledge of students in kindergartens using the *best practice* approach to early literacy described above. Assessment should take into consideration the developmental and personal characteristics of the four- to six-year-old. Current reading readiness tests clearly fail to provide useful information for teachers who consider reading and writing to be constructive and interactive processes.

Writing about reading readiness tests over 20 years ago, Robert Dykstra stated, "generally there appears to be little reason for administering a complete readiness battery if the only reason for its administration is the classification of pupils and the determination for each of when to initiate reading instruction."[17] Dykstra believed that the time spent in administering and scoring readiness tests could be better used for instruction. Ten years ago, when Jana Mason and Christine McCormick listed the specific skills that were tested in reading readiness tests, the following skills were represented.[18]

listening comprehension	letter recognition
auditory discrimination	visual discrimination
auditory blending	copying
following directions	word meaning
draw a man	learning rate

Of these, visual and auditory discrimination and letter recognition were most frequently included skills. Mason and McCormick reported that there was a lack of agreement on the specific skills of reading readiness as well as a lack of rigor in the tests themselves. They concluded that the reading readiness measures available in 1979 were not meeting the expectations of their users.[19]

More recently, a critique of six widely used standardized early reading tests found that the items on the subtests presupposed that reading consists of the use of isolated skills.[20] Consequently, these early reading tests are not directly related to the act of reading as conceived of by the most recent work in cognitive and developmental psychology. A formal test can only assess selected parts of the total knowledge and skill needed for reading and writing and may miss important elements, thereby severely limiting the teacher's ability to make important daily decisions. In addition, because the test makers appear to ignore the model of reading as a constructive and interactive activity, readiness tests require simulated, rather than real, reading.[21] For example, tests require children to respond to a decontextualized single word or sentence. Furthermore, Shepard and Smith point out that even assessment tools like the Metropolitan Readiness Test, which has the highest predictive correlation of any test of its kind, can misidentify up to one-third of the children it declares unready because the test is a fallible predictor.[22]

There is evidence that kindergarten or first-grade teachers rarely rely on information from standardized readiness tests in making instructional decisions in any event.[23] For kindergarten teachers the test information gathered at the end of the school year is returned too late to be useful. The test is useless for the myriad daily instructional decisions that must be made in kindergarten. For the first-grade teacher who teaches the children in September, the test administered several months earlier provides little useful information. First-grade teachers appear to prefer the kindergarten teacher's substantive comments regarding the child's reading and writing progress. They also rely on their own observations of the child in everyday reading/writing tasks.

ASSESSING EARLY LITERACY—FUTURE PROSPECTS

Researchers suggest that, instead of standardized tests, school-based assessment should be considered as a means of gathering information to fill the needs of a range of audiences from school boards and administrators to parents and teachers.[24] A variety of assessment tools would provide numerous developmentally appropriate strategies for measuring what children know in a variety of settings and across time. While standardized achievement tests might play a role in such an assessment framework, it would be a small one.

The starring role in such a systematic and reflective framework would be provided by what Yetta Goodman terms "kidwatching."[25] This term is used to describe a combination of systematically collected observational data, brief anecdotal records of classroom behavior, and performance samples—including samples of written, drawn, and oral work collected by means of portfolios and audio- and videotaping. Data collected in this manner can provide information for instructional decision making, for predicting future development, and for reporting to parents. A thoughtful, systematic, repeated, and thorough analysis of the data by means of such assessment tools provides the teacher with an individual record of each child's growth and development in literacy. Such things as the use of print conventions and cueing systems used, the ability to predict and the range of language exhibited, the invented spellings attempted, and other skills can be analyzed from data gained through observations, work samples, and anecdotal records. This information must be gathered in a variety of settings and across time to protect from overgeneralizations about a child's abilities.

Such assessment should be keyed to the insights into how children develop their reading and writing ability that research on emergent literacy provides. Teale suggests that systematic developmental data should be gathered on:

> young children's (1) concepts of the functions and conventions of written language, (2) text comprehension (i.e. their ability to understand and recall books read to them), (3) abilities to read print commonly found in their homes and communities, (4) emergent reading of storybooks (strategies children use to read books before they are able to read conventionally), (5) metalinguistic awareness (including word awareness and phonological awareness), (6) emergent writing strategies (including composing, spelling, and strategies for rereading their own writing), (7) knowledge of letters, letter sounds, and the relationships between them.[26]

Systematic direct observation, carried out using a variety of checklists and supported by oral and written performance samples, is a useful assessment tool with nonreaders, the young, and the handicapped. It has the advantage of being able to be used almost anytime, which permits teachers to identify their students' levels of development in the classroom environment in which the teaching and learning normally take place. In addition, this approach is less obtrusive and threatening than other types of assessment. Furthermore, it allows the teacher to provide direct feedback and immediate redirection to children.

This is not to say that direct observation is without disadvantages. Using a checklist may lead teachers to be too narrowly focused. Because certain behaviors are targeted for attention, observers may miss other important factors. This method may also provide biased information, insofar as observers may accept or reject information because of whether it fits what they already know. For example, teachers may be inclined to generalize or oversimplify. If they usually see a child in a favorable light in one area, they may expect the same response in other areas. Furthermore, there may be a tendency to arrive at conclusions based on only one or two observations. Good observational assessment is time consuming and takes considerable training.

ORGANIZING FOR ASSESSMENT IN EMERGENT LITERACY

As Goodman and others point out, expertise in observation is complex and does not come without planning and effort.[27] First, observers must have a framework for making sense of what they see. They must have knowledge of the reading and writing processes, of the developmental process, and of procedural knowledge that helps them know what to look for and become more aware of their biases and philosophical orientation. A format for recording early literacy behaviors in the classroom must be based on the school district's and teacher's philosophy and goals and objectives of literacy development.

Second, the teacher must be able to break those goals and objectives down into observable units including items that are significant and representative of the literacy processes of the children in that teacher's group. Teachers at the same grade level and across grade levels must meet and decide what kinds of behaviors will serve to demonstrate that the child is progressing toward the ultimate goal of reading and writing with understanding. A series of checklists based on various processes can be designed and used throughout the school year. Such a series, designed to fit specific needs, can provide an efficient and simple way of recording and retrieving the information collected. Experts in the areas of reading and writing might suggest items for the checklists, but the final decision about specific items must be made by the teachers so that they are aware of how each behavior functions in demonstrating progress toward the goals and objectives of their school district and classroom. This dialogue among teachers would take place as teachers were discussing their philosophy of instruction in early literacy and later as they discussed the abilities and needs of particular children. Peter Johnston suggests that this type of conversation allows teachers to reflect upon their knowledge-in-practice and engage in a process of self-education.[28] What a wonderful side effect!

Third, successful observers must be systematic yet flexible. If a teacher believes that a child must have an understanding of the concepts of print, then that teacher might use a checklist to record systematically a child's progress. However, there is no one *correct* or *all encompassing* observational list or set of lists. The observational inventory contains important concepts for which a teacher will watch; but it also should provide a mental set that heightens and sensitizes the teacher's awareness to the diagnostic and evaluative potential in all activities in which the children might participate. No matter what framework is used to organize the observational activity, teachers must be open to other behaviors that might provide additional information. If they substitute one or more static observational lists for a standardized reading test teachers are making little progress toward becoming astute diagnosers and evaluators, and in fact, they may only be substituting one inappropriate set of categories for another. Providing room for anecdotal written comments to accompany the checklists is critical to remind teachers to be aware of other important behaviors and to note them on the checklist. These more global or summary comments plus the specific items chosen for observation provide part of a well-rounded assessment format for measuring the child's total literacy performance.

Fourth, observers must be astute watchers and listeners who can reflect on what is seen and heard in order to extend the child's capacity to use language. To secure appropriate and adequate evidence, they must watch children often and in a wide variety of contexts. They must be patient rather than deciding prematurely that children do not know something or are unable to perform certain tasks. The informed observer recognizes what the child already knows, plans experiences to build on that knowledge, and then observes and listens on a timely basis with appropriate attention, patience, and thoughtful questioning. Samples of students' work that clarify observational data or illustrate their skill on a particular task are valuable additions. Writing folders that contain examples of children's writing, records of how they reread what they wrote, and developmental information about such things as their ability to spell, compose, and use punctuation provide teachers with an excellent resource for assessing progress. A performance sample of a child's emergent reading of a book is another example of a useful tool. After listening to a child read a book, the teacher can estimate how close to conventional literacy the child is. An audiotape of each reading can be stored for future comparisons illustrating development of skills.

The major advantage of an assessment framework, including observation, anecdotal records, and performance samples, is its flexibility, which allows teachers to design it for a special purpose and construct it around materials that are being used in everyday instruction. Such a framework built around a process-oriented philosophy of reading can provide teachers with the opportunity to evaluate a student's ability to use early literacy skills within the context of *real* reading situations. In addition, by looking closely at a classroom, such teachers also learn about the ways in which they are interacting with their students and the environment to facilitate the emergence of literacy. Such data provides teachers with the important knowledge that is the basis for the modification of instruction.

INFLUENCING EDUCATIONAL POLICYMAKERS

If researchers, teacher educators, professional organizations, teachers, and others interested in early childhood education hope to eliminate the use of standardized readiness and other types of achievement tests in early childhood classrooms and to initiate the use of an observation-based assessment framework, they must educate policymakers about several important issues. As already noted, early childhood educators have taken the position that standardized reading readiness tests have significant negative effects on young children and on the kindergarten curriculum. Few of the tests meet acceptable standards of reliability and validity for making predictions about children's future achievement in reading. In addition, because their format is often confusing to children accustomed to interaction and teamwork, the tests often yield inconclusive results for young children, who are inexperienced and erratic test takers. Furthermore, because young children grow and learn rapidly, the danger of misdiagnosis or mislabeling is greater at this age than at any other. And finally, the pressure to score well on such tests is stressful for both young children and their teachers. Consequently, teachers are often forced to substitute inappropriate drills with ditto sheets and workbooks for more developmentally appropriate activities.

Even if such paper-and-pencil reading readiness tests did not produce long-term negative effects on young children, their teachers, and the curriculum, the concept of early reading underlying current standardized tests is flawed. Most test makers conceive of reading as a set of separate skills, which the readers use to unlock the meaning of the printed page. In contrast, reading as reflected in the emerging literacy perspective is a complex interactive process of predicting meaning from cues offered by the print and the context in which the prints is found. Thus policymakers who use the results of current readiness tests to make curricular or other programmatic decisions are receiving information not about children's emergent reading ability but about how well children can perform isolated fragments of simulated reading tasks. Indeed, some children who score well on such a test may not be *ready*, while some low scorers may actually be reading already!

Third, the standardized, product-oriented reading readiness tests currently in use in most schools indicate at best in some global and artificial manner regardless of whether groups of children have made progress on isolated *reading* skills since the last testing period. In this way, the tests allow the school boards or administrators to compare progress on these isolated skills of students in different school systems. While these tests may conceivably provide some kind of information for those audiences, they do not meet the needs of classroom teachers.

At best such tests provide global information about how well one child can do tasks such as identifying letters or matching words when compared to other similar children. But what kind of instructional decision-making data does a stanine of 6 or a percentile of 66 provide? First, it is difficult, if not impossible, for classroom teachers to make instructional decisions based on test results often obtained weeks or months after the test was taken. Second, because such scores are norm referenced, they are irrelevant to criterion-referenced instructional decisions—even if the results could be returned the same day the test was taken.

In addition, such test results are not helpful to parents who wish to know what sorts of reading and writing strategies their children have developed and what kind of reading and writing competencies they have achieved. To be sure, many parents expect to hear their children's progress reported in terms of stanines or percentiles, having been trained by school systems to believe that such numbers offer objectives and real evidence of progress. And yet, the type of documentation that parents would intuitively accept as representing real progress in reading and writing does not consist of scores on drill sheets or achievement test pages. Parents are interested in whether their children like books, listen to stories, read along with the teacher, read at home, and write for real purposes—exactly the kind of evidence that a good observation-based assessment framework would produce.

Individual, process-oriented assessment by responsible teachers is indeed *real* evaluation. Observations, anecdotal summaries, and performance samples rely on what Johnston calls the teacher as evaluation instrument.[29] The purpose of such a framework is as much to teach as it is to assess. It is instructionally more relevant, timely, and useful to teachers than are the standardized, product-oriented approaches now in place.

It appears that assessment tools such as standardized reading readiness tests have significant negative effects on young children and on the curriculum in kindergarten. The concepts of early reading underlying them appear to be flawed. They provide little, if any, help to teachers as they make their daily instructional decisions, and they offer little *real* evidence to parents who are interested in knowing how their children are progressing in actual reading and writing abilities.

Given the many failings of standardized reading readiness tests, it appears that the only argument for administering such tests is that the results can be used to make comparisons for accountability purposes. If we accept the research based on the emergent literacy perspective and early childhood developmental studies, however, it is obvious that the objective and valid accountability results that school system administrators and school boards and local, state, and federal governmental officials believe they are obtaining are, in fact, not representative of the real status of their students' emergent literacy skills at all.

Over the past five years or so early childhood organizations and researchers in the fields of reading and writing have called attention to the inappropriateness of standardized tests of any type in early childhood classrooms. Yet school systems and governmental agencies persist in calling for the use of such tests for accountability purposes. It is obvious that additional steps need to be taken to educate policymakers.

First, researchers in the fields of reading and writing and early childhood education must carry out more longitudinal research on both the concepts that underlie early reading ability and on the potential negative effects of achievement testing. In the same vein, pilot projects sponsored jointly by researchers and school districts should be undertaken to clarify what is already known about emergent literacy instruction and assessment.

Second, information already gathered must be disseminated so that it will reach policymakers at all levels. Journal articles and conference presentations need to be aimed at audiences made up of principals, superintendents, school board members, and governmental officials.

Third, professional organizations such as the International Reading Association, the National Council of Teachers of English, and the National Association for the Education of Young Children need to go beyond the level of position papers. They must lobby at the local, state, and federal levels to inform policy-makers that standardized reading readiness tests may result in significant negative effects to young children and are based on an ill-conceived and inadequate notion of literacy.

Fourth, teacher educators must disseminate such information in their pre- and in-service education courses so that teachers of young children are alerted to the newest research and best practice in emergent literacy. In addition, because observation is so critical in forming instructional and placement decisions, teachers would profit from explicit training in observational techniques. Teacher organizations and teacher educators should also cooperate to educate parents to expect the kind of evidence of progress that parents might intuitively believe tells them their children are making progress in reading and writing. Workshops could be held at which parents would view videotapes of youngsters exhibiting emergent literacy behaviors and would hear educators discussing what is being viewed. Teachers and parents who have been educated in assessment could join together to influence local policymakers.

Finally, assessment experts must work with researchers and practitioners in the fields of early childhood and literacy to develop assessment techniques that are developmentally appropriate and to rethink the question of the potential reliability and validity of professional judgment as an alternative to standardized testing.

CONCLUSION

The criticisms leveled at reading readiness tests by a variety of early childhood groups and by reading researchers certainly appear valid. These tests are developmentally inappropriate and have not kept pace with advances in early literacy instructional techniques—such as those represented by the emergent literacy perspective. They assess isolated skills that may have very little to do with whether a child is able to gain meaning from print in the environment or to understand the purposes and functions of print.

An assessment framework consisting of systematized observation, anecdotal summaries, and performance samples gathered by responsible teachers with a knowledge of reading and writing processes, child development, and observational and record-keeping procedures and analysis would provide classroom teachers with the information for making daily instructional decisions. This approach also explicitly recognizes the growing professionalization of teaching.

Finally, policymakers must be educated to the fact that the tests upon which they place so much weight in evaluating their early reading programs are based on an inadequate and inappropriate conception of literacy. They must be convinced to support the development of more appropriate judgmentally based assessment techniques.

NOTES

1. George Madaus, "The Influence of Testing on Curriculum," in *Critical Issues in Curriculum: Eighty-Seventh Yearbook of the National Society for the Study of Education*, ed. Laurel Tanner (Chicago: University of Chicago Press, 1988), p. 83.

2. Sue Bredekamp, ed., *Developmentally Appropriate Practice* (Washington, D.C.: National Association for the Education of Young Children, 1986); International Reading Association, Early Childhood and Literacy Development Committee, "Literacy Development and Pre-First Grade," *Childhood Education* 63 (December 1986): 110–111; Joan Moyer, Harriet Egertson, and Joan Isenberg, "Association for Childhood Education International Position Paper: The Child-Centered Kindergarten," *Childhood Education* 63 (April 1987): 235–242; and National Asso-

ciation for the Education of Young Children, "NAEYC Position Statement on Standardized Testing of Young Children 3 through 8 Years of Age." *Young Children* 43 (March 1988): 42–47.

3. Educational Research Service, "Kindergarten Programs and Practices in Public Schools," *Principal* 65 (May 1986): 22–23.

4. Lorrie Shepard and Mary Lee Smith, "Escalating Academic Demand in Kindergarten: Counterproductive Policies," *The Elementary School Journal* 89 (November 1988): 135–145.

5. Dolores Durkin, "A Classroom Observation Study of Reading Instruction in Kindergarten," *Early Childhood Research Quarterly* 2 (1987): 275–300 and Elfrieda Hiebert and Linda McWhorter, "The Content of Kindergarten and Readiness Books in Four Basal Reading Programs," paper presented at the Annual Meeting of the American Educational Research Association, Washington, DC., April 1987.

6. Bredekamp, *Developmentally Appropriate Practice*, Moyer, Egertson, and Isenberg, "Association for Childhood Education Paper"; David Elkind, *Miseducation: Preschoolers at Risk* (New York: Knopf, 1987); and Linda Gibson, *Literacy Learning in the Early Years: Through Children's Eyes* (New York: Teacher's College Press, 1989).

7. William Teale and Elizabeth Sulzby, eds., *Emergent Literacy: Writing and Reading* (Norwood, N.J.: Ablex, 1986).

8. Gibson, *Literacy Learning*.

9. Gail Heald-Taylor, "Whole Language Evaluation," unpublished paper, Cambridge, Canada, 1987.

10. Marie Clay, *What Did I Write?* (Portsmouth, N.H.: Heinemann, 1975); Kenneth Goodman, "Acquiring Literacy is Natural: Who Skilled Cock Robin?" *Theory Into Practice* 16 (December 1977): 311; Don Holdaway, *The Foundations of Literacy* (Toronto: Ashton Scholastic, 1979); Yetta Goodman, "The Roots of Literacy," in *Claremont Reading Conference Forty-fourth Yearbook*, ed. M. P. Douglas (Claremont, Calif.: Claremont Reading Conference, 1980); Jerome Harste, Virginia Woodward, and Carolyn Burke, *Language Stories and Literacy Lessons* (Portsmouth, N.J.: Heinemann, 1984); Jana Mason and JoBeth Allen, *A Review of Emergent Literacy with Implications for Research and Practice in Reading*, Technical Report 379 (Urbana: University of Illinois, Center for the Study of Reading, 1986); Nancy Taylor, "Developing Beginning Literacy Concepts: Content and Context," in *Metalinguistic Awareness and Beginning Literacy*, ed. David Yaden, Jr., and Shane Templeton (Portsmouth, N.H.: Heinemann, 1986); and Lea McGee and Richard Lomax, "Young Children's Concepts about Print and Reading: Toward a Model of Word Reading Acquisition," *Reading Research Quarterly* 22 (Spring 1987): 237–256.

11. Teale and Sulzby, *Emergent Literacy*.

12. Elfrieda Hiebert, "The Role of Literacy Experiences in Early Childhood Programs," *The Elementary School Journal* 89 (November 1988): 161–171.

13. Leslie Morrow and Carol Weinstein, "Increasing Children's Use of Literature through Program and Physical Design Changes," *Elementary School Journal* 83 (November 1982): 131–137; Christine McCormick and Jana Mason, *Intervention Procedures for Increasing Preschool Children's Interest in and Knowledge about Reading*, Technical Report No. 312 (Urbana: University of Illinois, Center for the Study of Reading, 1984); Taylor, "Developing Beginning Literacy Concepts"; Hiebert, "The Role of Literacy Experiences"; and William Teale, "Developing Appropriate Assessment of Reading and Writing in the Early Childhood Classroom," *The Elementary School Journal* 89 (November 1988): 173–183.

14. Dolores Durkin, "Testing in the Kindergarten," *The Reading Teacher* 40 (April 1987): 766–770.

15. Doris Fromberg, "Kindergarten: Current Circumstances Affecting Curriculum," *Teachers College Record* 90 (Spring 1989): 392–403.

16. Constance Kamii, ed., *Achievement Tests in Early Childhood Education: Power in Need of Accountability* (Washington, D.C.: National Association for the Education of Young Children, forthcoming). Cited in Fromberg, "Kindergarten."

17. Robert Dykstra, "The Use of Reading Readiness Tests for Prediction and Diagnosis: A Critique," in *The Evaluation of Children's Reading Achievement*, ed. Thomas Barrett (Newark, Del.: International Reading Association, 1967), p. 47.

18. Jana Mason and Christine McCormick, *Testing the Development of Reading and Linguistic Awareness*, Technical Report No. 126 (Urbana: University of Illinois, Center for the Study of Reading, 1979).

19. Ibid., p.2.

20. Carol Hodges, "Has Reading Readiness Assessment Kept Pace with Advances in Developing Early Literacy?" paper presented at the 33d International Reading Association Annual Conference, Toronto, May 1988.

21. Carole Edelsky and Susan Harman, "One More Critique of Reading Tests—With Two Differences," *English Education* 20 (October 1988): 157–171.

22. Shepard and Smith, "Escalating Academic Demand."

23. Richard Stiggins, "Improving Assessment Where It Means the Most: In the Classroom," *Educational Leadership* 43 (October 1985): 69–74; Durkin, "A Classroom Observation Study"; and Carol Hodges, "Readiness Tests: An Obsolete Approach to Emergent Literacy Assessment," paper presented at the Annual Meeting of the American Educational Research Association, San Francisco, March 1989.

24. Peter Johnston, "Teachers as Evaluation Experts," *The Reading Teacher* 40 (April 1987): 744–748; William Teale, Elfrieda Hiebert, and Edward Chittenden, "Assessing Young Children's Literacy Development," *The Reading Teacher*

40 (April 1987): 772–777; Edelsky and Harmon, "One More Critique"; Hodges, "Has Reading Readiness Assessment Kept Pace?"; James Flood and Diane Lapp, "Reporting Reading Progress: A Comparison Portfolio for Parents," *The Reading Teacher* 42 (March 1989): 508–515.

25. Yetta Goodman, "Kidwatching: Observing Children in the Classroom," in *Observing the Language Learner* ed. Angela Jagger and Margaret Smith-Burke (Newark, Del.: International Reading Association, 1985).

26. Teale, "Developing Appropriate Assessment," p. 177.

27. Harste, Woodward, and Burke, *Language Stories*; Yetta Goodman, "Kidwatching"; Nigel Hall, *The Emergence of Literacy* (Portsmouth, N.H.: Heinemann, 1987); and Johnston, "Teachers as Evaluation Experts."

28. Peter Johnston, "Constructive Evaluation and the Improvement of Teaching and Learning," *Teachers College Record* (in press).

29. Ibid.

Part III

Early Childhood Education in Broader Social and Economic Context

WENDY S. GROLNICK

Chapter Ten

Targeting Children's Motivational Resources in Early Childhood Education

With increased concern over educational outcomes in disadvantaged children,[1] a general questioning of our current educational objectives, and research increasingly supporting the plasticity and malleability of children's development,[2] educators and politicians are looking to early childhood education as a source of equality and change. Some experts suggest that prekindergarten programs will soon become the standard in public education.[3] With such predictions, it is no surprise that much research is being directed toward evaluating early childhood education. However, this research has raised complex questions about the goals and long-term gains of such programs, and about mechanisms of effect.

The purpose of this article is to provide a rationale for reexamining the importance of affective goals in early childhood education. Using a model identifying specific "inner affective resources" associated with successful academic outcomes,[4] evidence for the importance of three specific resources is presented. Next, literature specifying factors in children's environments that are facilitative of these resources is examined. Finally, implications of this model for early childhood programs are discussed.

This article is not a review of the literature on early childhood programs, and thus only a brief summary of relevant findings follows. The most comprehensive evaluative project to date is the consortium organized by Irving Lazar,[5] which examined the results of 12 programs, each including long-term follow-up. While the results of the project are complex, some clear trends emerge. Both IQ and achievement results indicate short- but not long-term gains, though a decreased rate of special-education placement for participating children was found. Results suggest no program effects on occupational and educational aspirations or self-evaluation (where measured). Experimental-control differences in achievement were typically attenuated by the third or fourth grade. Results reported for other projects with long-term follow-up confirm these findings.[6] Follow-up studies of Head Start programs suggest postintervention increases in IQ, school performance, self-esteem, and social behavior followed by losses in each of these areas.[7] Most other studies show some difference between experimental and control children in retention and need for special services, while only a few suggest achievement differences persisting through the second grade.[8]

While the data from longitudinal studies clearly provide grounds for optimism and increased attention by educational policymakers, two issues merit special concern. First, the most pressing problem concerns maintenance of gains. While early effects are promising, gains are gradually being lost following program termination. thus, identification of factors that would increase maintenance of gains must become a focus. Second, there has been an almost exclusive reliance on cognitive outcomes in program evaluation. With some exceptions,[9] program outcomes have been limited to standardized measures of IQ and achievement.[10] Some suggest that this focus is the result of advocates' believing that they must demonstrate quickly the long-term effectiveness of preschool intervention to ensure support and funding.[11] Such pressure may account for the tendency to focus on intellectual factors rather than on social and emotional factors for which fewer reliable and valid measures are available.[12]

An emphasis on cognitive outcomes as goals and indicators of successful programs misses the importance of emotional and experiential factors that may affect children's performance in school.[13] First, even if it were possible to influence IQ scores, there is no guarantee that this change would translate into greater school performance. Motivational and affective characteristics of children may determine achievement behavior even controlling for ability.[14] Second, Edward Zigler has argued that subsystems other than intelligence may be more likely to be influenced than the intellectual system, especially those affecting socialization, motivation, and personality. It is suggested that the lower heritability ratios for socioemotional as opposed to intellectual variables[15] support their greater malleability. Further, these authors suggest that initial IQ gains may actually reflect changes in motivation as a result of program experience.

Following this reasoning, the question becomes, what are the affective and attitudinal characteristics facilitative of successful school performance? If such characteristics could be identified, they would be likely candidates as goals for intervention and prospects for measurement in program evaluation. A second question concerns the environmental factors promoting such attitudes and affective reactions. One recent conceptualization, drawing on developmental and educational literature, has identified three school-related "inner resources" facilitative of school success:[16] namely, perceived competence,[17] or the confidence one has in oneself as a learner and producer; self-regulation,[18] or the degree to which children self-direct their learning behavior through their own value for learning and learning goals; and perceived control,[19] or one's understanding of the sources of control at work in achievement contexts. These three resources have each been found to be linked to school success. Even the school performance of children with high ability has been found to be affected by levels of these inner resources.[20] It is argued in this article that policy for early childhood education would benefit from incorporation of relevant motivational research into goals and evaluation.

Clearly, this is not the first suggestion that affective goals merit attention, either in the educational literature or in early education policy. John Dewey suggested that enhancing self-perceptions is a primary educational need and that relevant goals should be explicit in educational practice.[21] However, authors of the *Taxonomy of Educational Objectives* noted the erosion of affective objectives in educational research.[22] They suggest that guiding notions assume that if cognitive goals are met, affective processes will follow. Arguing from their comprehensive review, they noted that this was only the case given an appropriate learning experience. Moreover, the development of cognitive skills in certain environments may actually destroy interest and motivation for later learning.[23]

Affective goals have been included in policy in early education since its inception. Head Start's seven original goals included

> helping the emotional and social development of the child by encouraging self-confidence, spontaneity, and self-discipline, . . . establishing patterns and expectations of success for the child that create a climate of confidence for future learning efforts . . . [and]increasing the sense of dignity and self-worth within the child and his family.[24]

Such goals indicate a commitment to the development of the whole child, including attitudes toward self and others. While intentions clearly indicate attention to self-perception issues, few programs translate vague goal statements (e.g., develop a positive sense of self-worth) into specific, measurable outcomes.[25] It is the goal of this article to provide a framework including affective goals that are specific and potentially measurable.

INNER RESOURCES: COMPILING THE EVIDENCE

Before summarizing evidence regarding inner resources for school achievement, it is important to clarify our view of the nature of psychological self-relevant structures in children. In our view, the child's psychological development occurs in interaction with the social surround—especially, the family and school contexts. Psychological structures such as self-image are seen as relatively enduring (or "semi-permanent")[26] but are effected by the behaviors and expectations of important others, which may themselves be a function of social factors such as economic conditions. While children may come into the classroom with beliefs about themselves and learning, these beliefs can be strongly impacted by the learning situation. The socializing impact of the learning environment may be especially strong for the young child who is encountering the structured learning environment for the first time and whose psychological structures and cognitive development are undergoing rapid change.[27] The formative nature of early childhood is underscored by the fact that by the end of third grade, children are on achievement trajectories they will follow through school.[28]

Given the myriad studies on motivation and school adaptation, it would be impossible to provide a thorough review of such studies. What follows is a brief review of work that may be applicable to early childhood programming. It is hoped that it will spark increased dialogue between researchers in motivation and those in early childhood education.

PERCEIVED COMPETENCE

It is increasingly recognized that one's impression of competence plays a strong role in school performance and is critical to adaptive functioning in the classroom.[29] Children higher in perceived competence have been found to be lower in anxiety and higher in preference for challenge than those lower on this dimension.[30] Self-efficacy in a given activity influences the choice of activity, effort expended, and task accomplishment.[31] Further, experimental interventions that increase perceptions of self-efficacy, such as verbalization of strategy use in problem solving, significantly increase task performance.[32]

While there has been controversy about the causal predominance of self-perceptions of competence and achievement, most researchers believe that the relationship between them is at least partially reciprocal.[33] Most studies of this causal relation have focused on elementary or older children. Because achievement is extremely stable by the early elementary years[34] many of the studies finding only that achievement leads to positive self-perceptions (and not the reverse) may be less applicable to early childhood.

Doris Entwisle and her colleagues examined self-perceptions as they develop during the transition to school. In examining factors affecting self-image and grades, these authors suggest that, at the start of schooling, children's achievement has less impact on later school marks than do affective variables such as self-expectations. These authors suggest that early in schooling affective status may shape cognitive status more than the other way around because marks generally do not predict the academic self-image in its earliest form.[35] This research suggests that programs may best impact on perceived capabilities early in schooling.

PERCEIVED CONTROL

Much research suggests that perceived control influences academic performance. Relevant studies focus on a variety of constructs including locus of control,[36] causal attributions,[37] and control perceptions.[38] While earlier conceptions focused on beliefs about internal versus external control only, more recent developmental conceptualizations make distinctions between such overall concepts as known versus unknown control[39] and controllability versus noncontrollability[40] as well as differentiating various internal (e.g., effort, ability) and external (e.g., powerful others) beliefs.

Children who report that they did not know what controls outcomes in school, for example, are rated by teachers as less engaged in school and are lower in achievement and grades relative to those with greater knowledge.[41] Beliefs in ability and luck as strategies for causing success and failure are also negatively associated with these outcomes. Similarly, attributing failure to ability can have debilitating effects on motivation and performance.[42] Attributing failure to effort promotes positive performance expectations and success-oriented behaviors. These findings suggest that control understanding is a key variable in successful school performance. In particular, young children, who may not yet discriminate between effort and ability as causes of outcomes,[43] without a sense that there are contingent and consistent relations between actions and outcomes, appear at risk for school problems.

MOTIVATIONAL ORIENTATION

A great deal of work has examined the role of motivational factors in academic adjustment. Work in this area has been described under the rubrics of achievement motivation,[44] mastery motivation,[45] and intrinsic motivation.[46] Recently researchers have differentiated two issues in motivation: the level or intensity and the type or orientation of motivation. The orientation issue focuses not on how motivated a person is but on what motives are at work in achievement situations.

A number of researchers have examined the concomitants of children adopting more intrinsic orientations (where learning is motivated by curiosity or interest) versus extrinsic orientations (where learning is initiated as a result of external rewards or prompts or focus on self or other evaluation).[47] Having an intrinsic orientation is positively associated with perceived competence, preference for challenge, and task persistence in elementary children.[48]

While intrinsic motivation clearly plays an important role in learning, particularly at young ages, not all classroom activities or information taught is inherently interesting. However, children's orientation to learning nonintrinsically motivating material will vary. Richard Ryan and his colleagues suggest that orientations to learning can be seen as lying along a continuum of autonomy or self-regulation ranging from external regulation, in which behavior is regulated by anticipated environmental contingencies such as rewards and punishments from teachers, to identified regulation, in which the child regulates behavior through internalized goals and acceptance of responsibility.[49] In related work, Carol Dweck suggests that goal orientations can be either mastery-oriented, where focus is one the learning process, or performance-oriented, where concern is with being judged and showing the ability to be successful with little effort.[50]

Differences in motivational orientations for school behavior appear to have important consequences. External styles have been found to be negatively associated with perceived competence and self-worth[51] as well as with greater use of defensive styles of coping with setbacks in school.[52] More self-regulated children tend to cope positively with failure and display better long-term retention of information and conceptual learning relative to more externally regulated children.[53] Children who are more mastery-oriented in their learning goals tend to persist in task-related behavior while those displaying performance goals tend to develop a "helpless stance" in the face of failure.[54]

ENVIRONMENTS AND INNER RESOURCES

Research on contextual factors and inner resources includes studies of factors such as rewards, evaluation, pressure and control, and styles of interpersonal communication. Within our motivational perspective we suggest that three contextual dimensions, which may subsume many of the above factors, are important facilitators of inner resources. First, environmental events that facilitate the experience of autonomy, choice, or self-determination are said to enhance perceived competence, perceived control, and self-regulation. Facilitation of autonomy involves providing opportunities for others to experience a sense of choicefulness, activity, and self-determination, while controlling communications creates the feeling of control, pressure, and lack of choice.[55] In our perspective, this dimension is labeled autonomy support versus control though other constructs such as origin climate[56] and authoritative-authoritarian[57] are also relevant.

A second facilitator of inner resources concerns environmental feedback. When the environment provides contingent, positive, competence-relevant feedback concerning one's performance, motivation and adaptive self-perceptions will be facilitated. We have included under the rubric of *structure* environmental qualities involving clear and consistent expectations and consequences for behavior and appropriate feedback for success.

Finally, we suggest that the degree to which the environment meets relational needs will also play a role in self-perceptions and motivation. An environment providing an experience of caring, warmth, and positive and active involvement is said to facilitate perceived competence and self-regulation.

Thus, in our theory, three contextual factors—autonomy support to control, structure, and involvement—are hypothesized to impact upon inner resources in children. Studies supporting and clarifying this framework follow. Though not all directly assess these factors, all include dimensions with direct relevance to the theory.

EARLY HOME INFLUENCES

There have been a number of studies pointing to the importance of home influences in early competence. One set of studies has examined contingent responsiveness, or the degree to which the environment responds to behavior in a manner that is quick, consistent, and discriminative.[58] Studies show that the probability of a contingent maternal response to the infant's cues is significantly related to infant cognitive performance.[59] Michael Lewis and Susan Goldberg found that infants with mothers who responded contingently to cries and vocalizations learned better in a habituation task than infants with less responsive mothers.[60]

Another relevant study measured mothers' tendencies toward supporting and encouraging their infants' initiations and autonomy versus directing or controlling the infants' behavior during play. Mothers' tendencies on this dimension were examined in relation to children's persistence in *indepen-*

dently trying to solve challenging tasks. Results suggested that more autonomy-supportive mothers had infants who were more persistent in solving tasks than those of more controlling mothers.[61]

Ellen Skinner examined the link between children's perceived control and mother-child interaction. Skinner rated mothers' behavior on dimensions representing sensitive initiation (allowing independent child response) and sensitive responding (contingent and appropriate response to child bids). In this work, positive relations between sensitive initiation and responding and attributions of internal responsibility and positive task engagement in children were found.[62] This study, like others, suggests that inner resources are developing from early childhood and focuses on feedback and support for autonomy.

PARENTING DIMENSIONS AND SCHOOL CHILDREN

Several studies have examined parenting and children's school performance. One parental dimension that has received much attention in this literature is parental control.[63] One study, for example, examined authoritarian (controlling and demanding), authoritative (noncontrolling and demanding), and permissive (nondemanding) parents and students' achievement. The findings indicated that lower grades were associated with more authoritarian, more permissive, and less authoritative parenting.[64]

A recent trend in this area is to focus on relations between parenting and affective and motivational factors rather than only on achievement outcomes. Grolnick and Ryan conducted interviews with parents of elementary children, after which they were rated on dimensions of autonomy support, structure, and involvement. More autonomy-supportive parenting was associated with greater self-regulation and higher grades and achievement test scores. Children from homes lacking in structure displayed the lowest levels of control understanding. Finally, maternal involvement positively predicted control understanding and achievement.[65]

CLASSROOM STUDIES

Within the literature, the undermining effects of rewards on intrinsic motivation have been well demonstrated. While many laboratory studies have demonstrated this effect,[66] work has also examined classroom and teacher orientations and children's inner resources. Edward Deci, John Nezlek and Louise Sheinman suggested that teachers may vary in their orientation toward controlling children or supporting their autonomy. In the former, teachers attempt to motivate children through reward, evaluation, and competition. Autonomy-supportive teachers support children in solving their own problems and use autonomy-supportive motivational techniques such as empathic limit setting. These authors demonstrated that teacher control orientations have significant relations with inner resources in children. Perceived cognitive competence, self-worth, and mastery motivation were all greater in classrooms of more autonomy-oriented teachers.[67] In a subsequent study, measures of motivation and perceived competence were taken on day one of the school year and eight weeks later. Change over the eight-week period was predicted by teachers' styles. In classrooms of more controlling teachers children displayed greater decrements in affective resources relative to those in classrooms of more autonomy supportive teachers.[68]

In another study, Ryan and Grolnick assessed the degree to which children perceive their classrooms as providing a "pawn" (control-oriented) or "origin" (autonomy-oriented) experience. Perceptions of more origin-enhancing teachers were positively associated with children's mastery motivation and perceived competence. In addition, children who perceived their classroom as controlling attributed control over outcomes to external or unknown sources more than did those in more autonomy-oriented classrooms.[69]

Classrooms may also be characterized by their emphasis on mastery versus performance goals. Classrooms emphasizing performance goals stress normative comparisons and competition while those with mastery orientations focus on the process of learning and nonnormative progress. Children rating the classroom as more mastery-oriented use more effective learning strategies, prefer tasks that offer challenge, and believe that effort and success covary.[70] Competitive environments tend to promote performance orientations while individualistic environments promote more mastery-oriented orientations.[71]

Richard deCharms trained teachers to be more supportive of autonomy and to promote active learning. Intrinsic motivation, self-esteem, and achievement were assessed in the children both of teachers who did and of teachers who did not receive this training. Results suggested increases in motivation, self-esteem, and achievement as a result of the intervention.[72] Other researchers have examined the effects of interventions that promote active learning. One example of such an approach is the "jigsaw procedure," in which small groups of children learn by teaching each other. Outcomes of this procedure include increases in self-esteem and interpersonal relations especially for low-achieving children.[73] Learning in small groups also provides more opportunity for self-regulation and responsibility and greater intrinsic motivation and performance.[74]

IMPLICATIONS FOR EARLY CHILDHOOD INTERVENTION

The preceding literature has focused on affective resources associated with positive school outcomes. While many of these studies were conducted with elementary children and thus may not be directly applicable to the preschool child with his/her cognitive level and learning style, it is suggested that these studies may serve as a starting point for a discussion about how early childhood programs can be tailored toward an impact on motivational and affective goals. The following are theoretical and program implications that have been drawn from the work reviewed.

Classroom Environment

The above research suggests that the classroom environment can play a crucial role in children's developing motivational and affective characteristics. The intrinsic motivation and positive attitudes of young children toward learning can be capitalized upon through a game-like atmosphere and opportunities for exploration. In addition, self-regulation, perceived competence, and control understanding seem to be most facilitated in an autonomy-supportive classroom where opportunities are provided for independent mastery and where there is a lack of reliance on rewards to motivate behavior. While, originally, Head Start programs were designed around a flexible schedule and child-initiated group learning experiences, recent approaches have included direct instruction in readiness skills.[75] While direct instruction *can* be conducted within an autonomy-supportive climate, opportunities for self-initiation and independent problem solving must be purposefully built into such activities if enhancement of inner resources is a primary goal.

Classroom structure may also play a crucial role in setting the foundations for inner resource development. Here, emphasis is on contingent relations between children's behavior and positive feedback. One survey suggests that praise is infrequently used by teachers.[76] Even kindergarten teachers use reprimand more often than praise—suggesting that negative behavior is more likely to receive a response than is positive behavior.[77] It should be noted, however, that even positive feedback can have differential motivational effects depending on the way it is communicated. Feedback emphasizing control and normative comparisons may undermine motivation while that focused on the task and nonnormative information will be more likely to facilitate motivation.[78] Contingent feedback, if used appropriately to indicate competent functioning, can be an integral part of training children high in inner resources.

Finally, while most trips to early-intervention programs find warm, supportive teachers interacting with enthusiastic children, conditions in schools must be created that provide teachers the opportunity to form intimate connections with children in their classrooms. Issues such as class size and reasonable pay to ensure continuity are relevant here. In addition, recent work suggests that conditions for teachers (see below) must receive attention.

Classroom Activities

Activities can be planned that stress choice, active participation, and self-initiation. Exercises pointing out each child's unique personality and skills are also frequently used to foster a positive self-image. Literature on curriculum for enhancing self-concept is available and has already become an integral part of many early childhood programs.[79] Specific strategies for incorporating immediate positive feedback into classroom activities are also available.[80] Computers may be a useful part of the motivation-enhancing early childhood program.[81]

Policy Facilitating Teacher Efficacy

Recent work on teacher motivation suggests that teachers who feel effective are able to facilitate student motivation and achievement. Patricia Ashton identified the following factors as affecting the sense of efficacy of teachers of low-achieving, low SES (socioeconomic status) students: salary dissatisfaction, status panic, lack of collegial and administrative support, uncertainty, and powerlessness.[82] If we are serious about putting our hope for change in early childhood programs, we must support teachers so that they can provide the types of learning experiences facilitative of inner resources.

Parent Participation

Research suggests that inner resources are being shaped in infancy, and not surprisingly, some of the most successful intervention programs have focused on parents. The Mother-Child Home Program is one such program. In this program, home visitors model for mothers play behaviors hypothesized to facilitate socioemotional and cognitive growth. The goals are not only to increase maternal stimulation but contingently responsive and independence-supporting interactions.[83] Another approach involves having parents take turns visiting their child's classroom. One such program is the Parent-in-the-Classroom Program, in which teachers trained to model for visiting parents specific interactional and management techniques and parents' experiences are later discussed in groups.[84] Such programs have been found to have benefits for both mothers' and children's self-images.

Interventions may also be targeted to enhancing parents' expectations for their children. Parental expectations have been found to have potent effects on school-related affective variables in children.[85]

Broader Goals and Measures in Program Evaluation

Ruby Takanashi has suggested that the goals of evaluation of early childhood programs have been narrowly limited to outcome evaluation. She suggests that, if conceptualized more broadly, evaluation may serve not just to support program efficacy but also program development and feedback to participants.[86] Evaluation of process (i.e., what works and what doesn't) can lead to programmatic change. In addition, the questions asked should not be limited to whether early childhood education promotes intellectual development only but on its impact on the whole child. The recent availability of models for understanding self-development (e.g., Susan Harter)[87] and measures to assess aspects of the self (e.g., Entwisle et al.)[88] in young children makes the possibility of including such measures more realistic. With this orientation, complex questions involving the aspects of programs that are key to enhancing various motivational, affective, and cognitive goals can be asked.

Increased Focus on Factors That Maintain Gains

Unfortunately, program gains may be overridden by ongoing school, home, and sociocultural factors. A process evaluation approach will help to move toward examining which children under what circumstances maintain gains. This type of approach will clearly proceed best through collaborative efforts between early intervention specialists and educational researchers specializing in motivational development.

SUMMARY

Because of the separation between researchers studying motivation and researchers and policymakers in early childhood education, the extensive literature on motivational processes in education has had little influence on policy development. While a number of conceptualizations for understanding motivational development could be used, the present analysis suggested that three inner resources—perceived competence, perceived control, and self-regulation for learning—may be prime targets for early childhood programming. Suggestions for creating programs facilitating inner resources include providing opportunities for self-initiation, focusing on tasks rather than outcomes, and using appropriate feedback. It is also suggested that many of the most successful programs have included parents. Clearly such suggestions require a modification of goals for the early childhood program but, perhaps more problematically, require expenditures consistent with such changes as the use of small groups and pay assuring teacher continuity. Further, the ongoing transaction between motivational development and the social context suggests that conditions within our schools must be attended to if maintenance of gains is to be expected. As successful school adaptation for all children is a shared goal of motivational and early childhood researchers, movement toward this goal can be best accomplished with a sharing of information and mutual influence.

NOTES

1. L. J. Schweinhart and J. J. Koshel, *Policy Options for Preschool Programs* (Ypsilanti, Mich.: High/Scope Educational Research Foundation, 1986).

2. J J. Gallagher and C. T. Ramey, *The Malleability of Children* (Baltimore: Brooks, 1987).

3. R. Haskins, "Beyond Metaphor: The Efficacy of Early Childhood Intervention," *American Psychologist* 44 (1989): 274–282.

4. W. S. Grolnick and R. M. Ryan, "Parent Styles Associated with Children's Self-Regulation and Competence in School," *Journal of Educational Psychology* 81 (1989): 143–154; W. S. Grolnick, R. M. Ryan, and E. L. Deci, "The Inner Resources for School Achievement: Motivational Mediators of Children's Perceptions of Their Parents" (New York University, 1989).

5. I. Lazar et al. "Lasting Effects of Early Education: A Report from the Consortium for Longitudinal Studies," *Monographs of the Society for Research on Child Development* 47, 2–3, serial no. 195 (1982).

6. E. K. Beller, "The Philadelphia Study: The Impact of Preschool on Intellectual and Socioemotional Development," in *As the Twig is Bent: Lasting Effects of Preschool Programs*, ed. Consortium for Longitudinal Studies (Hillsdale, N.J.: Erlbaum, 1983), pp. 333–376; S. W. Gray, B. K. Ramsey and R. A. Klaus, *From 3 to 20: The Early Training Project* (Baltimore: University Park Press, 1982).

7. R. J. McKey et al., *The Impact of Head Start on Children, Families and Communities*, Department of Health and Human Services Publication no. OHDS 85–31198 (Washington, D.C.: GPO, 1985).

8. B. M. Caldwell, "Sustaining Intervention Effects: Putting Malleability to the Test," *Malleability of Children*, ed. Gallagher and Ramey, pp. 115–126.

9. P. Levenstein, "The Mother-Child-Home Program," in *The Preschool in Action*, ed. M. C. Day and R. K. Parker (Boston: Allyn & Bacon, 1977), pp. 27–49;

C. T. Ramey and F. A. Campbell, "The Carolina Abecedarian Project," in *Malleability of Children*, ed. Gallagher and Ramey, pp. 127–139.

10. R. Takanashi, "Evaluation of Early Childhood Programs: Toward a Developmental Perspective," in *Current Topics in Early Childhood Education*, ed. L. G. Katz, vol. 2 (Norwood, N.J.: Ablex, 1977), pp. 27–49.

11. C. Hymes, *Early Childhood Education: An Introduction to the Profession* (Washington, D.C.: National Association of Educators of Young Children, 1975).

12. Takanashi, "Evaluation of Early Childhood Programs."

13. E. Zigler and J. Freedman, "Early Experience, Malleability and Head Start," in *Malleability of Children*, ed. Gallagher and Ramey, pp. 85–96.

14. D. Dweck and W. S. Elliot, "Achievement Motivation," in *Handbook of Child Psychology, Socialization, Personality, and Social Development*, ed. E. M. Hetherington, vol. 4 (New York: Wiley, 1983), pp. 643–691.

15. G. Kimble, N. Garmezy and E. Zigler, *Psychology* (New York: Wiley, 1984).

16. Grolnick, Ryan, and Deci, "Inner Resources for School Achievement."

17. S. Harter, "The Perceived Competence Scale for Children," *Child Development* 53 (1982): 87–97.

18. R. M. Ryan and J. P. Connell, "Perceived Locus of Causuality and Internalization: Examining Reasons for Acting in Two Domains," *Journal of Personality and Social Psychology* 57 (1989): 749–761.

19. E. A. Skinner and J. P. Connell, "Control Understanding: Suggestions for a Developmental Framework," in *The Psychology of Control and Aging*, ed. M. M. Baltes and P. B. Baltes (Hillside, N.J.: Erlbaum, 1986) pp. 35–69.

20. D. A. Phillips, "Socialization of Perceived Academic Competence among Highly Competent Children," *Child Development* 58 (1987): 1308–1320.

21 J. D. Dewey, *Democracy and Education* (New York: Macmillan, 1978).

22. D. R. Krathwohl, B. S. Bloom, and B. B. Masia, *Taxonomy of Educational Objectives: Handbook 2, Affective Domain* (New York: David McKay, 1974).

23. J. Condry and B. Koslowski, "Can Education Be Made 'Intrinsically Interesting' to Children?" in *Current Topics*, ed. Katz, pp. 227–258; W. S. Grolnick and R. M. Ryan, "Autonomy in Children's Learning: An Experimental and Individual Difference Investigation," *Journal of Personality and Social Psychology* 52 (1987): 890–898.

24. Zigler and Freedman, "Early Experience and Head Start."

25. J. A. Beane and R. P. Lipka, *Self-Concept Self-Esteem and the Curriculum* (New York: Teachers College Press, 1986).

26. D. R. Entwisle and L. A. Hayduk, *Early Schooling* (Baltimore: Johns Hopkins University Press, 1982).

27. A. Skolnick, "The Limits of Childhood: Conceptions of Child Development and the Social Context," *Law and Contemporary Problems* 39 (1977): 38–77.

28. K. L. Alexander and D. R. Entwisle, "Achievement in the First Two Years of School: Patterns and Processes," *Monographs of the Society for Research in Child Development* 53 (1988): 2.

29. S. Harter, "Developmental Perspectives on the Self-System" in Handbook of Child Psychology, vol. 4, *Socialization, Personality, and Social Development*, 4th ed., ed. E. M. Hetherington (New York: Wiley, 1983), pp. 275–386.

30. Harter, "Perceived competence Scale."

31. D. H. Schunk, "Verbal Self-Regulation as a Facilitator of Children's Achievement and Self-Efficacy," *Human Learning* 1 (1982): 265–277.

32. D. H. Schunk and P. D. Cox, "Strategy Training and Attributional Feedback with Learning Disabled Students," *Journal of Educational Psychology* 78 (1986): 201–209.

33. W. W. Purkey, *Self-Concept and School Achievement* (Englewood Cliffs, N.J.: Prentice-Hall, 1970).

34. G. Maruyama, R. A. Rubin, and G. G. Kinsbury, "Self-Esteem and Educational Achievement: Independent Constructs with a Common Cause?" *Journal of Personality and Social Psychology* 40 (1981): 962–975.

35. D. R. Entwisle et al., "The Emergent Academic Self-Image of First Graders: Its Response to Social Structure," *Child Development* 58 (1987): 1190–1206.

36. J. B. Rotter, "Generalized Expectancies for Internal versus External Control of Reinforcement," *Psychological Monographs* 80, 1 (1966): 1–28.

37. M. E. P. Seligman, "Fall Into Helplessness," *Psychology Today* 7 (1973): 43–48.

38. Skinner and Connell, "Control Understanding."

39. J. P. Connell, "A New Multidimensional Measure of Children's Perceptions of Control," *Child Development* 56 (1985): 1018–1041.

40. J. R. Weisz and A. M. Cameron, "Individual Differences in the Student's Sense of Control," in *Research on Motivation in Education, vol. 2, The Classroom Milieu*, ed. C. Ames and R. Ames (New York: Academic Press, 1985): pp. 93–140.

41. E. A. Skinner, J. G. Wellborn, and J. P. Connell, "What It Takes to Do Well in School and Whether I've Got It: A Process Model of Perceived Control and Children's Engagement and Achievement in School." *Journal of Educational Psychology* 82 (1990): 22–32.

42. C. I. Diener and C. S. Dweck, "An Analysis of Learned Helplessness: Continuous Changes in Performance, Strategy and Achievement cognitions following failure," *Journal of Personality and Social Psychology 36 (1978): 451–462.*

43. J. Nicholls, "Quality and Equality in Intellectual Development: The Role of Motivation in Education," *American Psychologist* 34 (1979): 1071–1084.

44. D. C. McClelland et al., *The achievement motive* (New York: Appleton-Century-Crofts, 1953).

45. L. Y. Yarrow, J. L. Rubenstein, and F. A. Pedersen, *Infant and Environment: Early Cognitive and Motivational Development (New York: Wiley, 1975).*

46. E. L. Deci, "The Effects of Contingent and Non-Contingent Rewards and Controls on Intrinsic Motivation," *Organizational Behavior and Human Performance* 8 (1972): 217–299.

47. R. M. Ryan, J. P. Connell, and E. L. Deci, "A Motivational Analysis of Self-Determination and Self-Regulation in Education," in *Research on Motivation in Education*, vol. 2, ed. Ames and Ames, pp. 13–51.

48. S. Harter, "A New Self-Report Scale of Intrinsic versus Extrinsic Orientation in the Classroom: Motivational and Informational Components," *Developmental Psychology* 17 (1981): 300–312.

49. R. M. Ryan, J. P. Connell, and W. S. Grolnick, "When Achievement is *not* Intrinsically Motivated: A Theory of Self-Regulation in School," in *Achievement and Motivation: A Social-Developmental Perspective*, ed. A. K. Boggiano and T. S. Pittman (New York: Cambridge University Press, in press).

50. C. Dweck, "The Role of Expectations and Attributions in the Alleviation of Learned Helplessness," *Journal of Personality and Social Psychology* 31 (1975): 674–685.

51. Harter, "Perceived Competence Scale."

52. P. F. Tero and J. P. Connell, "Children's Academic Coping Inventory: A New Self-Report Measure" (Paper presented at the Annual Meeting of the American Educational Research Association, Montreal, April 1983).

53. Grolnick and Ryan, "Autonomy in Children's Learning."

54. Dweck, "Role of Expectations."

55. Ryan, Connell, and Grolnick, "Self-Regulation in School."

56. R. deCharms, *Enhancing Motivation: Change in the Classroom* (New York: Irvington, 1976).

57. D. Baumrind, "Childcare Practices Anteceding Three Patterns of Preschool Behavior," *Genetic Psychology Monographs* 58 (1967).

58. M. E. P. Seligman, *Helplessness: On Depression, Development and Death* (San Francisco: Freeman, 1975).

59. M. Lewis and D. Coates, "Mother-Infant Interaction and Cognitive Performance," *Infant Behavior and Development* 3 (1980): 95–105; Yarrow, Rubenstein, and Pedersen, *Infant and Environment.*

60. M. Lewis and S. Goldberg, "Perceptual-Cognitive Development in Infancy: A Generalized Expectancy Model as a Function of Maternal-Infant Interaction," *Merrill Palmer Quarterly* 15 (1969): 81–100.

61. W. S. Grolnick, A. Frodi, and L. B. Bridges, "Maternal Control Style and the Mastery Motivation of One-Year-Olds," *Infant Mental Health Journal* 5 (1984): 72–82.

62. E. A. Skinner, "The Origins of Young Children's Perceived Control: Mother Contingent and Sensitive Behavior," *International Journal of Behavioral Development* 9 (1986): 359–382.

63. For example, see Baumrind, "Childcare Practices."

64. S. M. Dornbusch et al. "The Relation of Parenting Style to Adolescent School Performance," *Child Development* 58 (1987): 1244–1257.

65. Grolnick and Ryan, "Parent styles."

66. Deci, "Effects of Rewards."

67. E. L. Deci, J. Nezlek, and L. Sheinman, "Characteristics of the Rewarder and Intrinsic Motivation of the Rewardee," *Journal of Personality and Social Psychology* 40 (1981): 1–10.

68. E. L. Deci et al. "An Instrument to Assess Adults' Orientations toward Control versus Autonomy with Children: Reflections on Intrinsic Motivation and Perceived Competence," *Journal of Educational Psychology* 73 (1981): 642–650.

69. R M. Ryan and W. S. Grolnick, "Origins and Pawns in the Classroom: Self-Report and Projective Assessments of Individual Differences in Children's Perceptions," *Journal of Personality and Social Psychology* 50 (1986): 550–558.

70. C. Ames and J. Archer, "Achievement Goals in the Classroom: Learning Strategies and Motivation Processes," *Journal of Educational Psychology* 80 (1988): 260–267.

71. C. Ames, "Achievement Attributions and Self-Instructions under Competitive and Individualistic Goal Structures," *Journal of Educational Psychology* 76 (1984): 478–487.

72. deCharms, "Enhancing Motivation."

73. G. W. Lucker et al. "Performance in the Interdependent Classroom: A Field Study," *American Educational Research Journal* 13 (1977): 115–123.

74. J. L. Meece, P. C. Blumenfeld, and R. H. Hoyle, "Students' Goal Orientation and Cognitive Engagement in Classroom Activities," *Journal of Educational Psychology* 80 (1988): 514–523.

75. E. Evans, *Contemporary Influences in Early Childhood Education* (New York: Holt, Reinhart & Winston, 1975).

76. M. J. Dunkin and D. J. Biddle, *The Study of Teaching* (New York: Holt, Reinhart & Winston, 1974).

77. M. V. Berkeley, "Inside Kindergarten" (Ph.D. diss., Johns Hopkins University, 1978), cited in Entwisle et al., "Academic Self-Image."

78. R. Butler and M. Nisan, "Effects of No Feedback, Task-Related Comments, and Grade on Intrinsic Motivation and Performance," *Journal of Educational Psychology* 78 (1986): 210–216.

79. Beane and Lipka, "Self-concept."

80. J. Brophy, "On Motivating Students," in *Talks to teachers* ed. D. Berliner and B. Rosenshire (New York: Random House, 1987), pp. 201–245.

81. M. R. Lepper and J. W. Malone, "Intrinsic Motivation and Instructional Effectiveness in Computer-based Education," in *Aptitude, Learning and Instruction*, vol. 3, *Conative and Affective Process Analyses*, ed. R. E. Snow and M. J. Farr (Hillside, N.J.: Erlbaum, 1987), pp. 223–250.

82. P. Ashton, "Motivation and the Teacher's Sense of Efficacy," in *Research on Motivation in Education*, ed. Ames and Ames, pp. 141–171.

83. Levenstein, "Mother-Child-Home Program."

84. F. Eppsteiner, J. Fantuzzo, and W. Grolnick, "Parent Skills Training: Helping Children by Helping Their Parents" (New York State Council for Children, Rochester, N.Y., April 1985).

85. J. E. Parsons, J. F. Adler, and C. M. Kaczala, "Socialization of Perceived Academic Competence among Highly Competent Children," *Child Development* 58 (1987): 1308–1320.

86. Takanashi, "Evaluation of Early Childhood Programs."

87. Harter, "Developmental perspectives."

88. Entwisle et al., "Academic Self-Image."

JULIA WRIGLEY

Chapter Eleven

Different Care for Different Kids: Social Class and Child Care Policy

Entry to good jobs depends increasingly on academic credentials.[1] This has made educational equity an important goal for racial minorities and other dispossessed groups. The civil rights movement targeted school segregation in both the South and the North, and during periods of labor militancy some working-class groups have organized to combat class biases in the curriculum and control of the public schools.[2] Formally egalitarian organizations such as the public schools tend to generate such political pressures for equality, even though more privileged groups can often successfully maintain their advantages.[3]

The American child care market is rapidly growing, as more than half of all mothers of preschoolers now work outside the home. In child care, in contrast to the public schools, there has never been even the promise of egalitarianism. Once the state began providing public education, the schools became potential, and sometimes actual, targets of political mobilization. The child care market, however, remains so privatized and fragmented that, while millions of children receive some kind of care, race and class segregation of young children remains largely unchallenged. Of the approximately 10 million preschool children with working mothers in 1986, only about 1 million were in federally funded day care centers.[4] These children, chosen on the basis of their families' neediness, are isolated from middle-class peers.

The class segregation of child care goes beyond this, however, as children of different social class backgrounds not only do not mingle in day care centers but are often in quite different types of child care. While middle-class parents use family day care for infants and toddlers, they generally put their three- and four-year-olds in nursery schools or some other form of preschool.[5] Low-income parents cannot afford to make the switch to more formal, structured care for their three- and four-year-olds, unless they receive some type of subsidy. Most keep their children in family day care through their preschool years. This results in a major bifurcation of the child care market with middle-class children in preschools with trained teachers and developmental goals and low-income children more commonly in family day care with untrained providers.

While much race and class segregation occurs between different sectors of the child care market, this paper focuses on the dual market in formal group care, that is, the care provided in institutions such as nursery schools and day care centers. Proposals for child care reform and expansion often assume continued segregation. I will suggest this occurs in part because child care advocates, both historically and today, believe the deprived children need different kinds of child care programs than do middle-class children. While much inequity in public school programs exists, on a formal level most policymakers admit the desirability of children receiving the same types of schooling. No such consensus exists around child care.

To show the pervasiveness of the assumption that children from different social classes need different kinds of child care, I will look at day care programs in two historical periods, the early 1900s and the 1960s. In each of these periods reformers started group care programs for the children of the poor. The founders of day nurseries in the early 1900s primarily wanted to provide safe care for the children of working mothers.[6] They also argued, however, that poor children would learn new standards of hygiene and morality from their exposure to the nurseries. They saw the nurseries as superior to the children's homes in ways defined as critical by the experts of the era. By the 1960s, reformers were still concerned with the family defects of the poor, but they had shifted their attention from hygiene to cognitive development. They believed Head Start would give deprived children a cognitive boost that would improve their chances of school success.

In neither period did reformers or policymakers see any reason to mix middle-class with poor children. The middle-class children of the early 1900s were assumed to have reasonably orderly and hygienic homes; when group care developed for them in the form of nursery schools, quite different reasons were advanced for their attendance. Similarly, in the 1960s middle-class children were not thought to need the cognitive stimulation provided by Head Start. Put most broadly, care for children of the poor has focused on overcoming their families' deficiencies with those deficiencies defined differently in different eras; care for middle-class children has focused on maximizing their personal development. Given these different goals, it is not surprising that child care policymakers have accepted, often without question, the provision of different services in different institutions for children of different social class levels.

This article's first section will contrast day nurseries for the poor in the 1920s with the nursery schools gradually being introduced for middle-class children. I will examine the ideology supporting the introduction of these two types of group care, each designed for a different population. This article's second section will discuss the ideas governing the introduction of Head Start. While much changed in the child care field between the early 1900s and the 1960s, the belief that poor and middle-class children needed different forms of group care continued to govern child care policy. Head Start is not considered a child care program as it is not designed to allow mothers to work but rather to provide children with an enriched environment.[7] It is, however, the best known form of group care for disadvantaged children, and the destinctions between preschools and child care centers are increasingly arbitrary. This article's final section discusses the current child care market and how social class segregation would be affected, and perhaps intensified, if particular reform proposals went into effect. Throughout, the article relies on primary and secondary historical sources.

CUSTODIAL CARE FOR THE POOR IN DAY NURSERIES

In the first decades of the 1900s, reformers founded day nurseries in many of America's large cities. They hoped these nurseries would allow poor families to stay together by freeing needy mothers to go out to work. Destitute families had earlier faced removal of their children to orphanages. This policy, in addition to being inhumane, had proven to be very expensive. Historians estimate that in New York City in the 1890s at least 1 in every 35 children lived in a public orphan asylum.[8] By 1899 the city was caring for 15,000 children at a cost of $1.5 million.[9] Institutions that took on the complete care of whole families of children cost a great deal of money, and increasingly the outcome did not seem to justify the expense. The children taken from their families often tried to return to them at the earliest opportunity but seldom had the skills, connections, or emotional well-being to put their lives back together as they became young adults.

As the failure of the removal policy became clearer, philanthropists and middle-class reformers, mainly women, agitated for a less drastic solution to problems of family poverty. In particular, they suggested that, if day nurseries looked after children, mothers could work to support the family. The reformers deplored mothers' employment but argued it was better than breaking up the family or letting its members be thrown onto the streets. Day nurseries presented a solution and in addition would allow deprived and often neglected children a chance to eat good food and spend the day in orderly, hygienic surroundings.[10]

Day nursery founders generally defined those families that needed their services as pathological.[11] While some expressed sympathy for the hard-pressed families that used their services, many viewed their clientele with suspicion. They feared irresponsible mothers would try to shift the burden of their children's care to others. They reserved most of their suspicion for fathers, however, suggesting that they might be hoping to live off the labor of their wives. In a society where money was the measure of success, the poor were often seen as morally deficient or at least as lacking in competence and drive. The day nursery founders did not question the industrial order or the extremes of wealth and poverty in the society, but viewed poverty in individual terms.[12]

Day nursery workers adopted a social casework model. Those requesting services were required to present themselves to investigators who would explore their cases, including specifically their fitness to receive and benefit from aid. Only those who were deemed morally deserving and truly needy were to receive services. The matron in charge, warned a contemporary observer, had to "be a sufficiently keen observer to detect ordinary fraud, and experience has proved that the right kind of matron is the best possible investigator." Another critic urged that matrons carefully investigate mothers' circumstances, noting that such investigations required a "keen eye. Mothers seeking admission for babies are quick to learn the ropes. And with foreign standards of veracity to consider, even a trained social worker may be put to it to arrive at facts."[13]

The casework model emphasized the provision of services through charity rather than through any form of social entitlement. This was further emphasized by nursery workers' ability to withdraw services from those who disobeyed directives or rules of hygiene. In such situations parents had no recourse but to accept the unilateral decisions of the nursery workers. "There was little sense of accountability, either to the client or to the larger society. Since there were no public funds involved, there was no need for public accountability."[14]

The day nurseries did provide a genuine service. Their philanthropically geared sponsors tried to provide a high standard of care according to conventional ideas of the time, but they did not believe it necessary or appropriate to try innovative social or educational practices. The literature of the day nursery movement provides more information on the nurseries' administrative arrangements than it does on how the staff looked after the children. It appears, though, that the nurseries provided largely custodial care.[15] Contemporary accounts did not refer to educational goals but instead stressed the hygienic and moral value of the nursery program.

The emphasis on hygiene was typical of the era. In the early 1900s, middle-class mothers were also instructed that hygiene was of paramount importance in raising healthy infants. The parental advice literature paid little attention to children's intellectual or social development; instead, experts warned mothers to keep their children scrupulously clean, to feed them according to doctors' orders, and to maintain a strict and unvarying daily routine.[16] These ideas, not surprisingly, were applied in the group care settings of the day. It is possible that in an institutional setting they operated with greater force than in private homes. In family settings, grandmothers and other relatives could suggest other modes of care; doctors' frequent strictures against listening to female relatives makes it appear they found such women to be competitors for mothers' ears. Further, household routines are often hard to maintain in the face of daily exigencies and minor crises. In an institutional setting, however, bureaucratic rules acquire their own legitimacy and are less often upset by unexpected events. Thus care focused on children's cleanliness and on the strict scheduling of the day could probably proceed with little challenge.

Day nursery supporters believed their programs could help raise the household standards of whole families.[17] They hoped the nurseries could first change the children, by exposing them to higher standards of cleanliness and order than they experienced at home. Mothers could then be influenced, both by seeing the advantages accruing to the children and by direct instruction from nursery workers. The staff and volunteers ran evening classes for mothers, teaching them household skills and preparing them for employment, particularly as domestic workers.

As the day nurseries served only a needy population, the institutions never had to adapt to a heterogeneous clientele. There is reason to think that, even if the doors of the day nursery had been open to them, middle-class parents would have rejected this type of care as inappropriate for them and their children. A Mrs. Levitas wrote in 1913 that,

> The public nurseries are charitable institutions for the children of the poor. The middle-class working women, who earn enough to pay a little for the care of their babies, are not permitted to leave their babies in them. But even if they were given this permission, no intelligent mother would be willing to do so. For these nurseries attempt to minister only to physical wants. Although the needs of the child at infancy seem to be largely physical, we know that from the day of its birth, the infant is getting impressions and forming habits.[18]

Middle-class parents had no reason to accept the intrusive questioning of their family circumstances that needy parents had to endure. A form of care begun as a charitable service could not readily be adjusted to others.

The day nurseries, in short, served only one stratum of the society. They adopted a didactic and often patronizing tone toward their clientele and provided mainly custodial care. There were other models of care available, but the day nurseries had a limited clientele and limited objectives. They were largely shaped by their charitable purposes. At the same time as the day nurseries arose, however, group care for more privileged children was taking a different turn. Nursery schools gained a foothold in the 1920s, and they adopted a pedagogy far more geared to maximizing children's social and emotional development. The literature of the period makes it clear that there was little overlap, either institutionally or ideologically, between the care designed for the poor in the day nurseries and that provided for the more prosperous in the nursery schools.

NURSERY SCHOOLS AND MIDDLE-CLASS CHILDREN

Nursery schools had to appeal to a clientele that seldom had a practical need for child care. This meant the nursery schools had to have positive features that would draw parents to them. As the middle-class home was conventionally considered the ideal place for children to be raised, it was not at first obvious that nursery schools would have broad appeal. Early nursery schools had an experimental quality. They were often attached to universities and research institutes, and their adherents sought a new pedagogy suitable for preschoolers. Gradually, middle-class parents were won over to this new form of preschool experience. This, however, required a fairly concerted campaign by early childhood teachers and experts.

The nursery schools were sold on the basis of their ability to foster young children's social and emotional development.[19] In the literature of the period, there were sharp differences between how nursery schools and day nurseries were presented. With the day nurseries hygiene was extremely important. With the nursery schools teachers' skills in fostering children's social development were critical. Different justifications for group care of preschoolers were offered in each case. The day nurseries were designed to make up for two major parental deficiencies. The families served were primarily deficient in that they could not maintain a conventional home life for their children, with the father supporting the family and the mother staying home. For whatever reason (the father's death, desertion, alcoholism, injury, or unemployment), the mother had to take on the burden of family support. In addition, however, the mothers were often perceived by the day nursery staff as deficient in hygienic and nutritional skills. The day nurseries saw it as their mission to instruct the mothers in these arts. In the case of the nursery schools, the mothers faced no such implicit condemnation. Their culture was not suspect in the same fashion. Nursery school advocates argued, though, that young children would benefit from social interaction with their peers under the guidance of trained teachers.[20]

Day nursery advocates had not emphasized the staff's knowledge of child development. This, however, was the forte of nursery school teachers and directors. They were portrayed as having expert knowledge on how to foster young children's social integration while building the child's self-esteem. Mothers could learn from the teachers; the mothers, after all, had not had any training in how to maximize their children's developmental potential and emotional health. The mothers had to shed their view that only they could raise their children and had to be brought to recognize the advantages of professional knowledge. An early article on nursery schools made this point emphatically:

> But is it not better for mothers to train their own little children? No doubt, when they know enough of what experts know about the mental and physical hygiene of little children, are wise and patient, and have plenty of time for patience![21]

Nursery school pioneers thought middle-class mothers could learn from observing teachers' practices and skills in child management. These parents did not receive didactic instruction, on the order of that provided by the day nurseries, so much as professional advice and insights. Their children with all their individual variety were the focus of discussion. The mothers did not learn rules for care so much as they learned to observe the teachers and incorporate those skills that were applicable to their own home situations. Mothers were to be students; at some nursery schools they were expected to take notes on their children's behavior. Later they discussed these notes with the nursery school director. The nursery school was a laboratory, and the mothers, if they were apt students, could pick up some of the expert knowledge held by the teachers.[22]

Nursery school directors and teachers could often point to academic qualifications for their post. Some had received university training in child development. Such academic credentials tended to carry respect in a milieu where parents themselves valued education. The teachers had gained their expertise through recognized courses of study in recognized institutions; this had not been the case with day nursery workers who generally had administrative rather than academic skills.[23]

The nursery schools differed from the day nurseries in the qualifications of the staff, in the clientele served, in their relation to the parents, and in the stated goals of the institutions. In the one case, middle-class children were being prepared for entry into educational and occupational worlds where skills at getting along with people would be highly advantageous. In the other case, children from impoverished families were given shelter, food, and clean surroundings but were not encouraged to develop their own individuality. Their social interactions with their peers and their emotional lives were seen as of little consequence.

HEAD START

The 1930s and 1940s brought important changes in child care programs. For the first time the federal government became a major actor in the child care field, funding both depression and wartime child care. In the 1930s the federal government supported child care centers that had the primary goal of providing work for unemployed teachers. The centers were intended to serve needy children, but in the economic collapse of the period some children of middle-class backgrounds fell within their eligibility criteria. The new centers reduced the stigma of relief that had been associated with the earlier day nurseries as they were not run as private charities. Also, in the economic collapse of the depression the shame of being poor lessened. The government-funded centers also had a broader program than had the day nurseries.[24] Overall, however, a two-class system of preschool care continued, with the more privileged children going to private nursery schools and the poorer going to government-funded centers designed to serve only the needy.

After the crises of the depression and the war ended, government-sponsored child care programs faded. Only in the 1960s did the federal government become an important actor again, and it did so in a way that once again reinforced a dual system of preschool care. The story of Head Start's founding and purposes has often been told. I will therefore focus only on the social class implications of how Head Start was organized.

Robert E. Cooke, the chair of Head Start's original planning committee, wrote 15 years after its founding that the program's goal had been to interrupt and reverse the effects of poor parenting. Cooke attributed poverty itself to inadequate child rearing, writing that Head Start

> was a creative, innovative effort to interrupt the cycle of poverty, the nearly
> inevitable sequence of poor parenting which leads to children with social and
> intellectual deficits, which in turn leads to poor school performance, jobless-
> ness, and poverty, leading again to high risk births, inappropriate parenting,
> and so continues the cycle.[25]

Cooke continued that the "fundamental theoretical basis of Head Start was the concept that intellect is, to a large extent, a product of experience, not inheritance."[26] In these two statements, one emphasizing poor parenting and the other the plasticity of intelligence, he summed up a guiding rationale for group care of disadvantaged preschoolers. The children's deficiencies could be traced back to the parents, but hope lay in early intervention to provide a stimulating environment.

The emphasis on young children's intellectual development was new. We have seen that the early day nurseries did not view intellectual enrichment as part of their mission; in this, they were typical of their era. Nursery schools for middle-class children also did not emphasize cognitive development, focusing rather on the young children's social and emotional well-being. There was a broad trend over the course of the twentieth century toward greater social emphasis on young children's need for intellectual stimulation.[27] A content analysis of 1017 articles in the popular literature directed toward parents showed that, over the nine decades from 1900 through the 1980s, there was a marked upward trend in the proportion of articles that dealt with intellectual development. There was a particular spurt in the 1960s; Head Start was both a product of this spurt and helped reinforce it by vastly popularizing the idea of deliberately providing children with stimulating early experiences. What is most striking for our purposes, however, is that even as cognitive development became much more broadly acknowledged as an important goal, policymakers focused on the specific, and presumably unique, needs of disadvantaged children for early educational enrichment. When hygiene had been the sina qua non of good care in the early 1900s, the failures of their families had been securely located in their housekeeping defects. When intellectual development was the sina qua non, the families' deficiencies were identified with their cognitive failures. In each instance, group care was thought to offer part of the solution.

In the 1960s academic experts helped build a case for the importance of early experiences in preparing children for school success. Benjamin Bloom and J. McVicker Hunt were particularly influential in expounding this view. Hunt, in *Intelligence and Experience,* "abandoned the notion of fixed intelligence and abilities in favor of a new orientation emphasizing the power of a child's environment—particularly the quality of mothering—on intellectual growth."[28]

Given the stress on mothering, it is not surprising that Head Start's early planners decided that close ties with parents were crucial for early intervention to succeed.[29] As Edward Davens, a member of Head Start's original planning committee, put it, "Parents must be familiar with the philosophy, planning, and operation of the program so that they will be motivated to modify appropriately the home environment.[30] This stress on parent education was not so different from the didactic tone of the day nurseries, with their hope of changing whole families. It formed one important strand of Head Start's relations with parents.[31] It was not the whole story, however, as Head Start was not a charitable enterprise but a government program born in response to mass grassroots pressure for change. It was part of Lyndon Johnson's War on Poverty and was affected by the requirement of engaging the "maximum feasible participation" of the poor. Mobilized communities had organized and rioted against the stark inequalities of the society; the schools were a particular focus with demands for desegregation and community control. This gave the poor a brief moment in which they could, to varying degrees in different communities, influence the programs affecting their children. Head Start offered a political base for local activists and also provided jobs for many parents as teachers and aides. Over time, however, as activism waned, Head Start officials moved to restrict parental decision making, turning policy committees into advisory bodies.[32] As this happened, it was easier for those focused on family deficiencies, rather than on social inequalities and empowerment for the poor, to make Head Start into a more purely remedial program.

Head Start's curriculum varied a great deal from center to center, but there were many pressures contributing to a focus on cognitive development. The program, begun in great haste to be a showpiece for the War on Poverty, took its cues from earlier pilot preschool projects designed to improve poor children's cognitive functioning. In these programs administrators had initially tried to include the types of broad social and emotional, as well as intellectual, goals that had long been found in nursery schools for more privileged children. In the press to get cognitive results, however, the other goals tended to fall by the wayside. This made these early programs, the forerunners of Head Start, quite unlike those serving middle-class children. In the middle-class nursery schools and preschools, there was less sense of forcing development and achieving testable results. Instead children were to be provided with the means to develop their capabilities fully and naturally across the social and cognitive areas. The programs serving the disadvantaged became narrow:

> Academic preschools, strictly divorced from the social and emotional orientation of traditional middle-class nursery schools, focused on the language and cognitive skills needed to give disadvantaged children an equal footing with middle-class peers in the first grade.[33]

In retrospect, most of Head Start's early planners and administrators admit that the program was based on a simple ideology of family deficiency. As Edward Zigler, the first director of the Office of Child Development, and his coauthor, Karen Anderson, write, "The stereotype of the economically disadvantaged family was so bleak that it made intervention seem the obvious solution."[34] The early planners have backed away from a view of poor families as characterized by grossly inadequate parenting, and they have also become more skeptical about what intervention can accomplish. Head Start has left a larger legacy, however, because it provided a highly visible model of a program geared to one class of children. It promised to make these children more like their middle-class counterparts, and although that promise failed, the program implicitly reinforced the idea that different children needed different programs. As part of this, Head Start was never oriented toward mixing children from different social classes. While officially Head Start was to enroll diverse groups, in practice

> centers tended to serve homogeneous groups, reflecting segregated housing patterns, geographic isolation (Indians on reservations), and parental biases, which prevented children's participation in integrated facilities. Allocation of resources to the neediest also tended to reinforce racial segregation.[35]

This racial and social class homogeneity "continued to plague the program" over the course of its history.

Ironically even as Head Start continued to serve only one class of children, it helped influence the type of care deemed desirable for middle-class children. Head Start's broad influence helped legitimate cognitive goals for all young children in group care, whatever their social class level. Nursery schools and preschools for middle-class children were not, however, judged on how well their children did on cognitive tests. They generally maintained their child-centered curricula, holding to a traditional ideology long dominant in middle-class preschool provision, that children needed rich experiences that would encourage their intellectual curiosity but did not need rote learning.[36] Many early Head Start programs took over this traditional model, but there were strong external pressures to make the children *teachable* when they entered public schools.[37] While its founders were proud of the program's integrated cognitive, emotional, health, and social goals, arguing that for the first time deprived children were receiving broad care similar to that long provided middle-class children, in practice Head Start stood and fell politically on its cognitive component. The early planners' overoptimistic statements about the cognitive gains that could be achieved helped create just one standard for judging Head Start. When Head Start was evaluated according to a very narrow set of cognitive criteria, it was declared a failure. IQ gains were small and faded soon after the children began school.[38] Head Start's early advocates had opposed such a narrow form of evaluation, but their own statements had helped create a public sense that IQ scores represented a legitimate way of judging the program's success.

While Head Start no longer commands the nation's attention as it did in its infancy, the program has won continued funding. Observers report that mechanical forms of quasi-academic learning consume a large part of the curriculum. Eveline Omwake, a former president of the National Association for the Education of Young Children, comments on Head Start's curricular failures:

> Descriptions of classrooms suggest a picture of thousands of children spending half or full days in a relentless round of identifying shapes, matching colors, repeating the alphabet, and counting to ten. Such activities as dramatic play, block building, painting, and water play tend to be viewed by many teachers as special rewards for good behavior instead of important learning experiences.[39]

While sensitively exploring the larger context that helped make a Head Start program very different from a nursery school in the same community, Sally Lubeck paints a similar picture of a Head Start program that emphasized mechanical learning while having little creative content. She notes that, "Where the preschool teachers fostered individualism and self-expression, the center teachers expected obedience to authority and relative conformity.[40] In such formal programs, children spend much time learning letter recognition, numbers, and sound blends.[41] Teachers with little training often find it easier to master curricula that call for such highly structured activities. In addition the teachers bring their own values to their jobs; in the Head Start program Lubeck studied, the teachers, drawn from the surrounding community, formally accepted the supervisors' stress on the creative value of play, but in reality scorned play as mere babysitting. They wanted the children to learn preacademic skills they would need for school. While Head Start programs have always been very diverse and difficult to characterize,[42] Head Start's early cognitive focus has continued to influence the curriculum. This has been further reinforced by value differences related to social class.

CLASS SEGREGATED CHILDREN, SEGREGATED STAFF

The differences between care for poor and middle-class children can be seen not only in Head Start's explicit targeting to the poor, its definition of poor families as needing specific types of help in raising their children, and its narrow goals but also in the people who were chosen to staff it. As a rule, those with resources and power in the society try to find others as much like themselves as possible to look after their children. This often proves difficult as those with similar resources and class background generally have little interest in the low-paid, low-status job of child care. The wealthy have found ways to deal with this problem including hiring more culturally similar caregivers as their children grow older, employing caregivers from other countries who might be more culturally and educationally similar to themselves (as in the case of *au pairs*) than are the poor in their own society, and perhaps most importantly for educated middle-class parents, using nursery schools and child care centers with professionally trained and qualified staff.[43]

While the affluent could place priority on getting professionally trained teachers for their children, Head Start followed a different path. It was serving poor children, and such children are often looked after by those not much above them in social status. This general pattern became institutionalized when those directing the War on Poverty emphasized the employment aspects of Head Start programs. Head Start was to give the unemployed a start on a career ladder as child care workers. The larger political context not only helped shape the curriculum, but strongly affected the selection of staff. As rapidly trained paraprofessionals began to be employed in large numbers, many experienced teachers left, either resigning or being replaced in favor of the new staff.[44] The twin employment and program goals of Head Start have created lasting tensions. One observer criticizes Head Start's focus on jobs for the poor:

> Should adults' needs take precedence over those of children when these are in conflict to the extent that program quality is affected? Since 1967 the federal agencies administering Head Start have insisted that program quality and employment opportunity receive equal emphasis. Now it appears that the goal of providing jobs for the low-income unemployed has grown to be of more concern to sponsors than has the quality of the children's program.[45]

The effort to use Head Start as a jobs program arose out of the social movements of the 1960s. It initially was an ambitious effort to provide educational credentials and a career ladder for those hired. The original plan was to select community residents, usually women, and to have them attend regular educational institutions and receive regular academic credentials. The plan had some larger social implications. First, training community women to become child care workers ensured that salary demands would remain low. "Within day-care and Head Start programs, funded through client fees and limited federal funds, the concern has been with offering the most service to the most people for the least cost. This has resulted in minimal standards and low salaries for practitioners."[46] Second, it was not proposed that these rapidly trained community women would work in middle-class settings. The poor in essence were trained to work with the poor. Just as the children themselves were segregated so the caregivers were segregated. There was not a unitary market for child care personnel. There were several markets, and those trained in the crash programs of Head Start had little leverage in the world of the middle-class preschool. Its staff members generally came from different backgrounds and had different educational credentials. These differences became more pronounced over time as early ambitious goals of providing college training for Head Start staff faded.

Considerable numbers of people did receive college training through Head Start programs. Between 1967 and 1973, 25,000 Head Start staff attended college; 12,000 of these received college credit and 1,000 received degrees.[47] The program faltered, however, as the budget for training was cut. As the social movements of the 1960s receded, it became harder to sustain such programs. The Head Start staff also had trouble assuming the costs of their participation; they had to leave their homes and families for the schooling. The educational process soon drew fire as overly costly and ambitious.

In 1974 Edward Zigler, the head of the Office of Child Development (in charge of Head Start), ended the college-oriented staff training policy, instituting the Child Development Associate (CDA) credential in its place. Child care workers could earn this credential for demonstrated competencies in child development. They followed not a college curriculum but a training program that emphasized the specific skills they would need to work with children. The CDA was explicitly intended to be a credential that would "meet the needs of the poor and educationally disenfranchised—those who would not otherwise have access to "professional" status through normal educational channels."[48] As one commentator notes,

> One could say that the goal of the original career-development program was to take "indigenous nonprofessionals" and turn them into "indigenous professionals" who had received college training that made them certified teachers with B.A. degrees. The CDA program, on the other hand, could be seen as producing "indigenous paraprofessionals."[49]

The new program did not evoke great enthusiasm, as those seeking a way out of poverty had much more to gain by getting recognized B.A. degrees at recognized institutions than they did by getting a newly instituted, specific child care credential.[50] By remaining paraprofessionals, they also suffered in terms of salary and status. Head Start staff had never secured much professional legitimacy,[51] and they lost any chance of gaining it as their access to education diminished. The CDA credential has been secured primarily by those with little schooling; most CDA recipients have a high school diploma as their highest credential, and the vast majority have low family incomes.[52]

James L. Hymes, Jr., a member of Head Start's original planning committee and a past president of the National Association for the Education of

Young Children, has commented on how Head Start's planners believed professional training was largely unnecessary for most child care staff:

> In the [Planning] Committee we never did face up to the disadvantaged young child's need for skilled and trained teachers; we never did face up to the need for top-flight educational leadership in what was to be a massive educational program. In 1965 I detected a feeling that "anyone can teach young kids," and that feeling persists today.[53]

This, of course, contrasts with the unquestioned nature of educational requirements for teachers of older children in public and private schools. Such teachers must have at least four years of college and often more. There is a two-tiered system of standards between preschool and school care,[54] but beyond this there are also tiers within the child care system. The CDA credential continues to have limited legitimacy, receiving recognition within some child care centers and Head Start, but little elsewhere.[55] In child care centers and nursery schools serving middle- and upper-middle-class children, it is common to have aides with little training, but head teachers usually have educational credentials beyond those found among Head Start staff. Both those who receive care and those who deliver it are differentiated along lines of social class. What is considered acceptable for one population is, in practice, considered unacceptable for others.

POLICY IMPLICATIONS

The patchwork nature of America's child care system has led to many proposals for improved and expanded care. In an era of budget cutbacks and the destruction of many social programs, child care advocates are fighting an uphill battle, but they have won considerable public and legislative support. Those proposing expanded care have faced critical policy issues. These include whether the care should be delivered in child care centers or whether family day care homes should be encouraged, the extent and nature of government supervision and control, and whether the care should be linked with the public school system or provided outside that system as it largely is today.[56] While those debating child care policy tend to mention briefly issues of equity and class separation, there is little discussion of how these problems could be addressed. Above all there is little sense that this represents a critical problem, compared to what are seen as the larger problems of unavailable and inadequate child care.

Most of those proposing reforms continue to accept the idea that the children of the poor should receive different care from that provided for the middle class. Edward Zigler, one of the nation's most influential child care advocates, argues that early schooling makes economic sense only for the poor and is too expensive to be universally provided. He suggests that child care be made available in public schools with middle-class parents paying their way and other parents receiving subsidies. Those young children from the most deprived backgrounds should receive early schooling, which would differ from child care in that it would have an explicit educational component. Zigler writes that, while exemplary early schooling programs have benefited the very poor, "in contrast, there is a large body of evidence that indicates that there is little, if anything to be gained by exposing middle-class children to early education."[57] Early education programs should target the economically deprived, the handicapped, and the bilingual. Zigler concludes that "spreading education budgets to all four-year-olds would spread them too thin. Such an extension would not only have little effect on the more advantaged mainstream, but would diminish our capacity to intervene with those who could benefit the most."[58] This would, he acknowledges, reinforce a class-divided child care system, but is the only cost-effective possibility.

These types of proposals are in line with the long history of social class segregation in group care for preschool children. There are two main similarities: The care for the poor is designed to be qualitatively different from that offered in programs for more advantaged children, and care is provided on the basis of an income requirement, or means, test. While in the early 1900s day nurseries were run as private charities, the government is now the source of child care funding for those unable to buy private care. By having islands of subsidized care in the midst of a private, fee-for-service market, the child care available to nonpaying parents is immediately stigmatized. The care is limited to one socioeconomic group, both because institutionally it is available only to them and because ideologically others consider it unsuitable for their children.

Given the greater neediness of the poor, does it make sense, as Zigler argues, to target programs to them? In a narrow cost-benefit calculation this might be so, but in a broader one we can turn to child care history to see some of the costs. These costs can often include the maintenance of different standards for good care for the poor and the affluent. Universalistic programs, in contrast, tend to result in raised standards for those who have had the least care in the past. In a universalistic system there would have to be, for example, a uniform standard of teacher training. Currently teachers with little formal education tend to serve the poor, and more educated, middle-class teachers tend to serve middle-class children. These patterns are hard to break even within universal systems, but there is little or no chance of breaking them when they are institutionally and ideologically reinforced as at present.

The history of child care programs reveals another important cost in class-divided systems. By definition, such programs keep children from different backgrounds from mixing in heterogeneous centers. If, on the other hand, teachers had more uniform qualifications and if there were not sharp divisions between subsidized programs serving the poor and private programs serving the affluent, there would be at least a possibility of greater social class mixing of young children in child care. Many studies of school desegregation have shown that young children are far more flexible in adjusting to those of other races and backgrounds than are older children.[59] On the other side of the coin, as more and more children have experience in formal institutions of one kind or another before starting school, and as these are mainly one-race, one-class institutions, children may come to expect to encounter only those like themselves. This expectation might be fairly strongly developed in them by the time they start school. It could be countered by having a more heterogeneous child care clientele at individual centers.

A third major cost of class-divided systems concerns the stigmatizing of programs for the needy. For decades, *day care* carried a profound stigma because it conjured an image of neglected, poverty-stricken children who received minimal care in cold institutions.[60] Over the long run, such programs are subject to recurring political attacks just as the welfare programs in the United States have been attacked. They tend to divide voters, with *taxpayers* resenting those who are too easily defined as freeloaders. Such resentments receive extensive encouragement from politicians bent on cutting public programs. Social welfare programs based on a principle of universal entitlement do not have immunity from attack, but they are historically less likely to arouse stubborn, lasting opposition. Further, in programs with means tests or income criteria, even service providers themselves tend to adopt critical or disdainful views of those they serve. This happened both with the early day nurseries, and, in a somewhat more subtle way, with the Head Start program. In each era, families living in poverty were defined as culturally deficient and in need of middle-class intervention. If child care programs enroll a heterogeneous population, administrators and policymakers would not be able to make sweeping assumptions about those served.

The history of American public education shows that it took generations to solidify the principle that all children had the right to attend free public schools.[61] Those schools are now heavily and rightly criticized for their academic failures and their inequalities. Because of the earlier battles to win the principle of free public schooling, however, in times of rising political consciousness groups can and have struggled to make the schools more equal and more effective. Such groups begin from a higher level than did earlier reformers, who simply wanted a desk for each child. There is broad acceptance of the idea that children should receive equal schooling; there are no powerful competing ideologies that suggest that poor and middle-class children inherently should receive different forms of instruction in different kinds of institutions as there are with child care. We are not yet at the stage of accepting universalistic principles in the child care world, but they need to be kept on the political agenda. This can only happen when we recognize that good care for one set of children is likely to be good care for another. Segregated, remedial care has profound social limitations, including, most basically, a message of inferiority, however crudely or gently phrased.

NOTES

1. Randall Collins, *The Credential Society* (New York: Academic Press, 1979).

2. Richard Kluger, *Simple Justice* (New York: Knopf, 1975); Julia Wrigley, *Class Politics and Public Schools: Chicago, 1900–1950* (New Brunswick, N.J.: Rutgers University Press, 1982).

3. Martin Carnoy and Henry M. Levin, *Schooling and Work in the Democratic State* (Stanford, Calif.: Stanford University Press, 1985).

4. Alfred J. Kahn and Sheila B. Kamerman, *Child Care: Facing the Hard Choices* (Dover, Mass.: Auburn House, 1987), p. 249.

5. Ibid., pp. 248–249.

6. Margaret O'Brien Steinfels, *Who's Minding the Children? The History and Politics of Day Care in America* (New York: Simon and Schuster, 1973).

7. Susanne Martinez, "Childcare and Federal Policy," in caring for children: *Challenge to America*, ed. Jeffery S. Lande, Sandra Scarr, and Nina Guzenhauser (Hillsdale, New Jersey: Lawrence Erlbaum Associates, 1989), pp. 116–117; Hellen Blank, "Child Care: Issues at the State Level," in *Caring for Children*, pp. 146–147.

8. Catherine J. Ross, "Early Skirmishes with Poverty: The Historical Roots of Head Start," in *Project Head Start*, ed. Edward Zigler and Jeanette Valentine (New York: Free Press, 1979), pp. 21–42, 27.

9. Bernard Greenblatt, *Responsibility for Child Care* (San Francisco: Jossey-Bass, 1977), p. 37.

10. Marjory Hall, "For What Does the Day Nursery Stand?" *Charities* 12 (1904): 764–767; Steinfels, *Who's Minding the Children?*, p. 40; A. M. Dodge, "Neighborhood Work and Day Nurseries," *Conference on Charities and Corrections* (1912): 112–118.

11. Julia Wrigley, "Children's Caregivers and Ideologies of Parental Inadequacy," in *Circles of Care,* ed. Emily Abel and Margaret K. Nelson (Albany, N.Y.: SUNY Press, 199; Mary B. Hartt, "The Day Nursery Problem," *Good Housekeeping* 52 (January 1911): 21–27.

12. Greenblatt, *Responsibility for Child Care,* p. 23.

13. Dodge, "Neighborhood Work," p. 114; Hartt, "Day Nursery Problem," p. 25.

14. Bernard Spodek, Olivia N. Saracho, and Donald L. Peters, "Professionalizing the Field: The Tasks Ahead," in *Professionalism and the Early Childhood Practitioner,* ed. Bernard Spodek, Olivia N. Saracho, and Donald L. Peters (New York: Teachers College Press, 1988), pp. 189–194, 190.

15. Steinfels, *Who's Minding the Children?;* Greenblatt, *Responsibility for Child Care,* pp. 52–53.

16. Julia Wrigley, "Do Young Children Need Intellectual Stimulation? Experts' Advice to Parents, 1900–1985," *History of Education Quarterly* 29 (Spring 1989); 41–75; Nancy Weis, "The Mother-Child Dyad Revisited: Perceptions of Mother and Children in Twentieth-Century Child-Rearing Manuals," *Journal of Social Issues* 34 (Summer 1978): 29–45.

17. Dodge, "Neighborhood Work," p. 117; Hall, "For What Does the Day Nursery Stand," p. 766; Lillie H. French, "While the Mother Works," *Century Magazine* 65 (December 1902): 174–186.

18. A. Levitas, "Baby Garden," *Survey* 30 (26 April 1913), pp. 150–151, 150.

19. Wrigley, "Children's Caregivers."

20. Dorothea McCarthy, "The Nursery School and the Social Development of the Child," *Journal of Home Economics* 25 (January 1933): 13–18; John N. Washburne, "When Is a Child Too Young to Learn?" *Parents Magazine* 9 (April 1934): 17ff.

21. Ethel P. Howes, "The Nursery School," *Woman's Home Companion* 50 (December 1923): 34.

22. Dorothy Dick, "A Nursery School Based on Parent Cooperation," *Journal of Home Economics* 26 (January 1934): 15–16; May F. McElravy and Jean Van Note, "Laboratories for Parents," *Parents' Magazine* 19 (December 1944): 26ff.

23. Jean M. Kitchen, "When Babies Go to School," *Parents' Magazine* 10 (March 1935): pp. 16–17ff.

24. Wrigley, "Do Young Children Need Intellectual Stimulation?"

25. Robert E. Cooke, "Introduction," in *Project Head Start,* pp. xxiii–xxvi, xxiii.

26. Ibid., p. xxiii.

27. Wrigley, "Do Young Children Need Intellectual Stimulation?"

28. Edward Zigler and Karen Anderson, "An Idea Whose Time Had Come: The Intellectual and Political Climate," in *Project Head Start*, pp. 3–19, 7.

29. Ibid., p. 15.

30. Edward Davens, "Head Start, A Retrospective View: The Founders," in *Project Head Start*, pp. 88–91, 90.

31. Jeanette Valentine and Evan Stark, "The Social Context of Parent Involvement in Head Start," in *Project Head Start*, pp. 291–313.

32. Sar A. Levitan and Karen Cleary Alderman, *Child Care and ABC's Too* (Baltimore: Johns Hopkins University Press, 1975), p. 92; on parent involvement, see Bureau of Head Start and Child Service Programs, *Perspectives on Parent Participation in Project Head Start* (Washington, D.C.: U.S. Department of Health, Education, and Welfare, 1972).

33. Zigler and Anderson, "An Idea Whose Time Had Come," p. 11.

34. Ibid., p. 9.

35. Levitan and Alderman, *Child Care and ABC's Too*, p. 88.

36. Louise B. Miller, "Development of Curriculum Models in Head Start," in *Project Head Start*, pp. 195–220; Wrigley, "Do Young Children Need Intellectual Stimulation?"; Wrigley, "Children's Caregivers and Ideologies of Parental Inadequacy."

37. Miller, "Development of Curriculum Models," p. 199.

38 Levitan and Alderman, *Child Care and ABC's Too;* Zigler and Anderon, "An Idea Whose Time Had Come"; Greenblatt, *Responsibility for Child Care*, p. 211.

39. Eveline M. Omwake, "Assessment of Head Start Preschool Education Effort," in *Project Head Start*, pp. 221–228, 225.

40. Sally Lubeck, "Nested Contexts," in *Class, Race, and Gender in American Education*, ed. Lois Weis (Albany, N.Y.: SUNY Press, 1988), pp. 43–62, 47.

41. Miller, "Development of Curriculum Models," p. 199.

42. Ibid.

43. Julia Wrigley, "Servants and Cultural Transmission within English Families," paper delivered at the annual meeting of the American Sociological Association, San Francisco, August 1989.

44. Omwake, "Assessment of Head Start Preschool Education Effort," p. 223.

45. Ibid. p. 226.

46. Bernard Spodek, Olivia N. Saracho, and Donald L. Peters, "Professionalism, Semiprofessionalism, and Craftsmanship," in *Professionalism and the Early Childhood Practitioner,* p. 3–9, 5.

47. Levitan and Alderman, *Child Care and ABC's Too,* p. 93.

48. Donald L. Peters, "The Child Development Associate Credential and the Educationally Disenfranchised," in *Professionalism and the Early Childhood Practitioner,* pp. 93–104, 95.

49. Penelope K. Trickett, "Career Development in Head Start," in *Project Head Start,* pp. 315–336, 333.

50. Ibid., p. 333.

51. Levitan and Alderman, *Child Care and ABC's Too,* p. 93.

52. Peters, "The Child Development Associate Credential," p. 95.

53. James L. Hymes, Jr., "Head Start, A Retrospective View: The Founders," in *Project Head Start,* pp. 93–97, 97.

54. Spodek, Saracho, and Peters, "Professionalizing the Field," p. 192.

55. Peters, "The Child Development Associate Credential," p. 100.

56. Kahn and Kamerman, *Child Care;* Fred M. Hechinger, ed., *A Better Start: New Choices for Early Learning* (New York: Walker and Company, 1986); Sharon L. Kagan and Edward F. Zigler, *Early Schooling: The National Debate* (New Haven: Yale University Press, 1987).

57. Edward Zigler, "Formal Schooling for Four-Year-Olds?" in *A Better Start,* ed.. Hechinger, pp. 139–150, 143.

58. Ibid., p. 144.

59. Gary Orfield, "Why it Worked in Dixie: Southern School Desegregation and its Implications for the North," in *Race and Schooling in the City,* ed. Adam Yarmolinsky (Cambridge: Harvard University Press, 1987), pp. 22–44.

60. Florence A. Ruderman, *Child Care and Working Mothers* (New York: Child Welfare League of America, 1968).

61. Julia Wrigley, "Compulsory School Laws: A Dilemma with a History," in *Exit Age,* ed. Deborah Stipek and John Simon (New Haven: Yale University Press, forthcoming).

STEVE BARNETT

Chapter Twelve

Developing Preschool Education Policy: An Economic Perspective

Federal, state, and local governments are currently considering significant changes in public policies related to preschool education. Much of the impetus for these changes derives from evidence of the costs and benefits of such programs, and many of the issues being addressed have significant economic dimensions. This article examines four critical policy issues, with a focus on economic considerations.

- Is public preschool education a sound public investment and if so, for which target population?
- Which public policy options should be adopted?
- Who should fund the options adopted?
- What types of programs should be publicly supported?

In examining these issues, this article draws on one economic theory of family behavior and on the empirical research into the efficacy and economics of preschool programs. A central part of this issue is specifying the population for which these programs are a good public investment. This article considers only two groups, children from low-income families and all children. It does not consider the case for serving preschoolers with handicapping conditions, as programs for these children are now mandated by federal law (P.L. 99–457). In addition, it should be noted that this article does not deal with issues of child care arising from the needs of working parents as these are conceptually separate.

THE PUBLIC INVESTMENT IN PRESCHOOL EDUCATION

From an economic perspective, preschool education is an investment in the lives of young children that can be evaluated in terms of its pay-off. One reason for the recent interest in the economics of these programs is an increase in public concern that many public education and social programs may be ineffective and wasteful. This concern has been accompanied by funding restraints and debate over government spending for social programs. In addition, empirical studies show that preschool programs can produce important economic benefits.[1] Thus, advocates of publicly supported preschool programs have asserted that these are an economically sound public investment, at least for disadvantaged children.

The claim that public preschool education is economically efficient can be broken down into three parts. The first is that the economic benefits of preschool education justify its costs when compared with other public and private investment opportunities. The second is that the private sector will not provide the preschool programs necessary to obtain important potential benefits. The third is that government policies can obtain those additional benefits. However, given what is known about the problems that can beset public programs, it is no longer possible simply to assume that the public sector will succeed where the private sector fails. Each part of the claim is evaluated below using an economic model of family behavior and evidence from empirical studies.

A Theoretical Model

A simple economic model of family behavior appears to underlie much current thinking about public policy regarding preschool education and early childhood care and education more broadly. For example, Robert Samuelson's widely read 1988 *Newsweek* article implicitly uses such a model to argue that there is no public interest in government support for the care and education of young children on grounds of economic efficiency.[2] The only possible public interest he finds is that supporting programs for low-income families can be a means to redistribute income, and he appears to favor tax relief as a way to accomplish this redistribution.

In this economic model families are the primary source of investment in young children. Parents invest time, energy, money, and other resources in the development of their children. Parents make these investments because they pay off, and there is a strong presumption that parents make the best decisions about the amount and kind of investments to make, given the resources they have available. Thus, in general, if preschool education (either outside or within the home) is a good investment, parents will obtain it. In this simple model, there is no reason for government to become involved in any aspect of early childhood care and education on the grounds of economic efficiency.

Recent proposals for federal child care subsidies to lower-income families appear to be based on this economic model. They are in reality attempts to redistribute income in favor of poor to middle-income families with young children. However, subsidies are preferable to direct involvement in preschool education and child care because subsidies may be more efficient redistributors of income. Administrative costs are likely to be lower, and subsidies need not affect family decisions about early childhood care and education. In a subsidy program, no family is forced to accept choices it finds less desirable (e.g., sending a child to a preschool class when the family would rather have the child at home) in order to benefit from the program.

Not all economists would agree with every aspect of the simple economic model employed above (or indeed of any other theoretical model). The position of this article is that it is a useful approach but that a single critical oversight causes it to be misleading. The model implicitly assumes that in making decisions about investments in their children parents take all of the costs and benefits into account. This assumption can be expected to hold only if all of the important consequences for society are also of consequence for the family—otherwise parents cannot be relied upon to make the best decisions (from society's point of view) about investments in their children. Thus, significant differences between the costs and benefits for families and the rest of society would provide a reason for government intervention on behalf of young children. As will be made clear in the next section, this is not a purely hypothetical concern. There is evidence that there are substantial benefits to society from investment in preschool education that do not accrue to the children's families, at least in the case of disadvantaged children.

Empirical Evidence of Effectiveness

The literally hundreds of studies of preschool education make a traditional literature review practically impossible. An alternative is to conduct a meta-analysis or quantitative review of the literature.[3] Applying this methodology, Glen Casto and Margo Mastropieri find that a wide variety of programs have produced educationally meaningful cognitive gains for children from low-income families and handicapped children in the short run.[4]

Whether even short-term effects can be produced for nonhandicapped children from nonpoor families is at least an open question. Only three studies explicitly address the issue of effects on nonhandicapped children from middle- and upper-income families. (Other studies have included middle-class children in samples that were primarily disadvantaged, but data on these children have not been analyzed separately.)

The Brookline Early Education Project found differences in observer ratings of social behavior in kindergarten and of learning behaviors as well as differences in teacher ratings of reading problems in second grade.[5] These findings showed that middle-class children who had participated in the BEEP preschool program received higher ratings than did similar children not in the program. However, the BEEP researchers found no differences on achievement or school progress. In a study in which middle-class children were randomly assigned to preschool and control groups, Jean Larsen and Clyde Robinson found that preschool education had significant effects on second- and third-grade achievement test scores in reading and language for boys but not for girls.[6] One potential limitation in generalizing from this study is that family size in the sample was significantly larger than the national average.

Frank Palmer's Harlem study, which divided its sample into middle- and lower-class groups, found the effects of preschool education to be stronger for the middle-class group.[7] However, Palmer's definition of middle class does not correspond to common usage. Palmer states that less than 10 percent of the sample would be considered middle class by common standards. Most of Palmer's middle-class parents were in semiskilled employment. Moreover, in evaluating the evidence, it must be considered that Palmer's treatment group began with a significant IQ advantage over the comparison group.

Information about the long-term effects of preschool education for children from low-income families is provided by a dozen or so studies that have followed children well into the school years. The two methodologically strongest longitudinal studies are the Perry Preschool study and the Abecedarian study.[8] Both studies used random assignment to preschool and no-preschool groups. Both find immediate and persistent effects of preschool education. However, only the Perry study has been conducted over a sufficiently long time period and collected data on a sufficiently wide range of outcomes to provide a reasonable picture of the economic returns to preschool education. The findings of these two studies are supported by other long-term studies that find some of the same benefits and patterns of effects over time. Unfortunately, the other studies suffer from design limitations, severe attrition, or other problems that make their findings more difficult to interpret.[9]

TABLE 1

Selected Outcomes of the Perry Preschool Project

	Experimental	Control	p^a	N^b
Early Childhood:				
Post-Program IQ	96	83	$<.01$	123
Late Childhood:				
School years in special education	16%	28%	.04	112
Ever classified mentally retarded	15%	35%	.01	112
Adolescence/early adulthood:				
Age 15 mean achievement				
test score	122.2	94.5	$<.01$	95
High school graduation	67%	49%	.03	121
Postsecondary education	38%	21%	.03	121
Arrested or detained	31%	51%	.02	121
Employed at age 19	50%	32%	.03	121
Receiving welfare at age 19	18%	32%	.04	121
Some savings	62%	48%	.09	120
Median earnings at age 19	$2,772	$1,070	.06	121
Birth rate (per 100 women)	68	117	.08	49

[a]Two-tailed p-values
[b]Number of participants for analysis

Sources: W. Steven Barnett, "Benefit-Cost Analysis of the Perry Preschool Program and its Long-Term Effects," *Educational Evaluation and Policy Analysis* 7 (Winter 1985): 333–342. John R. Burrueta-Clement, Lawrence J. Schweinhart, W. Steven Barnett, Ann S. Epstein, and David P. Weikart, *Changed Lives: The Effects of the Perry Preschool Program on Youths Through Age 19* (Ypsilanti, Mich.: High/Scope, 1984).

The Perry study suggests a chain of effects linking preschool education's initial cognitive impact to adult educational and economic success, beginning with immediate increases in IQ test scores for the preschool group. In the early years of schooling, the children who attended preschool were found to be more capable and more motivated students, with better performance on standardized achievement tests. These school effects continued despite the disappearance of the IQ effect around third grade. By adolescence, there were differences in school placement. The preschool group continued to do better on standardized tests and was less involved in juvenile delinquency. At age 19, there were strong differences favoring the preschool group with respect to the total educational course and postschool social and economic adjustment. The preschool group had a higher grade-point average, less special education, a higher graduation rate, and more postsecondary education. Outside of school, they had a higher employment rate, higher income, greater likelihood of having savings, lower arrest rate, and lower rate of births—in the case of teenage girls. Detailed results are presented in table 1. Clearly, the preschool program had a meaningful impact on lives of disadvantaged children and on serious social problems, even though it was by no means a panacea.

The Abecedarian study, coming approximately a decade behind the Perry study, had a somewhat different program, but a similar population, and the same strong design—random assignment. The results are strikingly similar to those of the Perry study. There were initial IQ gains of about the same magnitude. In the early elementary grades, the preschool group was found to have less grade retention and higher achievement test scores.[10] Further data are not yet available from the Abecedarian study. As in the Perry study, the children entered the program in several waves; thus it takes a number of years for all children to pass a particular milestone.

As noted earlier, other longitudinal studies at least partially confirm the Perry and Abecedarian results. It is debatable how much weight to assign to these other studies since they typically have weaker designs. However, there are some interesting differences in findings among these studies, which may reflect differences in program and population.[11] It is also possible that some of the most important differences may arise from the social contexts of the studies.[12]

A primary insight from Urie Bronfenbrenner's ecological model is that long-term effects of preschool education should be expected to vary with differences in the families, schools, communities, and other social environments within which children live.[13] Thus, effects could differ among rural areas, small cities with large universities (settings for the Perry and Abecedarian studies), and large cities. Similarly, special education placement and grade-retention policies among local education agencies within a state and across states may account for the wide variation in the magnitude of preschool's effects. For example, it may be that large effects on grade retention tend to be accompanied by small effects on special education placement and vice versa. This would be consistent with schools using these as alternative methods for detailing with students who are failing in school or being failed by schools.

Costs and Benefits

The longitudinal data from the Perry Preschool study are the foundation for the most extensive benefit-cost analysis of preschool education for disadvantaged children yet conducted.[14] The results are presented in table 2. The analysis concludes that the Perry program was a good investment relative to other public and private investment opportunities. Note that the

TABLE 2

Present Value of Perry Program's Estimated Costs and Benefits per Child[a]

Category	Value of Benefits or Costs (1981 $s)		
	To Society	To Participants	To Taxpayers
Preschool program	−9,027	0	−9,027
Custodial child care	555	555	0
School cost savings	3,950	0	3,950
Crime reduction	905	0	905
Earnings increase	446	335	111
Welfare reduction	36	−358	394
Subtotal: benefits to age 19	−3,135	532	−3,778
College costs[b]	−483	0	−483
Crime reduction	1,077	0	1,077
Earnings increase	11,194	9,041	2,153
Welfare reduction	772	−7,718	8,490
Subtotal: benefits past age 19	12,560	1,323	11,237
Total net benefits	9,425	1,855	7,459

[a]Discounted present value at a 5 percent real rate.
[b]All attended state institutions and most of the cost was borne by the public. Costs to the students could not be estimated, except for "forgone earnings," which are accounted for in the "earnings increase" category.

Source: W. Steven Barnett, "The Perry Preschool Program and Its Long-Term Effects: A Benefit-Cost Analysis," *High/Scope Early Childhood Policy Papers,* no. 2 (Ypsilanti, Mich.: High/Scope Press, 1985).

figures presented in table 2 are *present values* calculated using a real (above inflation) discount rate of 5 percent. Present value is calculated to make costs and benefits from different years comparable at a single point in time, and the discount rate reflects an implicit estimate of the real-rate return to other investments. Although economists may quibble over the exact discount rate that should be used, the Perry program was shown to be a sound investment using real discount rates as high as 8 percent.[15]

Although the estimates presented in table 2 are based on the costs of two years of program participation, 13 of the 58 children in the treatment group attended for only one year. There are no statistically significant differences in outcomes between the two groups, which may be taken as evidence that about the same benefits can be produced at roughly half the cost. However, due the small sample size for one year, the study has little power to detect even fairly large differences between the two groups; thus one cannot have a great deal of confidence that there are no meaningful differences in benefits between one and two years. While it may be reasonable to speculate that more than half the benefits are as a result of the first year, it seems reckless to assume that one year yields essentially the same benefits as two years. One interesting implication of this argument is that the figures in table 2 (which have been widely reported in summary form) underestimate the benefits of two years of preschool education because they are based on the entire sample.

When the costs and benefits are broken down to show the distribution between preschool-program participants and the rest of society, who may be thought of as the "taxpayers," two interesting findings appear. As seen in table 2, taxpayers bear most of the cost of a publicly funded program but also receive most of the benefits. Thus, the program produces net benefits for both participants and taxpayers when publicly funded. In addition, it can be seen that the estimated monetary benefits to the participants are so small that their families have no economic incentive to purchase preschool education privately. Thus, even if low-income parents were given enough money to purchase a preschool program, rational economic behavior would lead them to spend most of it on other family needs. The reason that increased investment in preschool education is profitable for taxpayers but not for parents of disadvantaged children is that most of the economic benefits, such as reduced costs of schooling, reduced crime costs, and reduced welfare costs, are not benefits to the children and their families.

Summary of Economic Efficiency

Evidently, public preschool education can be a sound public investment, at least for children from low-income families. First, preschool education for children from low-income families has been found to have effects that generate adequate economic returns, comparing favorably with alternative investments. Second, private interest alone could not be expected to produce enough investment in preschool education for disadvantaged children (even if their parents had access to the resources) because much of the economic return is to society generally and not to the participants' families. Third, a wide variety of preschool programs (including government-operated programs) have been shown to produce the kinds of effects associated with long-term economic gains.

As the evidence of economic efficiency comes primarily from studies of small research programs, less is known about what happens when programs are provided on a large scale. The nation has some experience with large-scale public preschool programs. Unfortunately, these programs are on the whole not of the same quality as the research programs, and evaluations of Head Start and state preschool programs are not as methodologically sound, comprehensive, or long-term as those of the small research programs.

A few additional cautions about generalization are warranted. As suggested earlier, extending conclusions beyond children from low-income families to all children is problematic. Not only are the data inconclusive on the effectiveness for more-advantaged children, but the incidence of serious school problems, dropouts, arrests, unemployment, and welfare assistance is much lower for children from middle- and upper-income families.[16] Thus it would be implausible to expect universal preschool education to generate the same economic benefits as programs for disadvantaged children. In addition, it is difficult to justify generalization from quality programs with low child-staff ratios to most of the existing public preschool programs. Finally, the results of the benefit-cost analysis of the Perry Preschool study are frequently cited in a way that suggests that the conclusion is extremely precise, such as "a $4 return for every $1 invested." While this is a correct description of the study's results (in present value terms), it should be recognized that there is a wide margin of error around that estimate. Moreover, other studies suggest significant variation in the results from those found in the Perry study. Long-term economic benefits can be expected to vary with the type of program, child and family characteristics, and the broader social context.

WHICH PUBLIC POLICY OPTIONS SHOULD BE ADOPTED?

The most commonly advocated policy options at present are family subsidies, parent education, and public support for preschool programs. Each of these options can be evaluated using the economic model of family behavior presented earlier and evidence from empirical studies.

Family Subsidies

The case for pure family subsidies, or child allowances, is built upon the assumptions that there is no public economic gain from public investment in preschool education. Such subsidies allow parents to decide how much and what type of preschool investment should be made for their children. There is a fundamental flaw in this approach, given that important benefits go to society and not to the family. Families who receive subsidies will continue to respond solely to the private returns on investment in their preschool-age children, ignoring the additional returns to others that are the source of public interest. Low-income parents who receive even several thousand dollars per child are unlikely to invest more than a small portion of it in educating their young children. Parents can be expected to allocate the additional income to a variety of family needs, only one of which is preschool education. This is not necessarily a bad way to transfer income, but it is an ineffective way to increase the educational investment in preschoolers from low-income families.

Parent Education

The basic argument for parent education is that since parents (typically the mother) are the primary source of investment in young children, child outcomes can be improved by increasing or improving the parent's interaction with the preschool-age child. Implicit in this argument is the assumption that some parents invest less than others, either because they have inferior child-rearing knowledge or skills or because they have attitudes that lead them to invest less than other parents. Parent education attempts to alter the parent's interaction with the child by providing information, teaching skills, and new attitudes. This approach is based on the belief that parents are the best educators of their children, at least after their skills and attitudes have been improved, and that improved parenting continues to work far beyond the preschool years.

It may be granted that some parents have less education, information, and skills than do others. Also, some may have parenting behaviors that result in relatively poor educational outcomes for their children. A substantial body of evidence indicates considerable variation in parenting practices associated with differences in family characteristics.[17] However, it is difficult to determine the extent to which differences in parenting arise from differences in specific knowledge and skills that can be affected by parent education, as opposed to other parent characteristics such as general level of education, preferences, and income. In the latter case, parent education may not be very effective in changing parental behavior.

In terms of this article's economic model of family behavior, it is theoretically possible for parent education to be an effective policy. If such programs increase the effectiveness or enjoyability of parenting preschool children, then parents may increase the time and energy they invest in their children. Of course, parents who were offered parent education would still act in response to the consequences for the family alone. Thus, many parents would have little incentive to participate and even after parent education might invest less time and other resources in their preschool children's care and education than is desirable from the perspective of society as a whole. The seriousness of this problem is difficult to assess theoretically, however.

The empirical literature offers insights into the potential benefits and limitations of this approach. First, the well-researched parent education programs that provide evidence of positive effects on child outcomes rarely consist of parent education alone. There is usually some sort of structured program for the child, whether as a separate component or combined with activities for the parent. Second, the literature indicates that parent programs can produce positive changes in child outcomes but does not establish that parent education produces better or longer-lasting outcomes than center-based preschool education.[18] A strong warning about the efficacy of parent education comes from the Project CARE study, in which low-income families were randomly assigned to child center-based education and parent education programs; to parent education programs only; and to a no-treatment control group.[19] In the Project CARE study, the center-based plus parent education program produced cognitive gains for children while parent education alone did not. In another true experiment Julia Harris and Jean Larsen failed to find significant effects of parent education for children of middle-income parents.[20] Third, parents may be reluctant to participate, and many parent education programs have had serious problems in securing regular attendance. In the Parent Child Development Center studies, over 50 percent of the parents dropped out before program completion, and these were parents who had volunteered initially.[21] At two out of three PCDC sites, the dropout rate was twice as high for program participants as for controls; thus this does not appear to be simply a problem related to mobility.

It is not always recognized that parent education programs impose costs on parents, most importantly in time and, for out-of-home programs, transportation, and child care. Programs requiring extensive time commitments may conflict with work and other educational opportunities. Parents can be expected to weigh these costs against the potential benefits of parent education. Single parents and low-income parents may be least able to afford the costs of participation. Programs often try to increase the incentives for parents to participate by making programs socially enjoyable. Alternatively, parents can be paid for attending in order to offset their costs. (Of course, the extra time and effort that a parent education program requires of parents is a cost to society that must be evaluated against the program's benefits, whether or not parents are actually paid or otherwise compensated for it.) In addition to costs, there may be other obstacles to program participation for some parents, for example, substance abuse, mental health problems, fear and mistrust of public programs, or a reluctance to participate in programs that may be perceived as stigmatizing.

Publicly Supported Programs

Public support for preschool education is the last policy option to be examined. The premise is that direct investment in young children from low-income families can improve child outcomes and thereby generate public benefits. This policy option appears to have the strongest empirical support but does raise at least one potentially important problem. In the economic model of family behavior presented earlier, parents may react to publicly provided preschool education by reducing their own time, effort, and other resources devoted to the preschool-age child. Gary Becker suggests that this explains the fade-out of effects on IQ over time and that programs simply produce "a redistribution of family expenditures away from the children participating, with a small net increase in the total expenditure on these children."[22] However, this is not a necessary conclusion of the model (and is contradicted by other evidence of persistent effects). As Becker points out elsewhere,[23] whether parents decrease or increase their own efforts in response to a preschool program depends on how the program's effects on the child affect parenting. Parents might have better interactions with their children because of the attitudes and behaviors a child brings home from preschool and because a child is more knowledgeable, intellectually active, and successful. Moreover, the investment of a preschool program in a child may far exceed the potential parental reallocation of resources in poor families.

Considering the available evidence, it would seem that public support for center-based preschool programs for children from low-income families is the policy option most likely to secure the public interest. Parent education cannot be entirely ruled out as a useful approach on its own, and it is possible to deliver a child-focused program at home using visiting teachers. However, the results of the CARE study and low participation rates in other studies raise serious questions about a preschool education policy that depends on parent education alone. Whether the benefits to preschool education programs can be significantly increased by adding a parent education component is undermined at this time. Many of the preschool programs studied—including the Perry Preschool program—had both. It might even be argued that at this time, it is difficult to know how effective preschool education is without parent education.

It would seem desirable to obtain more empirical information about the effects of parent education and preschool programs on parental investment in their preschool-age children. This will require studies that provide measures of parent-child interaction into the early elementary years as well as in the preschool years, since allocation is intertemporal. A primary focus of such studies would be how much time parents spend in various activities with their children. One model for this kind of research is provided by economists' studies of family members' time use.[24] Another model is provided by studies of the home environment and the content of parent-child interaction.[25] A combination of methods could be quite productive as they appear to be complementary.

Public support for preschool education need not mean publicly operated programs. Parents could be allowed to select among public programs or be given vouchers to be spent on public or private programs. Some screening of programs would be required because parents might make trade-offs (longer days with lower quality, for example) that reduced the returns to taxpayers. The relative cost-efficiency of publicly and privately operated programs would depend on several factors, including costs of administration, costs of quality assurance, the availability of slack resources in the public (e.g., school buildings) and private (e.g., church buildings) sectors, and other public- and private-sector inefficiencies. Of course, even within the public sector, there is some potential for gaining benefits from competition, diversity, and parental choice by letting a variety of public agencies provide preschool programs.

One approach to public support unlikely to adequately serve the public interest is the expansion of child care tax credits. Like vouchers and direct payments to providers, tax credits are merely a means of payment. However, the current child care tax credit does not address the issue of preschool education, because it is limited to mothers who work outside the home, provides little incentive to purchase educational services, and does not target poor families. The proposal to make a child care tax credit available to everyone whether or not the mother works outside the home is no improvement. This tax credit is equivalent to a pure family subsidy and so will not effectively address the public interest in preschool education. For preschool education policy, it is a red herring. A tax credit for low-income families limited to preschool education programs would be roughly equivalent to a voucher, but less efficient. Tax credits are an ineffective way to reach low-income families. They are unlikely to have the money up front needed to pay for high-quality programs. Many do not file tax returns or owe any tax, and they may have difficulty complying with the procedures for obtaining the tax credit. In sum, tax credits are likely to be a poor choice for preschool education policy.

WHO SHOULD FUND PUBLIC PRESCHOOL EDUCATION?

It would be tempting to conclude that funding of preschool education for children from low-income families should be entirely a state and local responsibility. However, as with families, state and local governments appear to have inadequate incentives to invest as much as is desirable from the point of view of society as a whole. The benefits listed in table 2 are not entirely captured by state and local governments. While it is difficult to estimate accurately the portion of each benefit that would accrue to the federal level as opposed to the state level (and this varies by state), an estimate of the federal share can be made based on the Perry Preschool data.[26] It appears that about 50 percent of the taxpayer benefits would accrue to the federal government. Another factor that might limit the incentive of state and local governments to invest in preschool education is mobility. To the extent that recipients move outside the boundaries of the governmental unit that is funding the program before all of the benefits are produced, those benefits are lost to the funder. In our mobile society, state and local governments might tend to limit their investments in preschool education for this reason as well. Thus, it seems that adequate funding for public preschool education is most likely to be produced by combined federal, state and local efforts. One way for the federal government to take an expanded leadership role would be for it to offer to match state and local funding for disadvantaged children.

WHAT TYPES OF PROGRAMS SHOULD BE SUPPORTED?

Much of the literature suggests that the effectiveness of preschool education is fairly robust with respect to variations in program characteristics. Nevertheless, it is reasonable to expect the broad outlines established for government-funded programs to affect the efficacy and economic returns to those programs. It should be noted, for example, that many current preschool programs for disadvantaged children are much less well funded than the research programs that have provided most of the evidence of efficacy and economic returns. Realistically, underfunded large-scale programs cannot be expected to produce the same results as the research programs. While some may manage to produce quality programs with dedicated staff working for low wages, this is unlikely to be maintainable on a large scale. Recent research suggests that poor-quality programs may produce little if any of the potential benefits.[27]

It seems extremely risky to assume that current programs, which often last for only one year and have one teacher or a teacher and an aide for 18 to 20 students, minimal inservice training, and little administrative support, can produce the same benefits as the exemplary programs on which research has been carried out. The Perry Preschool program, for example, had two expert teachers for 8 to 13 children, and most children attended for two years. The Abecedarian program began before age one. Unfortunately, research does not provide a very precise guide to decisions about group size, teacher-child ratio, teacher training, curriculum, duration, program eligibility, and other characteristics of preschool education programs. Given this uncertainty, it may be advantageous to proceed incrementally and experimentally, and as Donald Campbell[28] has suggested, it may be more useful to adopt a process for developing optimal programs than to try to specify the optimal program from the start.

Developing Better Programs

Two alternative processes for developing effective and economically efficient publicly sported preschool education for disadvantaged children are suggested. The first is relatively conventional—to design programs based upon expert opinion, program evaluation, and the results of experiments within existing state and federal preschool programs. This information would be obtained by evaluation and used to direct program improvement. It would seem reasonable to begin with experiments that compare existing programs with better-funded programs. The increased funding could be spent in a variety of ways—among them, more qualified staff, lower class size, longer days, or teacher training. In response to the results of the experiments, programs could be gradually moved in the direction of increased efficiency.

The expert opinion/evaluation approach is not necessarily an easy one. It may be difficult to determine what works best. There may be no one best program for all children in all circumstances. Program success may be highly idiosyncratic—the same program may work well for one child but not for another, or for one family but not for another, or when followed up by one type of school program but not another. Ecological theory suggests that these kinds of interactions are important.[29] Thus, it is worth at least considering another option for addressing these problems.

One alternative is to let parent choice determine the optimal characteristics of programs. This could be done by allowing low-income families to select the preschool education programs. Parents might be allowed to choose from among preschool programs that meet standards for health, safety, and education. In this approach, parents are responsible for determining what type of program best suits their child, family, and community. Parents could be limited to a choice among public providers or be allowed to choose a private provider as well. Providers who compete for children would be expected to shape their programs in response to parents' wishes. Because decisions are individualized, this approach might be more successful in dealing with individual needs and circumstances. Moreover, satisfaction with the programs might be higher because parents could make choices about program characteristics that are not necessarily related to educational outcomes.

Among the options available for implementing a parent-choice approach to publicly funded preschool education are direct government payments to providers, as is done for Title XX child care, and vouchers. Nonpoor families could participate in such a system through the use of a sliding fee scale, according to which families in poverty paid nothing and higher income families paid a portion of the cost, with the subsidy completely phased out at some higher-income level. Families might be allowed to supplement the payment or voucher with their own funds to increase the quantity or quality of service so that parents would not be constrained to pay only as much as was in the public interest. The effects of the two payment systems would be similar. The only differences might be that one is cheaper to administer or that there is some psychological advantage to parents from having a voucher and paying the provider personally.

The terms *parent-choice* and *voucher* are politically sensitive because of the controversies about their roles in general education. However, many of the issues that make parent-choice controversial for education generally are irrelevant at the preschool level for two reasons.[30] First, most early childhood care and education is already in the private sector. Second, the broad social purposes of public education can be accomplished at the elementary and secondary levels without every child attending a public preschool program. Nevertheless, it might be politically desirable to avoid vouchers per se and employ something like preschool education "bonds." Such bonds could be made available for free or at very deep discounts to poor families, with the amount of discount rising with family income (i.e., a sliding fee scale). Preschool education bonds could be "purchased" by parents over a period of time, perhaps beginning with a child's birth, and redeemed later at face value for preschool education. Purchasing bonds might give parents an increased sense of participation in the educational investment in their young children.

One potential advantage of the parent-choice approach is that it might reduce the amount of segregation in preschool education by income and ability level. Many public preschool programs serve only, or primarily, low-income or academically at-risk children. The parent-choice approach could allow publicly funded children to apply to any approved program. With adequate funding, low-income families could purchase quality programs that are now within the reach of only higher-income families. In this and many other regards, the parent-choice approach to preschool education for low-income families may be quite different in its effects from proposals to introduce more choice in education generally.

Both the expert opinion/evaluation approach and the parent-choice approach to shaping publicly funded preschool education programs are imperfect solutions. If programs are publicly operated and experts determine program characteristics, diversity may be limited. "One size fits all" is an especially poor policy at the preschool level, and many parents may decide that public programs don't meet their needs. The benefits of preschool education could be eroded by poor matches between programs and children; such mismatching might cause some children not to attend. Although it is theoretically possible to make attendance compulsory, it seems unlikely that such a policy would be applied to low-income families alone.

The potential problem with the parent-choice approach is that parents might choose programs that meet the family's needs but not the public interest. This could be a serious problem as the basic economic rationale for public support is the existence of a difference between private and public interests in preschool education. Obviously, the public sector can try to protect its interest by allowing parents to choose from only approved centers that meet standards for quality (and other requirements such as nondiscrimination). Although this takes us back toward the expert/evaluation approach, it may be easier to set basic standards for all children and let parents try to find the best match for their family and children beyond the basics than to have experts define the best program for each child.

Neither theory nor existing research indicates which of the approaches discussed above for public support for preschool education of disadvantaged children would be more successful. Thus, it might be worthwhile to experiment with various amounts of parent-choice and examine the effects on participation rates, the types of programs that parents selected, and the effects of the programs parents choose on child development and school success. If such experiments were conducted in conjunction with increased funding for preschool education of disadvantaged children, they could be implemented so that no existing public program faced reductions.

SUMMARY AND DISCUSSION

Viewing the empirical evidence in light of a simple economic model of family behavior, it appears that preschool education can be an economically sound public investment for children from low-income families.[31] The rationale for this public investment is that low-income families invest less in their children's preschool education than is desirable for society as a whole because they have tightly limited resources and many pressing needs. The difference between this perspective and the "deficit model" held by some supporters of early intervention[32] is noteworthy. Whereas the deficit model assumes that low-income parents are culturally or otherwise inferior, the economic model applied in this paper assumes that low-income parents want (and try to obtain) the same things for their children as other parents and that the primary barrier to improving the success of their children is a lack of resources. From this perspective, the policy instrument most likely to secure the public interest is public funding of quality preschool education for disadvantaged children. Parent education is more problematic in terms of attendance, and its efficacy is not uniformly supported by the empirical evidence. Family subsidies, including recently proposed tax credits, appear to be the least promising approach to securing the public benefits of preschool education.

Despite the evidence of a public interest in preschool education for disadvantaged children, such programs not currently available to the vast majority of children from low-income families. Head Start serves only one in five of the eligible children. Greater public initiative appears to be warranted. Based on the estimated distribution of benefits to different levels of government, it is argued that the federal government should assume greater leadership in funding quality preschool education for children from low-income families. One way to do this would be to offer matching funds to state and local governments without allowing state and local governments to reduce their current efforts. Government should also be concerned with providing funding to increase the quality as well as the quantity of public programs. Current programs are grossly underfunded compared to the programs that are the basis for the estimates of the public benefits from preschool education. This is a high-risk policy. Doubling of current funding per child would be required to put within reach programs of the same quality as those demonstrated to produce long-term benefits.

Federal funding need not imply federally run and publicly operated preschool programs. Programs could be administered at the state and local levels, and direct payments to providers or some other system could be used to incorporate parent choice, competition, and diversity into the system. Any efforts to expand parental choice and reduce public control over program characteristics should be undertaken carefully (perhaps as small-scale experiments), for the rationale for public funding is that parents do not fully take into account the benefits to society from preschool education. Too much parental choice might lead to the erosion of the public benefits.

Further developments in public policy for preschool education will have to be made in the context of considerable uncertainty. If sufficient allowance is made for variation and experimentation in publicly supported preschool education, research and evaluation may be able to reduce some of that uncertainty. Among the most important topics for research and evaluation are policy variables with strong impacts on program costs but whose impacts on program benefits are not entirely understood. Among these are the level of program quality, number of years of attendance, and definition of the target population. With respect to the last of these, the possibility of public benefits from preschool education of nonpoor children who are not seriously at risk cannot be ruled out, although benefits are likely to differ from those for disadvantaged and otherwise at-risk children. Research on the economics of education indicates a wide range of public benefits from education that would create a public interest in universal preschool education, if all children benefited educationally.[33] Given the magnitude of potential costs and benefits to society, a greater investment in research on the consequences of universal preschool education seems desirable.

NOTES

Revised version of a paper presented at the National Conference on Early Childhood Issues: Policy Options in Support of Children and Families, 18 November 1988. The author wishes to acknowledge the many helpful comments received from Colette Escobar, Ellen Frede, Irving Lazar, Doug Powell, Bill Prosser, Edward Zigler, Gerald Musgrave, and two anonymous reviewers.

1. W. Steven Barnett and Colette M. Escobar, "The Economics of Early Educational Intervention: A Review," *Review of Educational Research* 57 (Winter 1987): 387–414.

2. Robert J. Samuelson, "The Debate Over Day Care," *Newsweek,* 27 June 1988, p. 45.

3. Gene V. Glass, "Primary, Secondary, and Meta-Analysis of Research," *Educational Researcher* 5 (November 1976): 3–8.

4. Glen Casto and Margo A. Mastropieri, "The Efficacy of Early Intervention Programs: A Meta-Analysis," *Exceptional Children* 52 (February 1986): 417–424.

5. Donald Pierson, Deborah Walker, and Terrence Tivnan, "A School-Based Program from Infancy to Kindergarten for Children and Their Parents," *Personnel and Guidance Journal* 62 (April 1984): 448–455.

6. Jean Larsen and Clyde Robinson, "Later Effects of Preschool on Low-Risk Children" *Early Childhood Research Quarterly* 4 (March 1989): 133–144.

7. Francis Palmer, "The Harlem Study," in *As the Twig is Bent . . . Lasting Effects of Preschool Programs,* ed. Consortium for Longitudinal Studies (Hillsadale, N.J.: Erlbaum, 1983), pp. 201–236.

8. John R. Berrueta-Clement, Lawrence J. Schweinhart, W. Steven Barnett, Ann S. Epstein, and David P. Weikart, *Changed Lives: The Effects of the Perry Preschool Program on Youths through Age 19* (Ypsilanti, Mich.: High/Scope, 1984); Craig T. Ramey and Francis Campbell, "The Carolina Abecedarian Project: An Educational Experiment Concerning Human Malleability," *The Malleability of Children,* ed. James J. Gallagher and Craig T. Ramey (Baltimore, Md.: Brookes Publishing, 1987), pp. 127–139.

9. Meena Balasubramaniam and Brenda J. Turnbull, *Exemplary Preschool Programs for At-Risk Children: A Review of Recent Literature* (Washington, D.C.: Policy Studies Associates, 1988); Barnett and Escobar, "Early Educational Intervention"; Consortium for Longitudinal Studies, *As the Twig is Bent;* Craig T. Ramey, Donna Bryant, and Tanya Suarez, "Preschool Compensatory Education and the Modifiability of Intelligence: A Critical Review," in *Current Topics in Human Intelligence,* ed. Douglas Detterman (Norwood, N.J.: Ablex, 1985), pp. 247–296.

10. Ramey and Campbell, "The Carolina Abecedarian Project."

11. Consortium for Longitudinal Studies, ed., *As the Twig is Bent;* Howard Garber, *The Milwaukee Project*, (Washington, D.C.: American Association on Mental Retardation, 1988); Ronald Lally, Peter Mangione, and Alice Honig, *Long-Range Impact of an Early Intervention with Low-Income Children and Their Families* (San Francisco: Far West Laboratory, Center for Child and Family Studies, 1987).

12. In most studies, the IQ gains disappear a few years after school entry. However, in the Milwaukee study (see Garber, *Milwaukee Project*) a strong IQ effect is maintained at least until age 10, the most recent measurement point. However, there are no strong persistent effects on school achievement. Several explanations for the unusual IQ finding of the Milwaukee study can be offered: the families were not simply low-income as most of the mothers' IQs were in the retarded range; it was by far the most intensive and far-reaching intervention; and it has been intensely criticized for methodological weakness, although criticisms have often been ad hominem and based on supposition (see Ellis Page, "The Disturbing Case of the Milwaukee Project," in *The Raising of Intelligence*, ed. Herman Spitz [Hillsdale, N.J.: Erlbaum, 1986]). As for the lack of effects on achievement: the sample size was small, achievement is more difficult to measure than IQ, and the environment may have been extremely hostile to children's school success.

13. Craig T. Ramey, David MacPhee, and Keith O. Yeates, "Preventing Developmental Retardation: A General Systems Model," in *Facilitating Infant and Early Childhood Development*, ed. Lynne A. Bond and Justing M. Joffe (Hanover, N.H.: University Press of New England, 1982), pp. 345–401; Martin Woodhead, "When Psychology Informs Public Policy: The Case of Early Childhood Intervention," *American Psychologist* 43 (June 1988): 443–454.

14. W. Steven Barnett, "Benefit-Cost Analysis of the Perry Preschool Program and its Long-Term Effects," *Educational Evaluation and Policy Analysis* 7 (Winter 1985): 333–342.

15. W. Steven Barnett, "The Perry Preschool Program and Its Long-Term Effects: A Benefit-Cost Analysis," *High/Scope Early Childhood Policy Papers*, no. 2 (Ypsilanti, Mich.: High/Scope Press, 1985).

16. Edward F. Zigler, "Formal Schooling for Four-Year-Olds? No." *American Psychologist* 42 (March 1987): 254–260.

17. Allison K. Clarke-Stewart and Nancy Apfel, "Evaluating Parental Effects on Child Development," in *Review of Research in Education*, ed. Lee Shulman (Itasca, Ill.: Peacock, 1978), pp. 47–119; C. Hill and Frank Stafford, "Parental Care of Children: Time Diary Estimate of Quantity, Predictability, and Variety," in *Time, Goods, and Well-Being*, ed. F. Thomas Juster and Frank Stafford (Ann Arbor: University of Michigan, Survey Research Center, 1985): pp. 415–435; Diana Slaughter and Edgar Epps, "The Home Environment and Academic Achieve-

ment of Black American Children and Youth: An Overview," *Journal of Negro Education* 56 (Winter 1987): 3–20.

18. Allison K. Clarke-Stewart, "Exploring the Assumptions of Parent Education," in *Parent Education and Public Policy,* ed. Ron Haskins and James J. Gallagher (Norwood, N.J.: Ablex, 1983), pp. 257–271.

19. Craig T. Ramey, Donna Bryant, Joseph Sparling, and Barbara Wasik, "Project CARE: A Comparison of Two Early Intervention Strategies to Prevent Retarded Development," *Topics in Early Childhood Special Education* 5 (Summer 1985): 12–25.

20. Julia Harris and Jean Larsen, "Parent Education as a Mandatory Component of Preschool: Effects on Middle-Class, Educationally Advantaged Parents and Children," *Early Childhood Research Quarterly* 4 (September 1989): 275–287.

21. Susan Andrews, Janet Blumenthal, Dale Johnson, Alfred Kahn, Carol Ferguson, Thomas Lasater, Paul Malone, and Doris Wallace, "The Skills of Mothering: A Study of the Parent-Child Development Centers," *Monographs of the Society for Research in Child Development* 47, 6, serial no. 198 (1982).

22. Gary Becker, *A Treatise on the Family* (Cambridge: Harvard University Press, 1981), p. 126.

23. Gary Becker, "Human Capital, Effort, and the Sexual Division of Labor," *Journal of Labor Economics* 3, 2 (July 1985): S33–S58.

24. Juster and Stafford, eds., *Time Goods and Well-Being;* W. Steven Barnett, F. Thomas Juster, and Colette M. Escobar, "Time Use, Well-Being, and Function in Families of Children with Down Syndrome" (Paper presented at the International Association for the Scientific Study of Mental Deficiency, Dublin, Ireland, August 1988).

25. Robert Bradley and Bettye Caldwell, "Home Environment, Social Status, and Mental Test Performance," *Journal of Educational Psychology* 69 (December 1977): 697–701; Allison K. Clarke-Stewart, "Interactions between Mothers and Their Young Children: Characteristics and Consequences," *Monographs of the Society for Research in Child Development,* 38, 6–7, serial no. 153 (1973); Robert Hess and Teresa M. McDevitt, "Some Cognitive Consequences of Maternal Intervention Techniques: A Longitudinal Study," *Child Development* 55 (December 1984): 2017–2030; Robert Hess and Victoria Shipman, "Early Experience and the Socialization of Cognitive Modes in Children," *Child Development* 36 (August 1965): 869–886; Martin Hughes, Barbara Tizard, Helen Carmichael, and Gill Pinkerton, "Recording Children's Conversations at Home and at Nursery School: A Technique and Some Methodological Considerations," *Journal of Child Psychology and Psychiatry and Allied Disciplines* 20 (1979): 225–232; Marion Radke Yarrow, John D. Campbell, and Roger Burton, *Child-rearing: An Inquiry into Research and Methods* (San Francisco: Jossey-Bass, 1968).

26. The distribution of benefits among levels of government is not easily determined. The estimates in this article were calculated by applying an estimate of the federal percentage (both direct expenditure and transfers to state and local governments) of total government expenditure by type of expenditure (education, welfare, criminal justice system) and of the federal percentage of tax payments associated with increased earnings to the percentage of total benefits from preschool education accounted for by each benefit category. Based upon data on government finance in the 1985–1986 fiscal year (see U.S. Bureau of the Census, *Government Finances in 1985–86,* series GF-86, no. 5 [Washington, DC: GPO, 1987]), the federal share of expenditures was estimated to be 14 percent for education, 12 percent for the criminal justice system, and 70 percent for welfare. To circumvent the problem of estimating the incidence of various taxes, the federal share of tax benefits was calculated using a low figure of 56 percent (the percentage of all revenue going to the federal government) and a high figure of 78 percent (the percentage of individual income tax and insurance trust payments going to the federal government). The relative importance of each type of benefit was estimated from the Perry Preschool study: 21 percent education, 53 percent welfare, 12 percent criminal justice system, and 14 percent tax payments from increased earnings. The resulting estimates for the federal share of total benefits range from a low of 49 percent to a high of 52 percent. Given the uncertainties involved in this estimation procedure and in the estimates of benefits and their distribution from the Perry Preschool study, this should be considered only a "ballpark" figure for the federal share.

27. W. Steven Barnett, Ellen C. Frede, Helal Mobasher, and Patricia Mohr, "The Efficacy of Public Preschool Programs and the Relationship of Program Quality to Efficacy," *Educational Evaluation and Policy Analysis* 10 (Spring 1988): 37–49.

28. Donald T. Campbell, "The Experimenting Society," in *Methodology and Epistemology for Social Science: Selected Papers of Donald T. Campbell,* ed. Samuel E. Overman (Chicago: University of Chicago Press, 1988), pp. 290–314.

29. Urie Bronfenbrenner, "Ecology of the Family as a Context for Human Development: Research Perspectives," *Developmental Psychology* 22 (November 1986): 723–742.

30. George R. LaNoue, *Educational Vouchers: Concepts and Controversies* (N.Y.: Teachers College Press, 1972); Henry M. Levin, *Educational Vouchers and Social Policy* (Palo Alto, Calif.: Stanford University, Institute for Research on Educational Finance and Governance, 1979); Daniel Levy, *Private Education: Studies in Choice and Public Policy* (N.Y.: Oxford University Press, 1986).

31. It is recognized that a positive economic return is not by itself a sufficient reason for an organization with fixed budget to make an investment. In this case, it is presumed that many other government expenditures have less favorable evidence of economic efficiency and that preschool education is competitive with some private sector activities.

32. Edward F. Zigler and Winnie Berman, "Discerning the Future of Early Childhood Intervention," *American Psychologist* 38 (August 1983): 894–906.

33. Robert H. Haveman and Barbara L. Wolfe, "Schooling and Economic Well-Being: The Role of Nonmarket Effects," *Journal of Human Resources* 19 (Summer 1984): 377–407.

SALLY LUBECK

Chapter Thirteen

A World of Difference:
American Child Care Policy
in Cross-National Perspective

... Alternative cultural inventions and differing directions of historical change constitute the great neglected resource for evaluating educational policy, because they raise fundamental questions about the status quo and provide empirical contact with possible futures.[1]

As the number of women in the workforce has escalated, a trend concurrent with declining birth rates in many countries, there have been increasing efforts to provide public supports so that both women and men can reconcile dual work and family responsibilities. These efforts constitute a basis for reform within and across nations and provide for American policymaking an international context in which proposals for early childhood care/education specifically and family and child policy more generally can be considered.[2]

In the United States and the industrialized nations of Europe, the segregated roles of men and women have undergone profound change over the last several decades.[3] Large numbers of women in OECD (Organization for Economic Cooperation and Development) countries have joined the labor force (see table 1). In the Communist bloc countries and in the Soviet Union participation rates are even higher.[4]

TABLE 13-1

Female Participation Rates in Employment (1985)[a]

Country	Percent	Country	Percent
Austria	51.1	Netherlands[b]	40.8
Belgium[b]	50.4	Norway	68.3
Denmark[b]	73.8	Sweden	78.0
Finland	75.0	Switzerland	53.3
France	55.0	United Kingdom	59.8
Italy	41.3	West Germany	50.4

[a]Defined as the total female labor force divided by the population of working age (15–64 years old).
[b]1984

Source: OECD Employment Outlook, Paris, 1986, reproduced in Organization for Economic Cooperation and Development, *Adults in Higher Education* (Paris: OECD, 1987), p. 43.

Public response to these changes has varied cross-nationally. In general, however, public support toward the care and welfare of children has come to be considered a basic social right. Most governments have made a strong commitment to families and have viewed children as a public responsibility and resource.

In the United States, female labor force participation rates have likewise increased dramatically since World War II. In 1986, 64 percent of all women were working full or part time.[5] Change has been most pronounced among married women—the largest group of adult women—particularly those with young (under age six) children.[6] For these women, rates have increased nearly fivefold, from 11 percent in 1948 to 54 percent in 1986.[7] Projecting from increases in maternal employment over the last 15 years, it has been estimated that, by 1995, 65 percent of American preschoolers and 77 percent of school-age children will have employed mothers;[8] at the same time, the "baby boom echo" is expected to result in a significant rise in the absolute number of children.[9]

Change on this scale reflects a myriad of social changes. Decreasing rates of fertility, a growing labor shortage, high divorce rates, and increased opportunity are only some of the factors cited by analysts. For many families, however, declining real wages are the significant factor, and the contribution women make to total family income is substantial. In 1980, the wages of women working full time accounted for 38 percent of family income, but contribution increases as family income decreases so that women in families making less than $10,000 per year provide 69 percent of total family income.[10] Increasingly, two incomes are required to maintain a family in comfort, but fully one-fourth of all working women with children was not married in 1985.[11]

Despite the number of mothers in the U.S. workforce, no family support legislation has been passed by Congress, and public support of extrafamilial child care/education has been limited and framed largely to support those least in need.[12] In point of fact:

> The United States is the only major industrialized nation other than South Africa that does not aid new parents upon the birth or illness of a child. Instead, new parents are often penalized by losing their jobs or wages or forfeiting critical benefits like health insurance when a new baby is born, adopted, or becomes critically ill.[13]

Excluding a nominal tax credit for child care, most Americans bear and rear young children without public supports of any kind. In this respect, the United States and South Africa are unique among the industrialized nations of the world.[14]

This article argues that a survey of the policies of other nations provides a resource for understanding American social history and a frame for evaluating a range of options for the future care and education of the young. As a basis for broadly conceptualizing policy alternatives, some of the public provisions made for children and families in other industrialized nations will be contrasted with those afforded working parents in the United States. The article begins with a comparative review of social policies, both *family-based* and *extrafamilial*. Different policy options are then examined as responses to a series of value dilemmas that are being resolved (or addressed) differently in different societies. Although conflicting views appear inevitable, an agenda tailored to the needs of families and children in the United States can benefit from examination of the policies of other nations: (1) the expanded range of choice; (2) the continuity of public provision over the early years of a child's life; (3) the efforts to foster gender equality; (4) equity across sectors and occupations; and (5) shared responsibility among parents, caregivers, employers, and government.

FAMILY POLICIES IN OTHER COUNTRIES[15]

In many nations, childbearing and rearing have come to be regarded as a societal responsibility as well as a source of personal satisfaction.[16] Accordingly, nations have enacted policies to protect women during all stages of reproduction and to provide children time with their mothers and, increasingly, fathers during the crucial early months of life. Family policies include: health care, paid job-protected leave, extended low-paid or unpaid leave, and sick leave. In addition, 67 countries, including all industrialized nations except the United States, provide family or child allowances to supplement the incomes of those raising children, thereby providing all children in the society with a floor of support.[17]

In a cross-national survey of legislative provisions conducted by the International Labour Office (ILO), 121 countries, characterized by different levels of industrialization, standards of consumption, and forms of government, were shown to provide maternal protection in the form of leave, wage replacement, job guarantees, and nursing breaks.[18] A majority of these nations have legislation and regulations that support paid leave, typically maternity leave, for some period of time. Despite important differences cross-nationally, the modal pattern is that countries mandated between 11 and 15 weeks maternal leave in 1984. In Europe, 5 months following childbirth is the typical leave.[19]

Fully 85 countries now provide health care and job protection during pregnancy and confinement.[20] The following statement about policies in Western Europe applies, in theory, on a broad scale:

> The safeguarding of [women's] health (and consequently that of the unborn child), the right to maternity leave at the time of birth, the guarantee that their income will be maintained during this leave, and their job security—all constitute fundamental and indissociable aspects of their protection.[21]

In short, such guarantees appear in legislation and regulations not only in advanced industrial societies but also in many Third World nations—Afghanistan, Ethiopia, Nicaragua, and Sri Lanka, among others.[22]

The most striking contrast exists between the United States and the industrial market economies and centrally planned economies of Europe. European nations have established a variety of policies to provide basic supports to mothers—and increasingly to fathers—during pregnancy, confinement, and the early months and years of childrearing (see Table 2). These family policies are then balanced by extrafamilial public provisions (preschools) that are available later in the child's life.

Qualifying Criteria

Legislation typically specifies how long a woman must work in a covered job before becoming eligible for maternity leave. In some cases, eligibility is defined in terms of employment for a specified period of time before childbirth; in other cases, the qualifying criterion is the amount of time that the employee has contributed to the social security/social insurance system. In Sweden, where a working parent is eligible for 90 percent of his or her wages during the leave period, even nonworking women receive a minimum cash benefit.

National Health Insurance

European nations have government-run health insurance programs. Under these auspices, prenatal, delivery, and postnatal medical care are guaranteed for every mother and child.[23] In general, such provisions result in lowered infant mortality rates.

By contrast, the United States ranked nineteenth in the world in infant mortality in 1985. In that year, 6.8 percent of all live births in the United States (over a quarter of a million children) were low birthweight babies, and 34.8 million Americans, 11.1 million of them children, had no health insurance.[24]

National health insurance in many countries also provides medical care and substitute income during the illness of a wage earner or child. All or part of a worker's salary is paid as a *sickness allowance* when a parent must stay home with a sick child. Sweden is noteworthy in this regard, guaranteeing parents 90 percent of their gross income to a maximum of 60 paid days per year per child who is ill.[25]

Unlike the universal health care systems of other industrialized nations, health care in the United States is tied to employment. Some American working women are now eligible for maternity benefits in the form of insurance coverage for maternity care and wage replacement (and, in two states, job protection), due in large part to the passage of the Pregnancy Discrimination Act in 1978. The act effectively prohibited sex discrimination due to pregnancy and childbirth and stated that pregnancy should be treated as any other disability. Thus women working in firms that provide disability and health insurance are now covered, and the five states that provide temporary disability insurance (California, Hawaii, New York, New Jersey, and Rhode Island) have expanded their programs to include working women at the time of childbirth.[26] The percentage of women covered has not changed substantially since the act was passed, however, and only about 40 percent of American working women have such coverage.[27]

Maternal/Parental Leave[28]

There is a great deal of variability in the maternity/parental leave policies of different nations, but typically, policies in Europe have come to have three principal components: job protection, cash benefit during the leave period, and, increasingly, a supplementary period of unpaid or low-paid leave. Some countries mandate specified periods of time pre- and post-

TABLE 13–2

Public Provisions for Children of Working Parents in Other Industrial Societies: Family-Based

Country	Qualifying Criteria	National Health Insurance Benefit	Job Protection/ Leave Period	Cash Benefit During Leave	Supplementary Low Paid/Unpaid Leave
Belgium	6 months social insurance coverage (120 days work)	Yes	14+ weeks; 2 weeks, paternity leave (1985)	Manual workers—100% for 7 days; others—100% for 1 month (paid by employer); rest (79.5%) social security	To 3 years
Denmark[a,b,c]	Insured and working 6 months in past; 40 hours in past 4 weeks	Yes	24 weeks (10 either parent); 2 weeks paternity leave at birth	Manual—90% of average earnings for 18 weeks; others—at least 50% of wages to 5 months	To 5 months
East Germany	6 months social insurance coverage during past year; 10 months during past 2 years	Yes	26 weeks[d]	Average net income during maternity leave	To 3 years
France	At least 10 months social security coverage + 200 hours employment 3 months preceding pregnancy	Yes	16 weeks	90% of wages (from maternity insurance)	To 2 years (either parent—if employed in firm of 100 or more workers)[b]

Country		Eligibility	Duration	Benefit	Extended leave
Hungary	Yes	At least 6 months employment during past 2 years	20 weeks[d]	100% of earnings during leave with 270 days insurance; decreasing benefit, if less[e]	To 3 years (35% average female wage);[b] to 6 years if child ill
Italy	Yes	Must be employed and insured at start of pregnancy	5 months (2 before; 3 after); prohibition of dismissal for 1 year	80% of wages (social security)	6 months additional at 30% of wages
Netherlands	Yes	Social insurance coverage	12 weeks	100% of earnings	6 additional weeks unpaid
Norway[a,c]	Yes	6 months national insurance coverage during previous 10 months	18 weeks; 2 weeks paternity leave	100% of earnings and paternity leave paid by national insurance	Yes
Poland	Yes	None	16 weeks—first child; 18 for second; 26—multiple births	100% of earnings	To 2 years (35% of average female wage); to 4 years unpaid; 10 years if child ill or handicapped
Sweden[b,c]	Yes	Working 6 months prior to confinement; 12 months during past 2 years	9 months (both parents equally)	90% of wages of parent on leave (9 months); 3 additional months at flat rate	To 18 months; right to parttime work until child is 8; sick leave—60 days/year

(continued)

TABLE 13-2 (continued)

Public Provisions for Children of Working Parents in Other Industrial Societies: Family-Based

Country	Qualifying Criteria	National Health Insurance Benefit	Job Protection/ Leave Period	Cash Benefit During Leave	Supplementary Low Paid/Unpaid Leave
USSR	None	Yes	16 weeks[d]	100% of earnings	1 year—partly paid to 18 months unpaid
United Kingdom[a,c]	National social insurance coverage + 2 years uninterrupted employment	Yes	6 weeks	6 weeks—90% weekly wage minus lump sum; at least 18 weeks—lump sum state allowance	To 40 weeks[d]
West Germany[b]	None	Yes	First 14 weeks limited to mothers; fathers thereafter	100% of earnings reduced monthly allowance during additional leave	To 1 year; 10 or more days sick leave for child

[a]ILO, "Protection of Working Mothers: An ILO Global Survey, 1964–84, *Women at Work* no. 2 (Geneva: ILO, 1984).

[b]Sheila Kamerman, "Parental Leave and Child Care: An Overview" (Paper presented at the Wingspread Conference on Parental Leave and Child Care, Racine, Wisc., September 1988) and Sheila Kamerman, "Maternity and Parenting Benefits: An International Overview," in *The Parental Leave Crisis: Toward a National Policy*, ed. Edward Zigler and Meryl Frank (New Haven, Conn.: Yale University Press, 1988.

[c]Sheila Kamerman, Parental Leave and Infant Care: U.S. and International Trends and Issues 1978–1988," in *Parental Leave and Childcare*, ed. Janet Hyde (Philadelphia: Temple University Press, in press).

[d]Extensions authorized for extenuating circumstances or if with same employer two years; see "At the Workplace," *Women at Work* no. 1 (Geneva: ILO, 1985).

[e]Also confinement allowance for each child; additional leave paid as a sickness or child allowance.

parturition, while others allow women themselves to decide on the period of leave. A number also authorize extensions if, for example, the woman has a difficult pregnancy, two or more children, or a sick infant.[29]

Job protection for a specified period of time is mandated in all European countries, ensuring that the same or a similar job will be held for the mother, without a loss of status or pay. Regulations surrounding cash payment or wage replacement during the leave period vary cross-nationally, although, in general, countries provide 80–100 percent of earnings for a minimum of six weeks (Great Britain) to a maximum of nine months (Sweden).[30] The Federal Republic of Germany provides either parent 75 percent of the average female wage (with employers paying the remainder) for one year.[31] Employment protection tends to be guaranteed through labor law, while income guarantees are generally under the auspices of the social security/social insurance system of each country. An interview study in three European societies found widespread support for such policies among employees, employers, and policymakers.[32]

More than half the mothers of all children born in the United States are now working by the time the child is one year of age.[33] Nonetheless maternity/paternity leave is poorly documented.[34] In one recent study of employee benefits by the Bureau of Labor Statistics, maternity/paternity leave policies in medium and large firms is not even reported.[35] In another study of practices in state and local governments, maternity leave was found to be available to a majority of women workers (57%), while paternity leave was less available (30%). Generally, leave was found to be unpaid.[36] A study that surveyed firms in the United States (n = 377), reported that 37 percent of the companies offered unpaid leaves to fathers, not generally as *parental leave* but rather as *leaves of absence*. Men in only nine companies had taken advantage of these leaves, however, because, the report suggests, the American corporate culture does not sanction their use.[37]

Supplementary Leave

Trends in Europe have been toward supplementing the leave period by means of an extended period of unpaid or low-paid leave and toward including fathers in the leave legislation in order to foster gender equality and shared parenting. In Hungary, a mother can receive 35 percent of the average female wage (after 20 weeks at full pay) for up to 3 years; in Poland, a woman is eligible for supplementary leave at 35 percent of average female wages until the child is 4 years of age, and, if the child is ill or handicapped, the mother's job will be guaranteed at this rate until the child is 10. In France, either parent can take the supplemental leave until the child is 2 years of age if the parent works in an establishment of 100 employees or more. All Nordic countries (Finland, Denmark, Sweden, Iceland, and

Norway), West Germany, and Belgium provide paid leave to fathers for at least some portion of the leave period, and Greece, Portugal, and Spain provide unpaid parental leave, with some qualifying conditions.[38]

Both temporally and conceptually, European family policies undergird preschool programs for young children. They serve as a tangible recognition of the importance a society places on the health and welfare of mothers and infants, on the father's role in childrearing, and on the necessity of parental attachment during the early weeks and months of life. Such policies enable young families to decrease the disjuncture between their work and family lives.

EXTRAFAMILIAL PROVISIONS IN OTHER COUNTRIES

European countries whose family policies were surveyed have also made complementary public provisions for extrafamilial child care and education for preschool-age children. Although public preschools begin as early as age two in some countries, parents typically must find care for some interim period before entry into public preschools and frequently during the preschool years as well. Nonetheless, parents in these societies have a broader range of options: parental leave for one parent, leave alternated between parents, supplementary leave, as necessary or desired, and the possibility of a public preschool for three or more years. Supplementary leaves have been extended in a number of countries (Belgium, East Germany, France, Hungary, and Poland), so that it is possible for a parent to be home with a child until entry into public preschool.

There is a good deal of variability in the types of public preschool programs offered in Europe. Programs differ according to the ages of children served, the length of time programs are in operation, the size of the group, teacher-child ratio, amount of teacher training, the degree of subsidization, and administrative affiliation[39] (see table 3).

Group-based child care and education programs in these societies generally do not include the very young. Typically children enter at age three, although France and the United Kingdom begin full-time care at age two and Belgium and Sweden, at age two and one-half.[40] In the USSR and in the Netherlands children enter when they are four. Since female labor force participation rates have generally been high in Europe and most women work full time, extrafamilial care must accommodate parents for extended periods.[41] Most programs are in operation full time, running from 10 to 13 hours each day.

Both group size and teacher-child ratio have been shown to be important factors in quality of care.[42] The European countries surveyed have groups as small as 12 and as large as 31.5 with the average about 21 children. Five countries—France, Hungary, the Netherlands, Poland, and the USSR—have ratios that would be considered high by American standards with 25 to 31.5 preschool-aged children per teacher. Once again Sweden is exemplary with ratios of 1 teacher for every 5 children.

Some postsecondary training is generally required of preschool teachers in each of these societies, but salaries remain low. In Sweden, teachers' salaries increase with the age of the children being taught, with preschool teachers making the least and secondary teachers the most. Public preschools are either administered by the Ministry of Education or by the Ministry of Social Affairs in each of these countries. In most countries, programs are run free of charge, with parents only paying for a child's food.

Nations have faced a host of problems in funding and implementing programs and, especially, in attempting to provide universal access. Nonetheless public preschooling (in all its diverse forms) has greatly expanded since the 1960s, generally serving all children, regardless of need and generally regardless of parental employment status.

In the United States, as in other industrial nations, children receive early care and education across a range of settings and arrangements.[43] Only a relatively small number of children receive free or subsidized care and education.[44] Currently there is federal funding for children from low-income families through Project Head Start (16% of eligible children are served) and through block grants to states under Title XX. Modest supports are also provided through other federal, state, and local programs. The lion's share of the cost of child care in the United States continues to be incurred by parents.[45] Low-income families pay a greater percentage of their income for such care, however,[46] and, while Title XX funds have declined in the 1980s, there has been an increase in the benefits accruing to families that are better off through the Dependent Care Tax Credit ($956 million in 1980 to $3.4 billion in 1986).[47]

EUROPEAN CHILD CARE POLICY

Governments struggle with significant dilemmas in addressing questions related to childbearing and rearing. In important ways, family policies (or the lack thereof) are intended to encourage or discourage certain behaviors and to promote or hinder certain choices. Policy options effectively exist as tensions within a society:

- Should problems regarding work and child care be addressed at the societal level or by individual families?

TABLE 13–3

Public Provisions for Children of Working Parents in Other Industrial Societies: Extrafamilial (Survey of Preschool Characteristics [approximate figures])

Country	Name of Program	Age Range	Hours Open (in hours/day)	Group Size	Age-Related Grouping	Teacher-Child Ratio	Teacher Training	Fees	Administrative Affiliation
Belgium	Ecole maternelle (nursery school)	2½–6	Mostly full time	21*	Homogeneous	1:12	Vocational school 3 years	Food only	Ministry of Education
Denmark	Børnehaver (nursery school, day nursery)	3–7	full time 10–12 hours part time 3–4 hours	Varies 20*	Heterogeneous	1:20	College level	22% of operating costs	Ministry of Social Affairs
	Børnehaver klasser (preschool classes)	5–7							
East Germany	Kindergarten (nursery school)	3–6	Full time 13 hours	21	Homogeneous	1:11	Vocational school 3 years	Food only	Ministry of Education
France	Ecole maternelle (nursery school)	2–6	Mostly full time	31.5*	Homogeneous	1:31.5	University	Food only	Ministry of Education

(continued)

Country	Name	Age	Schedule	Group size	Grouping	Ratio	Training	Funding	Ministry
Hungary	*Ovoda* (nursery school)	3–6	Full time 12 hours	25.9*	Homogeneous	1:13	Vocational school 2 years	Food only	Ministry of Education
Italy	*Scuola materna* (nursery school)	3–6	Full time, part time	Varies 15–30	Homogeneous	1:12	Vocational school 3–4 years	Food only	Ministry of Education
Netherlands	*Basisschool* (integrated preschool and primary school)	4–12	Mostly full time	25	Heterogeneous	1:28	College level 2 years	Food only	Ministry of Education
Norway	*Barnehage* (nursery school, day nursery)	3–7	Full time part time	Varies 4–18	Heterogeneous	1:8	College level	21% of operating costs	Ministry of Social Affairs
Poland	*Przedszkola* (nursery school)	3–7	Full time, part time	30 (often more)	Homogeneous	1:30	Vocational school 4–5 years	Food only	Ministry of Education
Sweden	*Daghem* (day nursery)	2½–7	Full time 10–12 hours	12–18	Heterogeneous	1:5	College level 2½ years	10% of operating costs	Ministry of Social Affairs
	Deltidgrupp (nursery school)	4–7	Part time	20		1:10			
USSR	*Detskij sad* (Nursery school)	4–7	Full time 9–12 hours	25	Homogeneous	1:25	Vocational school	Food only	Ministry of Education

(*continued*)

TABLE 13–3 (*continued*)

Public Provisions for Children of Working Parents in Other Industrial Societies:
Extrafamilial (Survey of Preschool Characteristics [approximate figures])

Country	Name of Program	Age Range	Hours Open (in hours/day)	Group Size	Age-Related Grouping	Teacher-Child Ratio	Teacher Training	Fees	Administrative Affiliation
United Kingdom	Nursery school	2–5	Full time	Varies	Heterogeneous	Varies 1:10	University 3 years	Food only	Ministry of Education
	Nursery classes	3–5	Part time						
West Germany	*Kindergarten* (nursery school)	3–6	Full time 10 hours Part time 4–7 hours	15–20 25	Heterogeneous	1:12.8	Vocational school 3 years	Varies between states	Ministry of Social Affairs

*denotes average group size.

Source: Reprinted, by permission, from W. Tietze and K. Ufermann, "An International Perspective on Schooling for 4-Year-Olds," *Theory into Practice* 28 (Winter 1989): 69–77.

- Should government adopt a pronatalist policy, elect to discourage childbearing, or assume a *laissez-faire* approach?
- Will government policy (or lack of policy) encourage or discourage female employment?

Tensions between opposing tendencies are great within and across societies, and emphases wax and wane to some extent with changing economic and political conditions.

The two Germanies are interesting examples of alternative stands. In a six-country comparison supported by the German Marshall Fund, the German Democratic Republic was found to have the highest incidence of female labor force participation (87% of all women between the ages of 15 and 60) and the most developed system of out-of-home child care. Since World War II, women have been needed in the workforce, because of the dearth of males. Policies have focused on improving extrafamilial child care and, with a birth rate below replacement level, on providing incentives to encourage women who work to bear children. Child care policy has thus had three objectives: "to assure children an optimum environment for growth and development and reduce the steady decline in fertility, while maintaining high and essential female labor force participation rates."[48]

By contrast, the Federal Republic of Germany imported foreign labor to meet expanding labor requirements. With significantly fewer mothers of young children in the labor force, the government has not encouraged the development of programs for children under the age of three. Fueled also by anxiety over the plummeting birth rate, a sort of "mother's wage" was being proposed to encourage women to stay home with children for one or more years, whether previously employed or not.

Although important differences exist, as evidenced in the examples above, European policymakers, in general, have taken action to direct or encourage desired social outcomes. Family policies have been formulated to varying degrees to reverse declining birth rates, to safeguard the labor force participation of mothers, to expand the availability of extrafamilial child care for children aged three to six, and to a lesser degree to foster equality between the sexes in both employment and child rearing.[49]

These foci have, at times, provided a rallying cry for advocates across the political spectrum. For example, when birth rates dropped below replacement levels, concern was registered that there would not be enough workers to support the retired population through social security or insurance systems. But even conservative politicians frequently supported family programs, because they wanted higher birth rates for nationalistic and militaristic reasons. Family supports and child care programs became part of the social welfare programs promoted by the Social Democratic parties of

Western Europe with the consequence that income has been redistributed to those bearing and rearing children.

AMERICAN CHILD CARE POLICY
IN CROSS-NATIONAL PERSPECTIVE

In rather stark contrast to the countries of Europe, there is a lack of broad-based social supports for families in the United States, and families are generally expected to be responsible for their own children. Individuals, however, cannot themselves alleviate problems that exist across a society such as inflexible work schedules and insufficient or inadequate child care resources. As Marvin Lazerson writes:

> By thinking of . . . dilemmas as exclusively or even primarily as problems to be faced and resolved by individual families, we refuse to acknowledge that the difficulties encountered by working families are shared by millions and require collective not individual responses. Choosing adequate child care facilities is a responsibility of each parent, but making sure that sufficient and adequate child care facilities are available is a social responsibility. Balancing the relationship of job and family life is a parental responsibility, but assessing how employment and working conditions affect parents and children and establishing policies that would ease the tension between job and home is a social responsibility.[50]

Nonetheless, despite dramatic shifts in social and economic conditions, little has been done at the national level to provide basic supports to families. Social policy, moreover, has had the effect of redistributing income to the wealthy, the childless, and the elderly.[51]

The United States, drawing on a different social history, has reconciled the tension between private and public responsibility very differently than have the nations of Europe. The American construction of public responsibility to families has taken two forms. The first, premised on the English tenet of *parens patriae,* has been to justify public action only when there is evidence that parents have failed. The second "has been to sidestep the economic and social basis of family life by creating children's institutions, that in theory compensate for parental deficiencies without intruding into private families and without intervening into the private economy to change the material conditions of family life."[52]

As the need for extrafamilial child care and education has grown, therefore, it is not surprising that arguments for expansion are frequently predicated on the assumption that more and more parents have failed and that more and more children are *at risk*. For example, a recent report by the Council of Chief State School Officers makes the case for universal access to preschool programs based on "an emerging awareness that all children are at risk to some degree and therefore will require prevention or intervention services at one point or another."[53]

Analysts of the American scene, however, are not necessarily skeptical about the future. Some point to the fact that there is an international diffusion of social policies as nations, in time, borrow one from the other.[54] Moreover the conditions that gave rise to social reform in Sweden specifically and in Europe more generally are increasingly evident in the United States.[55] Indeed in the U.S. birth rate is now below replacement level, although the increased number of births attributed to the large cohort of baby boomers has temporarily mitigated the effect of the decline. Women have entered or returned to the labor force in record numbers, and the workforce will become increasingly feminized until the year 2000 when women will account for fully 47 percent of all workers.[56] In this context, the need for extrafamilial child care will continue to escalate. And, finally, although the women's movement in the United States initially focused on changes in women's roles, there is a new interest in *men's liberation,* and a concern, as voiced in Sweden, for developing *the whole human being.*

Yet conditions do not inevitably result in desirable political action, and policies cannot so easily be transferred whole cloth into a different social, political, and economic fabric. A more subtle argument suggests that the state has been successful in ameliorating the most damaging effects of capitalism, by assuming responsibility for universal schooling for children aged 6–18, by assisting those in extreme poverty, and by providing for those members whose needs their families cannot or will not meet—the mentally retarded, delinquent, and aged.[57] This expansion of public responsibility, however, has not undermined the U.S. ideological commitment to private responsibility:

> Above all, the issues Americans will face over the next decades are whether it will be possible to move away from the fragmented, self-interested, unprincipled, and highly unequal form of democracy they now have to a form more worthy of their democratic aspirations; whether the state continues to expand on the basis of the principles that have dominated public policies for more than a century or more progressive principles can emerge. . . .[58]

Harking back to the American colonial past, there is a desire to recreate

> a society more egalitarian and less class-divided, a society that more nearly balances private interests and public responsibility, individual freedoms and collective decision making, liberalism and democracy.[59]

The crisis in child care in itself contains seeds of transformation.[60]

LESSONS FROM ABROAD

When looked at in broad comparative perspective, several lessons can be learned from an appraisal of the policies and programs that have been established to provide for young children in other countries.

A Balance between Familial and Extrafamilial Arrangements

Many child developmentalists have stressed the importance of attachment, and although it is a construct difficult to measure, enough evidence has accrued to make noted researchers register concern about the efficacy of infant day care.[61] In the countries reviewed here, a period of recuperation for the mother and care for the child universally precedes the period of out-of-home care, and legislation and regulations guarantee that there is no loss of employment or income during these times (see table 2). The trend in Europe is now toward including the father in leave legislation, and generally the same or similar provisions are made for parents who adopt. The rapid expansion of public preschools has helped to provide for many children 2–6 and 3–6.

Relative Continuity of Care

In recent years there has been an upward extension of leave, both through expanding the regular leave period and through the addition of supplementary low-paid or unpaid leave. At the same time, there has been a downward extension of public preschools so that in some countries (for example, Belgium, East Germany, France, and Hungary) it is possible for a parent to be home with the child until entry into preschool. Efforts are now underway to expand toddler care in Europe, while by 1991 Sweden expects to extend parental leave to 18 months for those who want it and to guarantee places in day care centers and preschools for all children 18 months and over in need of care.[62]

Promotion of Gender Equality

Many of the measures discussed above are tied to international efforts to promote equality of opportunity and treatment for women workers. Maternity leaves, once intended solely to acknowledge the physiological demands of giving birth, are increasingly seen as important to the care and rearing of children.[63] However, analysts point to the impact of restricting parental benefits solely to women:

> Such benefits, while offering some kind of protection, continue to assign to women the primary responsibility for home and family tasks and as a result

leave them overburdened generally and also at a significant disadvantage in the work world. It seems clear that until these ''benefits'' are available to men as well as women . . . and men are expected to use them, women will remain disadvantaged even though they may be better off than they would be if no such benefits existed.[64]

It is therefore at the level of national policy that countries such as Sweden, France, and West Germany are actively promoting parental leaves. Significantly the European Economic Community has proposed that all workers in all member countries be guaranteed a minimum three-month leave (countries would be free to offer more extended leaves) after the birth of a child. In a two-earner family, the leave would be granted consecutively to each parent and would be nontransferable.[65]

Equity Across Sectors and Occupations

Although some U.S. corporations are now offering parental leave and more flexible schedules, it has typically been women at the corporate executive level who have benefited from these innovations.[66] A few nations (notably Belgium and Denmark in Europe and some Third World countries) provide differential benefits for women in different sectors of the economy. For example, in Belgium manual workers receive 100 percent of their salary for one week, while other workers receive 100 percent for one month. During this period of time, the salary is paid by the employer. During the remaining leave, social security provides the cash benefit at a rate of 79.5 percent.

In general, however, national policies ensure that women in all sectors and occupations receive equal benefit. Because benefits derive from the social security system, even women who are self-employed receive them.

Shared Responsibility

The countries discussed here have mobilized a variety of supports, both human and monetary, in the service of children. Parents are able to stay home with their children for some period of time without the loss of income from employment, and professional caregivers later provide care in public preschools for three or more years.

Child care allowances provide a floor of support under all families. Maternity care and the costs associated with delivery are paid as a national health insurance benefit. Parental leaves are financed through both public and private means. Benefits are generally paid through the social insurance or social security system, with both employees and employers paying into the system. In some cases, employers are required to pay wages during the leave period for a specified period of time, and in addition to the costs of feeding, clothing, and housing children, parents in some countries pay a percentage of the operating costs for preschool programs. Such measures effectively enable the costs of childbearing and rearing to be shared across the society. Fundamental to these provisions then is the social construction of childrearing as both a social and a personal good.

SUMMARY AND CONCLUSIONS

Two broad types of policies characterize the child and family policies of other industrialized nations. One type, here referred to as *family-based*, focuses on parents and involves pre- and postnatal care, paid parental leave, extended low-paid or unpaid leave, and sick leave. Job-sharing, flexible schedules, and flexible benefits would also fall into this category.[67] The second, potentially complementary, type involves support for *extrafamilial* care, primarily through the provision of publicly supported preschool programs. A dual approach of family support and extrafamilial provisions has been adopted with many permutations in virtually every industrialized nation except the United States.

Industrialized societies, once characterized by a bifurcation of work and home, are witnessing a major restructuring, in which families, child care, and work all have the potential to be transformed. To varying degrees—and to some extent for different reasons—European governments have struggled with the tensions that massive social change has wrought: how to increase the life chances of individuals while at the same time supporting the connections among people that give life meaning.[68]

No arena of modern life exemplifies this central dilemma more clearly than efforts to define a reasonable balance between work and family. For Sheila Kamerman and Alfred Kahn

> The ultimate policy choice—for societies which need children and need them to be well cared for if the society is to survive—must reflect concern not only with women and child care, but with the income of families with children, the availability of jobs and the nature of work, the allocation of time to work and home. In other words, the ultimate concern must be with the development of alternative ways for adults, regardless of gender, to manage both family and work roles simultaneously, without undue hardship for themselves or for their children.[69]

A comparison of the policies of other industrialized nations reveals, perhaps most of all, how much there is to learn.

NOTES

1. Robert LeVine and Merry White, *Human Conditions: The Cultural Basis of Educational Developments* (New York: Routledge & Kegan Paul, 1986), p. 20.

The authors write explicitly about the prototypes for education and other life chances that have emerged or been transformed in non-Western societies. I am attempting to extend their argument by suggesting that much can be learned by analyzing the "alternative cultural inventions and differing directions of historical change" within western societies.

2. In 1919, during the first session of the International Labour Conference, the Maternity Protection Convention (no. 3) was adopted. It was not until 1975 that the International Labour Office included maternity protection in a broader plan to promote equality of opportunity and treatment for women workers. See Chantal Paoli, "Women Workers and Maternity," *International Labour Review 121*, (January–February, 1982): 13. In 1981, an ILO Convention and a Recommendation specifically urged that persons with family responsibilities not suffer job discrimination and be granted job guarantees during a period of parental leave. See International Labour Office [hereafter ILO]. *Convention (no. 156) and Recommendation (no. 165) Concerning Equal Opportunities and Equal Treatment for Men and Women Workers: Workers with Family Responsibilities* no. 2 (Geneva: ILO, 1981).

The first international conference on women was convened in Mexico City in 1975, leading to the United Nations Decade for Women (1976–1985). In 1979, the UN General Assembly adopted the Convention on the Elimination of All Forms of Discrimination Against Women, and in 1980, over 60 nations, the United States included, signed the convention. With the ratification of the twentieth member nation late in 1981, the convention became an international treaty. By 1987, over 90 countries had ratified it, and another 20 countries had signed it. Signing indicates that a country will not work against the principles set forth, while ratification binds a country to implement them. The treaty—an international equivalent of the Equal Rights Amendment—has never been ratified by the United States. See "Maternity Leave Policies: An International Survey," *Harvard Women's Law Journal* 11 (1988): 172–173. Countries that signed but did not ratify the convention are: Afghanistan, Benin, Bolivia, Burundi, Cameroon, Chile, Democratic Kampuchea, Gambia, Grenada, India, Israel, Ivory Coast, Jordan, Lesotho, Luxembourg, Madagascar, Netherlands, Switzerland, and the United States.

3. Sheila Kamerman, "Child Care and Family Benefits: Policies in Six Industrialized Countries," *Monthly Labor Review* 103, 11 (1980); Sheila Kamerman and Alfred Kahn, *Child Care, Family Benefits, and Working Parents: A Study in Comparative Policy* (New York: Columbia University Press, 1981) and Marion Janjic, "Women's Work in Industrialized Countries: An Overview from the Perspective of the International Labour Organization," in *Women Workers in Fifteen Countries*, ed. Jennie Farley (Ithaca, N.Y.: ILR Press, 1985), pp. 1–12. Janjic writes: "In the 1950s and 1960s women's contribution to the increase in the labor force in the Organization for Economic Cooperation and Development (OECD) countries was slightly more than half (51.7 percent in the 1950s and 52.9 percent in the 1960s), in the 1970s their contribution amounted to 62.6 percent."

4. ILO, "At the Workplace," *Women at Work*, no. 1 (Geneva: ILO, 1985) and Gail Lapidus, "The Soviet Union," in *Women Workers in Fifteen Countries*, ed. Farley, pp. 13–32.

5. Organization for Economic Cooperation and Development (OECD), Centre for Educational Research and Innovation, *Adults in Higher Education* (Paris: OECD, 1987).

6. U.S. Department of Labor, *Time of Change: 1983 Handbook on Women Workers,* Women's Bureau Bulletin 298 (Washington, D.C.: U.S. Government Printing Office, 1983) and U.S. Bureau of the Census, *Fertility of American Women: June 1987,* Current Population Reports, series P–20, no. 427 (Washington, D.C.: U.S. Government Printing Office, 1988), p. 8.

7. B. J. Wattenberg, *The Statistical History of the United States from Colonial Times to the Present* (New York: Basic Books, 1976); U.S. Bureau of the Census, *Statistical Abstract of the United States, 1986* (Washington, D.C.: U.S. Government Printing Office, 1987), p. 383; and Sally Lubeck and Patricia Garrett, "Child Care in America: Retrospect and Prospect," in *Family Policy,* ed. Richard Hula and Elaine Anderson (Westport, Con.: Greenwood, in press).

8. Sandra Hofferth and Deborah Phillips, "Child Care in the United States: 1970 to 1995," *Journal of Marriage and the Family* 49 (1987): 559.

9. Ann Rosewater, "Child and Family Trends: Beyond the Numbers," in *Caring for America's Children,* ed. Frank Macchiarola and Alan Gartner (New York: Academy of Political Science, 1989), p. 5.

10. U.S. Department of Labor, *Time of Change,* table 1–12.

11. Martin O'Connell and David Bloom, *Juggling Jobs and Babies: America's Child Care Challenge,* Population Reference Bureau, Bulletin no. 12, February 1987, p. 2.

12. Several states, however, have legislated *unpaid* parental leave: Minnesota, Oregon, California, Montana, Rhode Island, Maine, Wisconsin, Iowa, Tennessee, Massachusetts, Connecticut, and Maryland. Eligibility requirements vary. For example, Minnesota requires employers to offer leave to both fathers and mothers—up to six weeks for employees in firms of 21 or more workers. Tennessee's law provides for women only, in firms with at least 100 employees, and Connecticut and Maryland have laws that affect state employees only. See Sheila Kamerman, "Parental Leave and Child Care: An Overview" (Paper presented at the Wingspread Conference on Parental Leave and Child Care, Racine, Wisc., September, 1988) and Sheila Kamerman, "Parental Leave and Infant Care: U.S. and International Trends and Issues 1978–1988," in *Parental Leave and Child Care,* ed. Janet Hyde (Philadelphia: Temple University Press, in press).

13. Rosewater, "Child and Family Trends," p. 11.

14. Sally Lubeck and Patricia Garrett, "Child Care 2000: Policy Options for the Future," *Social Policy* 18 (May 1988): 31–37.

15. The data on which this paper is based are the most up-to-date available through major secondary sources but may not reflect recent changes in the policies of the countries cited.

16. For example, Sheila Kamerman, "Maternity and Parenting Benefits: An International Overview," in *The Parental Leave Crisis: Toward a National Policy,* ed. Edward Zigler and Meryl Frank (New Haven, Conn.: Yale University Press, 1988), p. 236.

17. Kamerman, "Child Care and Family Benefits," p. 24.

18. ILO, "Protection of Working Mothers: An ILO Global Survey, 1964–84," *Women at Work,* no. 2 (Geneva: ILO, 1984) and Patricia Garrett, Sally Lubeck, and DeeAnn Wenk, "Maternal Employment, Childbirth and Child Care: Comparative and Empirical Perspectives" (Paper presented at the Wingspread Conference on Parental Leave and Child Care: Setting a Research and Policy Agenda, Racine, Wisc., September 1988).

19. Kamerman, "Parental Leave and Infant Care."

20. Kamerman, "Maternity and Parenting Benefits," p. 237.

21. Paoli, "Women Workers," p. 2.

22. See, for example, ILO, "Protection of Working Mothers" and "At the Workplace."

23. Alfred Kadushin, *Child Welfare Services* (New York: Macmillan, 1980), p. 649.

24. Children's Defense Fund, *A Children's Defense Budget: FY 89* (Washington, D.C.: Children's Defense Fund, 1988), pp. 63, 253, and 70.

25. The Swedish Institute, *Fact Sheets on Sweden* (Stockholm: The Swedish Institute, 1987).

26. Sheila Kamerman, Alfred Kahn, and P. Kingston, *Maternity Policies and Working Women* (New York: Columbia University Press, 1983) and William Schwartz, "Comments as a Member of the State Government Panel" (Paper presented at the Wingspread Conference on Parental Leave and Child Care: Setting a Research and Policy Agenda, Racine, Wisc. September 1988).

27. Kamerman, "Parental Leave and Infant Care."

28. As the terms imply, *maternity* leave can be taken only by the mother, while *parental* leave can be taken by one or both parents.

29. ILO, "Protection of Working Mothers." Maternity protection is considered to be an issue different from the discriminatory protective measures (separate work environment, prohibition of night work, and employment limitations) that are increasingly coming under scrutiny. It is generally recognized that pregnancy and childbirth warrant limitation and protection, and special treatment fosters rather than inhibits the promotion of equality of opportunity and treatment. See, for example, ILO, "Women Workers: Protection of Equality," *Conditions of Work Digest*

vol. 2 (Geneva: ILO, 1987), and Janjic, "Women's Work." For an opposing view, see Patricia Spakes, "A Feminist Case Against National Family Policy: A View to the Future," in *Family Policy*, ed. Richard Hula and Elaine Anderson (Westport, Conn.: Greenwood, in press).

30. In the United Kingdom, mothers receive maximum benefit (90% of weekly wage) for 6 weeks and a minimum benefit in the form of a lump sum state allowance for up to 18 weeks. It is possible to have a leave for up to 40 weeks, the remaining weeks without pay. The average leave is about 18 weeks duration. See ILO, "Protection of Working Mothers" and Paoli, "Women Workers."

31. FRG policy states that the first 14 weeks of leave are limited to mothers. Legislation guarantees 75 percent of an average female salary to either parent for up to 1 year. Since men typically make considerably higher wages, however, few men have availed themselves of extended leave, because it means a dramatic decrease in total family income.

32. J. Allen, "European Infant Care Leaves: Foreign Perspectives on the Integration of Work and Family Roles," in *The Parental Leave Crisis*, ed. Zigler and Frank, pp. 245–275.

33. Bureau of the Census, *Fertility of American Women.*

34. Patricia Garrett, DeeAnn Wenk, and Sally Lubeck, "Working Around Childbirth: An Empirical Perspective on Parental Leave and Child Care Policies," (under review).

35. U.S. Department of Labor, Bureau of Labor Statistics, *Employee Benefits in Medium and Large Firms, 1986*, Bulletin no. 2281 (Washington, D.C.: U.S. Government Printing Office, 1987).

36. U.S. Department of Labor, Bureau of Labor Statistics, *Employee Benefits in State and Local Governments, 1987*, Bulletin no. 2309 (Washington, D.C.: U.S. Government Printing Office, 1988).

37. Catalyst, *Report on a National Study of Parental Leaves* (New York: Catalyst, 1986).

38. J. Pleck, "Fathers and Infant Care Leave" and Sheila Kamerman, "Maternity and Parenting Benefits: An International Overview," in *The Parental Leave Crisis*, ed. Zigler and Frank, pp. 177–191 and 235–344.

39. Wolfgang Tietze and Karin Ufermann, "An International Perspective on Schooling for 4-year-olds," *Theory into Practice* 28 (Winter 1989): 69–77. The Tietze and Ufermann data are produced in table 3. See also, Sheila Kamerman, "An International Overview of Preschool Programs," *Phi Delta Kappan* 71 (October 1989): 135–137. Earlier syntheses appear in OECD, Centre for Educational Research and Innovation, *Caring for Young Children: An Analysis of Education and Social Services* (Paris: OECD, 1982) and Kamerman and Kahn, *Child Care.*

40. Great Britain, like the United States, targets disadvantaged children for public programs. In this and some other respects, Britain appears more similar to the United States than to the countries of continental Europe. See, for example, Gilbert Steiner, *The Futility of Family Policy* (Washington, D.c.: Brookings Institution, 1981), pp. 182–185 and Jerome Bruner, *Under Five in Britain* (London: Grant McIntyre, 1980), chaps. 1 and 2. The extensive system of playgroups in Britain, however, is unique.

41. P. McMahon, "An International Comparison of Labor Force Participation," *Monthly Labor Review* (May 1986): 3–12 and OECD, *Adults in Higher Education*.

42. Deborah Phillips, *Quality in Child Care: What Does Research Tell Us?* (Washington, D.C.: National Association for the Education of Young Children, 1987).

43. U.S. Bureau of the Census, *Who's Minding the Kids? Child Care Arrangements, Winter, 1984–85*, Current Population Reports, series P–70, no. 9 (Washington, D.C.: U.S. Government Printing Office, 1987).

44. For reviews, see Richard Clifford and Susan Russell, "Financing Programs for Preschool-aged Children," *Theory into Practice* 28 (Winter 1989): 19–27 and Ron Haskins, *Summary of Federal Provisions for Child Care* (Washington, D.C.: U.S. House of Representatives, January 1988).

45. Clifford and Russell, "Financing Programs."

46. Sandra Hofferth, "The Current Child Care Debate in Context" (Revised version of paper presented at the Annual Meeting of the American Sociological Association, Chicago, January 1988) and U.S. Bureau of the Census, "Child Care Costs Estimated at $14 Billion in 1986, Census Bureau Survey Shows," press release (Washington, D.C.: U.S. Department of Commerce, 1989).

47. Alfred Kahn and Sheila Kamerman, *Child Care: Facing the Hard Choices* (Dover, Mass.: Auburn House, 1987), table 1.8.

48. Kamerman and Kahn, *Child Care*, p. 13.

49. For example, Kamerman and Kahn, *Child Care*, Steiner; *Futility of Family Policy*, pp. 177–192; Pleck, "Fathers and Infant Care Leave"; and Linda Haas, "Equal Parenthood and Social Policy—Lessons from a Study of Parental Leave in Sweden" (Paper presented at the Wingspread Conference on Parental Leave and Child Care: Setting a Research and Policy Agenda, Racine, Wisc., September 1988).

50. Marvin Lazerson, "The Dilemmas of Public Responsibility" (Paper presented at the Bush Colloquium on Family Policy: Issues and Concerns, Chapel Hill, N.C., May 1988, p. 11).

51. Marion Wright Edelman, *Families in Peril: An Agenda for Social Change* (Cambridge, Mass.: Harvard University Press, 1987) chap. 4.

52. Norton Grubb and Marvin Lazerson, *Broken Promises: How Americans Fail Their Children* (New York: Basic Books, 1982), p. 43.

53. Council of Chief State School Officers, *A Guide for State Action: Early Childhood and Family Education* (Washington, D.C.: Council of Chief State School Officers, November 1988), p. 40.

54. The essential argument appears in Steiner, *Futility of Family Policy,* pp. 177–178.

55. Haas, "Equal Parenthood," p. 20.

56. H. Fullerton, "Labor Force Projections: 1986 to 2000," *Monthly Labor Review* 110, 9(1987): 19–29.

57. Grubb and Lazerson, *Broken Promises,* p. 271.

58. Ibid, p. 273.

59. Ibid, p. 296.

60. It is perhaps significant that a Lou Harris poll in 1986 found that three-quarters of the American public were willing to pay higher taxes for day care and education; fully 88 percent were in favor of increasing health benefits and providing day care for children of the poor. See Lisbeth Schorr, *Within our Reach: Breaking the Cycle of Disadvantage* (New York: Anchor Press, 1988), p. 294.

61. For a review, see Thomas Gamble and Edward Zigler, "Effects of Infant Day Care: Another Look at the Evidence," *American Journal of Orthopsychiatry,* 56 (January 1986): 26–42.

62. Kamerman, "International Overview," pp. 135 and 137.

63. Paoli, "Women Workers."

64. Kamerman and Kahn, *Child Care,* p. 75.

65. Kamerman, "Maternity and Parenting Benefits," p. 243.

66. See, for example, Elizabeth Ehrlich, "The Mommy Track: Juggling Kids and Careers in Corporate America Takes a Controversial Turn," *Business Week,* 20 March 1989, pp. 126–134.

67. Lubeck and Garrett, "Child Care in America."

68. Ralf Dahrendorf, *Life Chances* (Chicago: University of Chicago Press, 1979).

69. Kamerman and Kahn, *Child Care, Family Benefits,* pp. 2–3.

About the Editors

LOIS WEIS is Professor and Associate Dean of the Graduate School of Education, State University of New York at Buffalo.

PHILIP G. ALTBACH is Professor of Education and Director of the Comparative Education Center, State University of New York at Buffalo.

GAIL P. KELLY was Professor and Chair in the Department of Educational Organization, Administration, and Policy, State University of New York at Buffalo.

HUGH G. PETRIE is Dean of the Graduate School of Education, State University of New York at Buffalo.

Contributors

LAURA E. ATKINSON is instructor of educational psychology at the University of Manitoba, Canada. Currently she teaches courses in early child development and early child language. Her research has focused on the determinants of the quality of teacher-child interactions in child care centers and their relationship to career and gender issues.

WILLIAM AYERS is assistant professor and director of elementary education at the University of Illinois at Chicago.

STEVE BARNETT is associate professor of economics and policy in the Graduate School of Education, and a Senior Research Fellow, Eagleton Institute of Politics at Rutgers, The State University of New Jersey. His interests include economics and public policy of early childhood programs and, more generally, educational programs for disadvantaged and handicapped children.

BRONWYN DAVIES is a Senior Lecturer in the Department of Social and Cultural Studies in Education at the University of New England, Australia, and author of *Frogs and Snails and Feminist Tales. Pre-school Children and Gender* and *Life in the Classroom and Playground*.

WENDY S. GROLNICK received her Ph.D. from the University of Rochester. She is currently Assistant Professor of Clinical Psychology at New York University. Her research efforts focus on self-regulation and adjustment in students. Other work explores effects of parenting styles on the social and emotional development of young children and developing strategies for preventing school problems.

CAROL ANN HODGES is associate professor and coordinator of the Graduate Reading Program in the Department of Elementary Education and Reading at the State University College at Buffalo. She has published articles in such journals as *Reading Research Quarterly, Reading Psychology,* and *Journal of Teacher Education*. Her professional interests focus on assessment of emergent and early literacy issues.

MARY A. JENSEN is associate professor of early childhood education, State University of New York—Geneseo, is Series Editor for *Early*

Childhood Education: Inquiries and Insights (SUNY Press). She also has recently co-authored *Issues and Advocacy in Early Education.*

SALLY LUBECK is a senior investigator at the Frank Porter Graham Child Development Center and clinical assistant professor in the School of Education at the University of North Carolina at Chapel Hill. She is the author of *Sandbox Society,* which received *Choice Magazine's* Outstanding Academic Book Award in 1987.

ANTHONY D. PELLEGRINI is professor of early childhood education and a research fellow at the University of Georgia. He has examined dimensions of children's play from the early preschool through the middle-school periods. He is currently engaged in a longitudinal study of the rough-and-tumble play of middle-school students.

DEBORAH PHILLIPS, Ph.D., is Director of the National Association for the Education of Young Children (NAEYC) Child Care Information Service, which offers resources and referrals on national child care issues.

MARIAJOSÉ ROMERO is a doctoral student in sociology of education in the Department of Educational Organization, Administration, and Policy at the State University of New York at Buffalo. Her research interests involve socialization processes and class and gender cultural forms in early childhood education.

KELVIN L. SEIFERT is professor of educational psychology at the University of Manitoba, Canada, where until recently he coordinated the early childhood teacher training program. Currently he teaches courses in child development and learning. His current research focuses on teachers' and students' thought processes, viewed from an ethnographic perspective.

MATIA FINN-STEVENSON is a research scientist at Yale University and associate director for program development at the Yale Bush Center in Child Development and Social Policy. She is conducting research on school-based child care and on the safety of children in child care and serves as special consultant and adviser to state and federal policymakers on matters pertaining to work and family issues.

ELIZABETH BLUE SWADENER is assistant professor of early childhood education at Kent State University. She has worked in the areas of social policy, child care, multicultural education, and cross-cultural issues in early education and care. Other research has focused on peace and global education and on preschool programs and policies in Senegal and The Gambia.

MARCY WHITEBOOK, M.A., is Director of the Child Care Employee Project, a resource clearinghouse for child care staff seeking to upgrade their wages, status, and working conditions.

JULIA WRIGLEY is associate professor in the Department of Sociology and the Department of Education at the University of California, Los

Angeles. The article in this volume is part of a larger study she is doing on child care. She is particularly interested in social class differences between parents and their children's caregivers and how these effect parents' strategies for transmitting their class cultural advantages to their children. She works in the sociology of education, political sociology, and gender studies.

EDWARD F. ZIGLER is Sterling Professor of Psychology at Yale University and director of the Yale Bush Center in Child Development and Social Policy. He testifies before congressional committees as an expert in child care research and policy. He served as first director of the Office of Child Development (now Administration for Children, Youth, and Families) and as chief of the U.S. Children's Bureau.

Index